# Introducing Theological Interpretation of Scripture

# Introducing Theological Interpretation of Scripture

Recovering a Christian Practice

## Daniel J. Treier

**Baker Academic**

a division of Baker Publishing Group
Grand Rapids, Michigan

© 2008 by Daniel J. Treier

Published by Baker Academic
a division of Baker Publishing Group
P.O. Box 6287, Grand Rapids, MI 49516-6287
www.bakeracademic.com

Second printing, July 2009

Printed in the United States of America

Library of Congress Cataloging-in-Publication Data
Treier, Daniel J., 1972–
    Introducing theological interpretation of scripture : recovering a Christian practice / Daniel J. Treier.
        p.   cm.
    Includes bibliographical references and indexes.
    ISBN 978-0-8010-3178-6 (pbk.)
    1. Bible—Hermeneutics. 2. Bible—Criticism, interpretation, etc. 3. Bible—Theology. I. Title.
BS476.T74 2008
220.6—dc22                                                                   2008003931

To Paul Beals, Joe Crawford, Jim Grier, Carl Hoch, David Kennedy, John Lillis, and David Turner—seminary teachers who taught me basic biblical and theological skills, and whose friendship nurtures my vocation. (2 Tim. 2:2, 14–26)

# Contents

# Acknowledgments

This book truly originates in community. It is an effort to give more tangible shape to a movement that I care about, thereby honoring a number of countercultural writers who have shaped my life. It is also an ecumenical effort, to emphasize agreements where possible and to name disagreements accurately so that theological interpretation of Scripture can press forward.

The teachers to whom I dedicate this book will not agree with, or find equally interesting, all that it says. But in the mystery of providence they share responsibility for my calling anyway, and I treasure them.

Still others also deserve a grateful mention. My teaching assistant, Michael Allen, did preliminary research and ran down numerous details, saving me countless hours and errors. Chris Atwood helped to generate the index. In addition, Darren Sarisky and my colleagues Tim Larsen and Steve Spencer read each chapter carefully and wisely; their encouragement means much, along with that of Mark Bowald and Kevin Vanhoozer. Students and other colleagues provided useful comments on the introduction and chapters 1–2 in the Wheaton Postgraduate Systematic Theology Seminar. Matthew Levering became a great pen pal, generously

9

sharing his work before publication while offering helpful feedback and support.

Before departing for Notre Dame, Mark Noll prompted me to write this book and, especially, to work hard at writing in English while observing a strict quota on uses of the word "narrative." The ongoing friendship of additional Wheaton faculty, especially the Café Padre gang, infuses my work with a sense of delight. Supportive administrators—Jill Peláez Baumgaertner, Jeff Greenman, and Stan Jones—made possible the necessary time and energy, particularly due to an Aldeen Grant that provided a course reduction.

Collaborating with longtime friend Brian Bolger as my editor has been an additional delight. I can point to tangible corrections and suggestions through which the good folks at Baker Academic made this book much better than it would have been otherwise. So did the reviewer Stephen Fowl, whose gracious comments gave me much to ponder along with considerable encouragement. Stephen and the many others mentioned here deserve no blame for the book's remaining faults and its author's stubbornness.

Finally, I composed most of this project in our first house, in a spacious office, while listening to birds and looking at rabbits (too many rabbits, actually). Without the love and gifts of my wife, Amy, and our parents, I could not experience such a joyful vocation. May God increase the church's faithfulness to Scripture, along with my own, as its fruit.

# Introduction

## From Karl Barth to "Postmodern" Theory

In the 1990s the quest to recover distinctively theological interpretation of Scripture began in earnest. Books by Francis Watson, Stephen Fowl, Kevin Vanhoozer, and others poured forth advocating this new, yet old, way of engaging the Bible. The purpose of the book that you hold in your hands is to tell the story and map the major themes of this movement (part 1), as well as to address some tough questions to clarify its future direction (part 2). Part 1 therefore tends to focus on what advocates of theological interpretation hold in common, while part 2 faces some of the movement's internal arguments. Before we pursue major themes and challenges of theological exegesis, however, we need some background regarding the story of its renewal. Therefore this introductory chapter begins by briefly sketching how theological interpretation of Scripture declined in the first place, due to the rise of "critical biblical scholarship." Then we examine Karl Barth as the forerunner of its recovery, before focusing on two groups of Christians who, having retained some aspects of theological exegesis despite its modern decline, are poised to join the recovery efforts. Evangelical Protestants and Roman Catholics both found themselves caught "between faith and criticism" for much of the twentieth century, but now some of them seem ready to join a small band of mainline Protestant scholars who are on a quest to renew Scripture interpretation theologically.

## Criticizing Critical Biblical Scholarship

Exegesis of the Bible—the effort to understand or interpret its meaning—is a centuries-old endeavor. Often we contrast it with eisegesis, which "reads into" a text something that is not there rather than leading out (the etymology of "exegesis") what the text says. Even before the modern age, figures such as Protestant Reformers Martin Luther and John Calvin believed that early Christian practices of engaging Scripture were frequently guilty of eisegesis. Catholic interpretation understood Scripture to have four senses, or dimensions, of meaning. Founded on the one literal sense (e.g., the word "Jerusalem" as the actual city), one also sought the three spiritual senses: (1) the allegorical, whereby the text somehow points us to Christ (e.g., Jerusalem as the church); (2) the tropological, or moral, import of the words for our lives (e.g., Jerusalem as the faithful soul); (3) the anagogical, or future, reference of the text (e.g., Jerusalem as the heavenly city, center of the new creation). The Protestant tendency to reject allegory—in theory, even if not entirely in practice, sticking with the "plain sense" as the only legitimate dimension of Scripture's meaning—appropriated Renaissance humanism in part. In addition, it continued developments from within medieval Roman Catholicism itself, such as the increasing value placed on the literal sense by Thomas Aquinas and others. Yet Protestant critiques did not establish the Reformers' approach(es) to Scripture as a new European norm for long: soon came the Enlightenment, and a newly "critical" age.

We have just surveyed some exercises in hermeneutics—efforts to understand the nature of human understanding. In this case, hermeneutical reflections concern what it would involve to read and exegete the Bible meaningfully. In that sense, Christians have engaged hermeneutics, and have done so theologically, from the beginning. Among the dominant thinkers who influenced the premodern Catholic approach were Origen and Augustine. Origen was one of the church fathers who interacted with Greek philosophy; while pursuing careful interpretation using the literary tools of his day, he also appropriated allegory for reading Scripture as a spiritual practice. In *On Christian Teaching* Augustine continued in this vein, carefully plundering his culture's rules of reading and rhetoric for Christ's sake, as the Israelites had done with the gold of the Egyptians. The resulting hermeneutics influenced Christian practice for a thousand years and beyond.

In all its variety, such practice was theological: Christians read the Bible as Scripture, authoritative as God's Word for faith and life; thus, to interpret Scripture was to encounter God. This remained true for the Protestant Reformers, but not for all Europeans when hermeneutics began to grow more formal two centuries later. In 1787 the German scholar J. P. Gabler delivered a lecture entitled "An Oration on the Proper Distinction between Biblical and Dogmatic Theology and the Specific Objectives of Each." The title sets forth his agenda clearly: a new distinction between biblical theology as a historical enterprise and dogmatic theology as a normative one. Gabler was not interested in the history of religions alone; rather, apparently he thought that this distinction would allow the Bible to speak more clearly without theology drowning out its voice.[1]

These were the heady days that led to the formation of the modern university at Berlin in 1801. The German model quickly set standards for the founding of American research universities such as Johns Hopkins, influencing before too long schools in the British Empire as well, some of which could trace their heritage back to the medieval university in Paris. Very soon, for interpretation of the Bible to result in knowledge of the truth, it had to be critical—scientific in the only sense that people felt possible for an enterprise of the humanities dealing with texts to attain (the German word for such an academic discipline is *Wissenschaft*). To

1. For introductory reflections on Gabler's significance, see Charles H. H. Scobie, *The Ways of Our God: An Approach to Biblical Theology* (Grand Rapids: Eerdmans, 2003), 5, 15–16; Craig G. Bartholomew, "Biblical Theology," in *Dictionary for Theological Interpretation of the Bible* (hereafter *DTIB*), ed. Kevin J. Vanhoozer et al. (Grand Rapids: Baker Academic, 2005), 84–90.

be critical, in this case, meant focusing on the historical, exploring the cause-and-effect relationships behind events and actions. The causes that we can explore critically, however, seem to be human—natural or social—not divine. Historical criticism of the Bible, therefore, meant focusing on the times and places of the texts' production as well as their historical references, and doing so objectively: seeking results to share with everyone, unbiased by personal experience or perspective.[2] What would such objectivity exclude? It would rule out interpreting the Bible as Scripture, with positive reference to beliefs in or encounter with God.

Today a new movement, often under the banner "theological interpretation of Scripture," seeks to reverse the dominance of historical criticism over churchly reading of the Bible and to redefine the role of hermeneutics in theology. Here I will tell the story of that movement, before offering in later chapters an interpretation of its key tenets and exploring its possible future. We begin by examining the crucial stimulus for recovering theological exegesis.

## Karl Barth: Pioneer of Theological Criticism

In 1915 Karl Barth found himself pastoring a church upon graduation from university. Distressed by the lack of anything to preach from the liberal verities of his theology teachers, and dismayed that those teachers signed on to the German war effort, Barth began to rediscover the Bible. This resulted in the launch of his Romans commentary, famously labeled a "bombshell dropped on the playground of the theologians." Barth continued to revise the work, which went through six editions; the second edition particularly, published in 1921, involved substantial reworking.

2. It is important to note the variety of meanings for the term "historical criticism"; the label does not denote a single approach. For an overview, see Richard E. Burnett, "Historical Criticism," *DTIB* 290–93. Karl P. Donfried suggests that the general phenomenon discussed here should be called "'historical biblical criticism,' by which is meant the attempt to understand what the biblical author wished to convey to the audience for which he wrote" ("Alien Hermeneutics and the Misappropriation of Scripture," in *Reclaiming the Bible for the Church*, ed. Carl E. Braaten and Robert W. Jenson [Grand Rapids: Eerdmans, 1995], 22).

Barth also drafted several versions of a preface for the original. There, as well as in letters to friends, he anticipated the reactions that his commentary would receive.

### The Romans Commentary

Many have viewed Barth's *Der Römerbrief* not as a commentary but rather as a virtuoso performance of theology or as a piece of spiritualized interpretation. Biblical scholars in particular have often felt that Paul's letter is largely absent or at least distant from Barth's vision, while historical critics have seen Barth's exegesis as "pneumatic," or spiritual (which, for them, is not a compliment). Yet, as John Webster insists, we must attend to Barth's self-understanding, at least initially: he sought to write a *commentary*.[3] In his original preface Barth wrote, "If we rightly understand ourselves, our problems are the problems of Paul," and he spoke of being "bound to labour with Paul." He also affirmed that "the historical-critical method of Biblical investigation has its rightful place," although he acknowledged that "were I driven to choose between it and the venerable doctrine of Inspiration, I should without hesitation adopt the latter, which has a broader, deeper, more important justification."[4] However, Barth felt that he did not have to choose.[5]

It is not as if Barth was unaware of modern developments in hermeneutics. As Richard Burnett shows, Hans-Georg Gadamer was not off the mark to call *Der Römerbrief* a "virtual hermeneutical manifesto," and Barth did not fail to comment regarding the pioneering work of Friedrich Schleiermacher on hermeneutics.[6]

---

3. John Webster, "Karl Barth," in *Reading Romans through the Centuries: From the Early Church to Karl Barth*, ed. Jeffrey P. Greenman and Timothy Larsen (Grand Rapids: Brazos, 2005), 205–23.

4. "The Preface to the First Edition," in Karl Barth, *The Epistle to the Romans*, trans. Edwyn C. Hoskyns, 6th ed. (Oxford: Oxford University Press, 1933), 1.

5. Barth affirmed this in his preface; his retention of a place for historical criticism is emphasized in Bruce L. McCormack, "Historical-Criticism and Dogmatic Interest in Karl Barth's Theological Exegesis of the New Testament," *Lutheran Quarterly* 5 (Summer 1991): 211–25.

6. Webster rightly cautions us against appreciating Gadamer's remark to the point of thinking that Barth's work is about hermeneutics rather than being

Yet Barth emphasized exegesis, dealing with the actual content of the text, as having priority. Apparently, he held this principle generally for all texts, not just Scripture.[7] According to Burnett, four basic commitments follow. First, Barth focused on the "subject matter" or "content" or "substance" of the text—and therefore, in this case, the being of the eternal God—as having hermeneutical control.[8] Hence, second, he held that one must enter into or participate in its meaning.[9] Some of this language might sound like Schleiermacher's, but given its emphasis on a human subject feeling connected to the past, the starting point was theological rather than anthropological. For Barth, we do not read "religiously," as a practice that is located in a pious feature of our generic humanity; instead, rather than conjuring up empathy for the author's mind-set, we respond to divine gift. Third, then, one must read "with more attention and love" than do the modern scientists, the mere historical critics.[10] And fourth, Barth insisted "upon a reading of the Bible that is more in accordance with 'the meaning of the Bible itself.'"[11]

What might this mean? Barth kept the Bible's language and content together instead of using hermeneutics as a justification for moving behind the text or for translating its words into general, rational principles held to be true on other grounds. This is not to deny the importance of textual criticism in particular.[12] Still, historical criticism is not comprehensive of interpretation but rather is preparatory for it—it is servant, not master. The subject matter

---

a commentary about Romans. Nevertheless, Burnett's analysis of the preface drafts shows that Barth was methodologically self-aware, even in his opposition to forms of "hermeneutics." (It is also important to note that Schleiermacher contributed to hermeneutics not only a focus on anthropology but also appreciation of grammatical and other technical matters.)

7. Richard E. Burnett, *Karl Barth's Theological Exegesis: The Hermeneutical Principles of the Römerbrief Period* (Grand Rapids: Eerdmans, 2004), 64.

8. Burnett, *Karl Barth's Theological Exegesis*, chap. 3.

9. Burnett, *Karl Barth's Theological Exegesis*, chap. 4.

10. Burnett, *Karl Barth's Theological Exegesis*, chap. 5.

11. Burnett, *Karl Barth's Theological Exegesis*, 221.

12. See, e.g., "The Preface to the Second Edition," in Barth, *Epistle to the Romans*, 6–7.

must have freedom to speak. Therefore, refusing any two-stage views of past versus present, or of what the text "meant" versus what it "means"—for how could we recognize the difference from where we stand, if we are connected to the text at all?—Barth put a priority on paraphrase. What the text says must be restated in other words, which requires making use of concepts and issues contemporary to the interpreter. For Barth, the model exegete is Calvin, however different their work might appear to us. From Calvin we learn a type of criticism that takes the humanity of the biblical text seriously, while, or even for the sake of, keeping its subject matter primary.[13]

### Barth as Motivation and Model

It is important to note that Romans was by no means Barth's only biblical preoccupation. Not only are the volumes of his *Church Dogmatics* saturated with scriptural exegesis—studies of which continue and perhaps are increasing—but he also taught a number of courses on biblical texts: Ephesians, James, 1 Corinthians 15, 1 John, Philippians, Colossians, the Sermon on the Mount, John's Gospel, 1 Peter (several of these more than once). In addition, he held a combined chair in dogmatics and New Testament exegesis for a time.[14] The point of this list is to overwhelm: if one wants to follow Barth in pursuing theological exegesis, that will mean not a loose relationship to Scripture but rather an overwhelming amount of detailed study. Moreover, Barth did not eschew critical study in favor of "practical" or "pneumatic" exegesis; he saw himself as being more properly critical than the historical critics![15] In Bruce McCormack's words, "Barth's approach would have us raise serious questions about whether the scientific approach is truly 'scientific' and whether the practical

---

13. Burnett, *Karl Barth's Theological Exegesis*, chap. 6.

14. Bruce L. McCormack, "The Significance of Karl Barth's Theological Exegesis of Philippians," in Karl Barth, *The Epistle to the Philippians*, trans. James W. Leitch, 40th anniversary ed. (Louisville: Westminster/John Knox, 2002), v–vi.

15. "The critical historian needs to be more critical"; see "The Preface to the Second Edition," in Barth, *Epistle to the Romans*, 7. This is one reason why many of the recent "postmodern" readings of Barth probably miss the mark.

can be truly 'practical' if it is not also 'scientific' in the sense he advocates."[16]

This is not to say that Barth achieved perfection or that theological interpretation of Scripture today means simply following Barth's path. The need for ongoing growth is suggested not only by his constant revisions but also by the differences between his Romans and Philippians commentaries. For example, Francis Watson finds in *Der Römerbrief* still "an apparent *disjunction* between what Paul said and what Paul says"—evidence of a critical breach between the past and the present that was largely abandoned by the time Barth treated Philippians.[17] Barth is therefore neither the sole model nor a static exemplar, but he has provided contemporary inspiration for theological exegesis.

We may briefly trace several lines of Barthian influence. One strand of inspiration begins with the longtime Yale University Old Testament scholar Brevard Childs, who often manifests appreciation for Barth and Calvin. Childs's "canonical" approach retains historical criticism while giving hermeneutical priority to the "final form" of the biblical text as we now have it. To trace the shaping of the canon is to engage the church already having done theological exegesis in the act of passing the texts on to us.[18] A second strand of Barth's influence also emerges from Yale, despite Childs's relative lack of connection to it. When David Kelsey authored *The Uses of Scripture in Recent Theology*,[19] he profiled Barth's theological focus on the biblical narratives' depiction of God's identity in Jesus Christ. Hans Frei, meanwhile, explored the hermeneutical loss of biblical narratives' meaning due to modern obsessions with their "historical"

16. McCormack, "Karl Barth's Theological Exegesis of Philippians," xxv.

17. Francis B. Watson, "Barth's *Philippians* as Theological Exegesis," in Barth, *Philippians*, xxix–xxx (italics in original).

18. We will study the work of Childs later, in chap. 4. For an overview, see Christopher Seitz, "Canonical Approach," *DTIB* 100–102. For essays honoring Childs, see Christopher Seitz and Kathryn Greene-McCreight, eds., *Theological Exegesis: Essays in Honor of Brevard S. Childs* (Grand Rapids: Eerdmans, 1998).

19. *The Uses of Scripture in Recent Theology* (Philadelphia: Fortress, 1975); reissued as *Proving Doctrine* (Harrisburg, PA: Trinity Press International, 1999).

truthfulness.[20] Appreciation for Calvin and Barth is evident not only in Frei but also in George Lindbeck, another Yale theologian whose methodological writings shaped a generation of thinkers often labeled "postliberal."[21] Whether or not a "Yale School" exists, many mainline Protestants interested in theological exegesis display visible affinities with Barth's work.[22] Third, while others in the movement accord more with Stanley Hauerwas than with the Yale School, focusing upon the virtues of the interpretative community, Hauerwas, whose PhD is from Yale, still manifests indebtedness to Barth as well.[23] Finally, Francis Watson's crucial contributions to theological hermeneutics, though eclectic and even iconoclastic, likewise demonstrate deep engagement with Barth and with these thinkers from Yale.[24]

To summarize, then, in the words of Mary Kathleen Cunningham,

> Barth's approach, in which theological commitments and exegetical insights are so tightly interwoven, leads to scriptural interpretation that is often counter-intuitive and departs from the standard

20. See especially *The Eclipse of Biblical Narrative: A Study in Eighteenth and Nineteenth Century Hermeneutics* (New Haven: Yale University Press, 1974).

21. Most relevant here is George A. Lindbeck, "Postcritical Canonical Interpretation: Three Modes of Retrieval," in Seitz and Greene-McCreight, *Theological Exegesis*, 26–51.

22. See David Lauber, "Yale School," *DTIB* 859–61; also George Hunsinger, "Postliberal Theology," in *The Cambridge Companion to Postmodern Theology*, ed. Kevin J. Vanhoozer (Cambridge: Cambridge University Press, 2003), 42–57.

23. See, e.g., Stephen E. Fowl, *Engaging Scripture: A Model for Theological Interpretation*, Challenges in Contemporary Theology (Oxford: Blackwell, 1998), and his earlier book coauthored with L. Gregory Jones, *Reading in Communion: Scripture and Ethics in Christian Life* (Grand Rapids: Eerdmans, 1991). An example of Barth's influence on Hauerwas is the latter's *With the Grain of the Universe: The Church's Witness and Natural Theology* (Grand Rapids: Brazos, 2001). Hauerwas's Barthian resistance to natural theology seems to fit well with his and others' confessional resistance to critical biblical scholarship.

24. See Francis Watson, *Text, Church and World: Biblical Interpretation in Theological Perspective* (Grand Rapids: Eerdmans, 1994); *Text and Truth: Redefining Biblical Theology* (Grand Rapids: Eerdmans, 1997). For an emphasis on interpretative virtue that is critical of aspects of both Childs and Watson, see Fowl, *Engaging Scripture*.

practices of professional biblical scholars. While Barth's concerns at times intersect those of historical critics of the Bible, enabling him to make eclectic and unsystematic use of their insights, he frequently diverges from their methods and observations altogether because he is operating with a different set of rules and interests. Instead of committing him to the pursuit of extra-biblical sources and textual reconstruction as a means of interpreting biblical concepts, his hermeneutical principles tie him to the linguistic world of the Bible itself. Hence we find him treating texts in their final form, juxtaposing widely separated texts, and appealing to passages in close proximity to the text under consideration. In so doing, he claims to be reading Scripture as it is intended to be read, namely, as a unified witness to its true object, Jesus Christ.[25]

For modern biblical criticism, historical distance between the text and the present is a problem, while critical distance between text and interpreter must be preserved in the name of objectivity. For those who would follow Barth, by contrast, true objectivity comes in God's gift of Christian freedom, which crosses Lessing's famous "ugly, wide ditch" of historical distance and enables the interpreter to enter lovingly into the text's subject matter. For still others, Barth provides inspiration for checking the dominance of historical criticism over the church, yet he and his followers are overly sanguine about the clarity of the Bible's subject matter. The Christian freedom to which Barth points is a gift from God *in and through the church*; many disagreements among advocates of theological interpretation of Scripture concern how this churchly reception of divine grace works.

### "Between Faith and Criticism": Evangelical Protestants and Roman Catholics

While Barth was undergoing his break from liberalism, Anglo-American evangelical Protestants and Roman Catholics worldwide found themselves in between flash points of a larger battle with

25. Mary Kathleen Cunningham, *What Is Theological Exegesis? Interpretation and Use of Scripture in Barth's Doctrine of Election* (Valley Forge, PA: Trinity Press International, 1995), 83.

"modernism." Both groups sustained certain traditional practices during the twentieth century that offer resources for theological interpretation, yet they also made mistakes in the ways they resisted modern culture. Now some thinkers in each context are poised to engage Barth constructively as well as critically, along with the hermeneutical renaissance that has accompanied his theology.

### Evangelical Protestants: Recovering Scholarly Engagement

Resisting the "liberal" idea that the Bible's plain-sense claims about the supernatural must be reinterpreted to suit what modern people could believe, American conservatives proclaimed their adherence to "the fundamentals" of Christian faith. First in the 1880s and then from the 1920s onward, controversies ensued within several Protestant denominations. At an institutional level fundamentalists lost, and they retreated not just from these churches but also from cultural engagement generally. Thus a deep breach grew between evangelical Christians and critical biblical scholarship, as Mark Noll summarizes:

> The story of these clashing communities is, however, really two stories. Of most interest to outsiders is the record of traditional Bible-believers first competing in the intellectual marketplace as full partners in the academic discussion of Scripture (roughly 1880 to 1900); then retreating from that world to the fortress of faith (roughly 1900 to 1935); then slowly realizing the values of some participation in that wider world (1935 to 1950), finding the strategies to put themselves back in the professional picture once again (1940 to 1975), and finally confronting new spiritual and intellectual dilemmas because of success in those ventures (1960 to the present). . . . The first story, in other words, concerns mostly the connected history of late nineteenth-century American Protestant conservatism, the fundamentalist movement, and the emergence of a new evangelicalism out of fundamentalism.
>
> The second involves the interplay of cultures, first British-American and second immigrant-American.[26]

26. Mark A. Noll, *Between Faith and Criticism: Evangelicals, Scholarship, and the Bible in America* (New York: Harper & Row, 1986), 7.

For our present purposes, a few implications follow from this evangelical story. First, because "theological interpretation of Scripture" is basically a movement within the academy (so far), there is a degree to which it addresses concerns that are most at home or at issue among "mainline" Protestants rather than evangelicals. Certain traditional denominations have been profoundly and rather pervasively affected by "critical" assumptions, reading practices and conclusions, all the while enjoying the academic influence and other benefits that stem from a longer track record of engaging scholarship. These Anglicans, Lutherans, Methodists, and Presbyterians (to name a few) have been the locus of recent discussions about recovering the Bible as Scripture.[27]

Second, Noll highlights the differences between British and American biblical scholarship in general, which had particular significance for evangelicals. British "practitioners of modern scholarship were never as rationalistic or anti-supernaturalistic as the best-known critics in Germany and the United States."[28] Meanwhile, British evangelical scholars tended to embrace more critical positions than did their American counterparts, finding themselves somewhere between the modernists and the conservative Americans; ardent conservatives in Britain never contributed serious biblical scholarship that could rival the more critical evangelicals. Behind these distinctions lay different church-state relationships, which placed British evangelical and modernist scholars in more frequent and fruitful contact while keeping British universities and the church in closer partnership as well. Study of "classics" retained some cultural and educational force in the United Kingdom while declining in the United States, and this accorded with British possession of distinct intellectual possibilities for mediating "between conservative theological convictions and the practice of modern scholarship." Moreover, "learned study of the Bible

27. An example of this claim is the introductory frame and conclusion of a widely cited essay by David S. Yeago, "The New Testament and the Nicene Dogma: A Contribution to the Recovery of Theological Exegesis," in *The Theological Interpretation of Scripture: Classic and Contemporary Readings*, ed. Stephen E. Fowl (Oxford: Blackwell, 1997), 87–100.

28. Noll, *Between Faith and Criticism*, 86.

and an intense interest in the Spirit had never been sundered" in Britain as they were by revivalism in America.[29] Today, then, "theological interpretation of Scripture" may find relatively more adherents in the United Kingdom than in the United States, or at least takes on a slightly different character: among evangelicals or conservative Protestants, such a phrase seems to enjoy a heartier British embrace.

Yet, third, certain aspects of theological interpretation persisted among evangelicals during their eclipse within wider academic and ecclesiastical cultures. For instance, evangelicals have long interpreted particular words of the Bible in light of other passages in which they appear,[30] as part of the larger practice—inherited from Augustine by way of the Protestant Reformers—of "interpreting Scripture with Scripture." In both good and bad ways, evangelicals read the Bible canonically—as one book—even when others would not, and their different varieties were open to developing particular forms of "spiritual" interpretation. As an example, we could point to typology, connecting earlier persons, institutions, or events in Scripture with later fulfillment. Until recently its modern academic practitioners were few, but forms of this theological approach thrived among evangelical interpreters for some time.

All the while, conservative Protestants have not been afraid to interpret Scripture with reference to doctrinal concerns. Unfortunately, they are well known for "proof-texting"—selectively using biblical passages to support theological points (often with individual verses listed in parentheses at the end of a sentence). As we hear in many a course on biblical interpretation, "A text without a context is a pretext for a proof text,"[31] and such a tendency has,

29. Noll, *Between Faith and Criticism*, 89.

30. On this point regarding how the words that fund our interpretative discourse (and whether they are abstract or concretely biblical) can shape its theological nature, see R. R. Reno, "Biblical Theology and Theological Exegesis," in *Out of Egypt: Biblical Theology and Biblical Interpretation*, ed. Craig Bartholomew et al., Scripture and Hermeneutics 5 (Grand Rapids: Zondervan, 2004), 385–408.

31. For a more thorough discussion, see Daniel J. Treier, "Proof Text," *DTIB* 622–24.

arguably, done violence not just to the Bible but also to the readers of plodding theology books. In reaction, many evangelical scholars have now lauded "biblical theology" as a responsible bridge between the task of exegesis and the concerns of systematic theology—a historically oriented critical check upon the proof-texting inclinations of theologians that will nevertheless retain Scripture as the ground for making doctrinal claims.

Since Noll published his history in 1986, evangelicals have continued increasing their acceptance of historical criticism. But the issue is not primarily wider openness to "higher" critical theories, such as multiple sources besides or instead of Moses authoring the Pentateuch.[32] The evangelical embrace of modernity runs deeper, in the distinction between a text's "meaning" as single and determinate and its "significance" or "application" as multiple and context-sensitive. The dominance of this approach is obvious to anyone who surveys hermeneutics textbooks.[33] As a result, evangelical scholars have used some of the same presuppositions used in the wider university: if biblical theology connects first of all with "what the text meant" rather than "what it means," then it requires the objectivity that can come only from critical distance. With such two-step hermeneutics the scientific pretensions of "inductive Bible study" continue while tensions increase over the relation between academy and church, the significance of "the priesthood of all believers," devotional practices, the work of the Holy Spirit, and so forth.[34] Hence, later we must examine various definitions of biblical theology and seek its place within theological interpretation of Scripture. In certain ways, the dominance of both popular proof-texting and academic biblical theology within evangelicalism reflects its theological weakness; a tendency exists to substitute the

32. A somewhat controversial recent example is Peter J. Enns, *Inspiration and Incarnation: Evangelicals and the Problem of the Old Testament* (Grand Rapids: Baker Academic, 2005).

33. In particular, evangelicals have appropriated E. D. Hirsch Jr., *Validity in Interpretation* (New Haven: Yale University Press, 1967). They have neglected the problems of this earlier work and the changes that Hirsch made later.

34. To demonstrate this, examine treatments (or lack thereof) of the Holy Spirit in evangelical hermeneutics texts.

selective use of biblical exegesis and philosophical epistemology for robust engagement with church doctrine.

For now, a final historical point deserves mention: both the decline of evangelical scholarship in the early 1900s and the renewal that followed did not manifest themselves immediately but rather emerged from latent subtleties under the surface.[35] By no means have evangelicals retained or attained all that theological interpretation of Scripture could embrace. Nor does the idea necessarily occupy them, at present, in the way that it interests others.[36] Nevertheless, having practiced some of its possible elements, evangelicals could be positioned to excel at these practices even more and to pursue other dimensions that they have lacked. Developments have occurred so quickly that we must be reluctant to predict the future.

### Roman Catholics: Recovering Spiritual Exegesis

Mark Noll's phrase regarding evangelicals and the Bible, suggesting perceived tensions "between faith and criticism," is also apt when we turn our attention to Roman Catholicism.[37] Indeed, the Catholic reaction to the Protestant Reformers at the Council of Trent (1546) "upheld the authority of both Scripture and the 'unwritten . . . traditions concerning both faith and morals, as coming from either Christ's spoken words or from the Holy Spirit' (First Decree). It further asserted 'that no one, by relying on their own judgment in matters of faith and morals, . . . shall dare to interpret the Sacred Scriptures in opposition to what has been and continues

35. On this point see, e.g., Noll, *Between Faith and Criticism*, 61.

36. It is interesting, however, that J. I. Packer described his theological method in terms of theological exegesis as long ago as "In Quest of Canonical Interpretation," in *The Use of the Bible in Theology: Evangelical Options*, ed. Robert K. Johnston (Atlanta: John Knox, 1985), 35–55.

37. I will use "Catholic" and "Roman Catholic" interchangeably. In so doing, I seek to acknowledge the claim of the Roman Catholic Church to represent or even constitute the universal church in an important sense, a claim that is important to its hermeneutical understanding, as one can see in, e.g., the overview by Peter S. Williamson, "Catholic Biblical Interpretation," *DTIB* 102–6. Yet Protestants such as myself must use different descriptions as well.

to be taught by Holy Mother Church . . .' (Second Decree)."[38] Such a principle of authority obviously meant fundamental conflict with the spirit of the modern age, and in 1870 Vatican Council I reacted with a staunch reaffirmation of the traditional "magisterium," or teaching office, by embracing the dogma of papal infallibility.[39] However, Catholic biblical interpretation changed nevertheless.

Matthew Levering does not begin his narrative with the Enlightenment, as some conservative Protestants might, when chronicling the loss of theological exegesis.[40] He agrees with Luke Timothy Johnson, who says,

> The most imaginative and original and important biblical interpretation of Scripture in Christianity's 1500 years . . . did not take place in biblical commentaries, but in other literary and liturgical expressions. Biblical commentaries tended to have an explanatory function. In them, the literal sense of Scripture was explicated. Commentaries then, as now, quickly became encyclopedic, as one generation borrowed lexical and grammatical and historical information from another. Commentaries rarely had anything original to say. This is one reason why modern scholars find so little of interest in ancient interpretation. They assume that the commentary is where interpretation is to be found. But it is not. The most vibrant forms of interpretation in antiquity occur when the Scripture is *used* to explicate the Christian life.[41]

Detailed study of the Bible was the basic practice of all leading premodern theologians, and, Johnson's generalization not-

---

38. Williamson, "Catholic Biblical Interpretation," 103.

39. For bibliography and brief discussion on how to understand this teaching properly in contrast to Protestant approaches, see Daniel J. Treier, "Scripture and Hermeneutics," in *The Cambridge Companion to Evangelical Theology*, ed. Timothy Larsen and Daniel J. Treier (Cambridge: Cambridge University Press, 2007), 35–49.

40. Matthew Levering, *Participatory Biblical Exegesis: A Theology of Biblical Interpretation* (Notre Dame, IN: University of Notre Dame Press, forthcoming).

41. Luke Timothy Johnson and William S. Kurz, *The Future of Catholic Biblical Scholarship: A Constructive Conversation* (Grand Rapids: Eerdmans, 2002), 44–45. Levering first highlighted this for me.

withstanding, their commentaries are often strikingly different from ours. Yet commentary by leading theologians became relatively rare after Bonaventure and Thomas Aquinas. Even if such commentary had been less formal, more related to use of Scripture in church life as Johnson suggests, the decline already indicates a shift, long before the Enlightenment. The forward march of time, or the linear flow of history, became separate from the traditional, vertical practices of Scripture interpretation as participation in God. Even before the final demise of patristic-medieval exegesis, history and theology were becoming extrinsic to each other. Levering shows that different types of commentaries, and different sections within them, became more distinct from each other.

The Enlightenment and its aftermath finalized this metaphysical separation between history and God. Ever since, time and space no longer seem to participate in the divine but rather have "natural" autonomy. Connection to the sacred mysteries of Scripture no longer involves spiritual insight received through Christian practices and especially the liturgy; instead, the Bible counts solely as evidence for understanding the causal relationships between events in linear sequence. Those events and the texts themselves must be studied with the scholarly rigor of "history," which precludes the need, and perhaps even the opportunity, for spiritual practice to shape one's perspective. Indeed, one cannot assume that the "real" events are sacred mysteries; there may be no divine actor behind the world stage. Instead of a player-coach, the interpreter now becomes like the color commentator—an armchair critic. The shift from participant to spectator, in terms of how we view the nature of interpretation, follows from the new assumption of distance between God and history.[42] Nowadays, "We are so accustomed to think of context as literary or historical that we forget that

42. For a discussion complementary to these themes from Levering, see Francis Martin, *Sacred Scripture: The Disclosure of the Word* (Naples, FL: Sapientia, 2006), especially chap. 12. See also the work of Robert Sokolowski, surveyed in William M. Wright IV, "The Theology of Disclosure and Biblical Exegesis," *The Thomist* 70 (2006): 395–419.

the words of the Bible have a life that transcends their original setting."[43]

Catholic acceptance of modern biblical studies ebbed and flowed for a while. In 1893 Pope Leo XIII saw primarily apologetic value in fostering critical study, and the subsequent modernism of some provoked a reaction against higher criticism. However, Pope Pius XII granted greater freedom for and encouragement of critical study in 1943, and the Second Vatican Council built upon this in the 1960s. Its *Dogmatic Constitution on Divine Revelation*, or *Dei Verbum*, fostered interaction with biblical scholarship outside the Roman Catholic Church, where a number of Catholic scholars became quite well known.[44]

Levering summarizes the overall trajectory as follows. First, in the fourteenth and fifteenth centuries the literal and spiritual senses began to split in ways that were connected to the disjunction between biblical exegesis and university theology. Second, in the sixteenth century, while university theologians sought to recover the Bible, they understood "history" in a primarily linear fashion—one event after another. As a result, they were embarrassed about the spiritual senses and engaged less and less with them. Third, then, from the seventeenth century to the twentieth, the ability to do historical work (understood without engaging the vertical dimension of divine action) continued to increase, while the spiritual senses became merely pietistic resources and were largely discarded. By the middle of the twentieth century this resulted in mostly historicist Catholic biblical scholarship lacking theological depth.[45]

Thus, the work of scholars such as Raymond Brown, given the extent of their solidarity with historical criticism, has been

43. Judith L. Kovacs, "Interpreting the New Testament," in *1 Corinthians: Interpreted by Early Christian Commentators*, trans. and ed. Judith L. Kovacs, The Church's Bible (Grand Rapids: Eerdmans, 2005), xvi.

44. This summary depends heavily on Williamson, "Catholic Biblical Interpretation," 103.

45. Levering, *Participatory Biblical Exegesis*, chap. 2. For a broader history without Levering's theological agenda, see Gerald P. Fogarty, *American Catholic Biblical Scholarship: A History from the Early Republic to Vatican II* (San Francisco: Harper & Row, 1989).

controversial among theologians such as Levering, but it seems to be the mainstream standard of practice among Catholic biblical scholars. Addressing such issues, a group of exegetes constituted as the Pontifical Biblical Commission produced a hermeneutical evaluation in 1993 entitled *The Interpretation of the Bible in the Church.* "Received" by Pope John Paul II, with his successor, Pope Benedict XVI, involved, the study reaffirms faithful use of the historical-critical method and other potential approaches while also emphasizing "that Catholic exegesis must 'maintain its identity as a theological discipline' (Conclusion, e)."[46] What that might mean, however, remains under discussion.

Luke Timothy Johnson and William S. Kurz have recently attempted not only to foster but also to embody such a conversation. In sequential sections of their book, each scholar offers several essays combining programmatic suggestions with attention to figures in the history of Catholic biblical interpretation (Johnson's focus) and to biblical case studies (Kurz's focus); both sections end with responses from the other. The joint conclusion offers short answers from each to ten conversation starters, which provide a useful overview of contemporary theological concerns in this tradition.

The first three questions concern specifically Catholic identity, celebrating its possible contributions of "a more explicit and congenial partnership between faith and reason and between Scripture and tradition (including all aspects of church worship, pastoral care, and life)."[47] Indeed, for Roman Catholicism there is a living institutional link to the premodern interpretative community. Moreover, the Catholic tendency toward "both/and" approaches

46. Williamson, "Catholic Biblical Interpretation," 104. For an overview of this document's approach to history, see Peter S. Williamson, "The Place of History in Catholic Exegesis: An Examination of the Pontifical Biblical Commission's *The Interpretation of the Bible in the Church*," in *"Behind" the Text: History and Biblical Interpretation*, ed. Craig Bartholomew et al., Scripture and Hermeneutics 4 (Grand Rapids: Zondervan, 2003), 196–226. Among those critical of *The Interpretation of the Bible in the Church*, see Lewis Ayres and Stephen E. Fowl, "(Mis)Reading the Face of God: *The Interpretation of the Bible in the Church*," *Theological Studies* 60 (1999): 513–28.

47. Johnson and Kurz, *Catholic Biblical Scholarship*, 265.

that respect the goodness of creation and the contributions of culture can be consistent with use of historical criticism and openness to spiritual senses as well as intra-ecclesiastical variety.[48]

The fourth and fifth questions explore the nature of critical study and history. For Kurz and Johnson, it seems, criticism ought to involve not excessive distance from or an attitude of superiority over the biblical texts but instead careful attention to them and to how history might assist in understanding their words. At the same time, neither scholar is willing simply to identify the texts' "literal sense" with or derive it from their "historical sense."[49]

The sixth question concerns the relation between Scripture scholarship and church authority, while questions eight through ten turn to the role of Catholic biblical scholars in different aspects of church life; question seven, concerning "the proper critical function of Scripture scholarship vis-à-vis theology and church life,"[50] connects these issues. Though scholars enjoy considerable "academic" freedom for the sake of the church, they remain subject to their bishops and the pope. At least they ought to be honest and clear about their disagreements with Catholic teaching instead of misleading the faithful or the unaware. Kurz is more concerned about inappropriate scholarly dissent, while Johnson seems more concerned over an authoritarian or suspicious hierarchy. Inappropriate censorship can come from both directions.[51] Moreover, mundane realities such as the time pressures on busy lives also limit academic contributions to the church.[52] Yet scholars ought to provide resistance against liturgical compromises of Scripture (for instance, shortening the length of readings) along with readable study resources and careful teaching.

Many of these concerns, of course, should be common to Protestants as well.[53] Potential Catholic distinctiveness when it

48. Johnson and Kurz, *Catholic Biblical Scholarship*, 265–68.
49. Johnson and Kurz, *Catholic Biblical Scholarship*, 269–73.
50. Johnson and Kurz, *Catholic Biblical Scholarship*, 278.
51. Johnson and Kurz, *Catholic Biblical Scholarship*, 274–80.
52. Johnson and Kurz, *Catholic Biblical Scholarship*, 281–82.
53. Overdoing the contrast between Catholics and Protestants is one of the critiques of Johnson and Kurz in the symposium on their book from *Nova et*

comes to theological interpretation of Scripture, then, follows from the unique claims of the church, resulting in a particular set of concerns about tradition and ecclesiastical authority, formalizing distinctively the issues of "faith and criticism" that also face Protestants. Nevertheless, a specifically Catholic resource exists alongside such tension: a longer tradition that remains more open to spiritual exegesis. Accordingly, in some ways certain strands of Catholic biblical scholarship may enjoy distinctive openness to theological interpretation, along with more established depth of doctrinal reflection.

Levering's advocacy of "participatory exegesis," using Thomas Aquinas as an exemplar, can illustrate my point. Study of the texts' original contexts can be affirmed, but doctrines and spiritual practices are also essential for participating in the realities of which the Bible speaks. This requires rejecting a strictly linear notion of history connected to the modern valorization of human autonomy, concepts that Levering blames on medieval "nominalism."[54] In his view, this philosophical turn broadened from a position on universals (they exist in name only) to a radical emphasis upon God's freedom and the dependence of creatures upon the (seemingly arbitrary) divine will. No longer were humans viewed as participating somehow in the divine perfections that are definitive for all reality: whereas the sacred mysteries of God's teaching had been constitutive of true knowledge, they became suspect as mere assumptions external (if they are even actual) to the linear march of ordinary time.

However, objectivity need not mean autonomous human neutrality, for in that case, rejection of a participatory metaphysics regarding creation's relation to God makes it very difficult for redemption to relate us to God either: grace would leave history alone. Yet if one follows Levering this far, then, following Dietrich Bonhoeffer, Christ and his church are ultimately the "center" of history. Churchly efforts to penetrate the realities of which the

<hr>

*Vetera* 4, no. 1 (Winter 2006). For another response, see Levering, *Participatory Biblical Exegesis*, chap. 4.

54. Levering, *Participatory Biblical Exegesis*, chap. 1.

Bible speaks actually illuminate its meaning, as the spiritual sense bridges between past and present, between human and divine authorship.[55] We need not only "historical-critical research into the linear past" but also "participatory 'wisdom-practices' (liturgical, moral, and doctrinal)" that relate people to the God of whom Scripture speaks.[56]

This highlights "the relationship of truth to power," for modern commitment to "'objectivity' established by 'history' understood as *strictly* linear" stems from "the suspicion that ecclesial tradition and authority lead down a corruptive path in which the Church's authority threatens either human freedom or (by constricting God) divine freedom."[57] Catholics must resist that suspicion to some degree. Broadening out to our concerns in this book, we might ask whether, or, in what sense and to what extent, non-Catholic Christians can pursue biblical interpretation that fully participates in God's creating and redeeming activity, given the church's claims. For all church contexts, ecclesiology proves to be a crucial issue regarding theological interpretation of Scripture. Indeed, mainline Protestants can claim a complex hybrid of the "evangelical" and "catholic" concerns that we have examined.[58]

The doctrine of the church is vital for ("Eastern") Orthodox Christians as well. On the one hand, they claim an unbroken ecclesiastical relationship to the theological exegesis of the earliest Christians, and seek to perpetuate that tradition, in ways that parallel a Catholic approach. On the other hand, Orthodox churches have not undergone "modernity" or faced the challenges of appropriating Enlightenment thought in a manner similar to the other communions. Nor have Orthodox thinkers been very significant within

55. On this point, in addition to Levering, see David M. Williams, *Receiving the Bible in Faith: Historical and Theological Exegesis* (Washington, DC: Catholic University of America Press, 2004).

56. Levering, *Participatory Biblical Exegesis*, 14.

57. Levering, *Participatory Biblical Exegesis*, 15.

58. The ecumenical trend toward "evangelical-catholic" or "catholic-evangelical" theology manifests itself especially in the journal *Pro Ecclesia*. Of course, the extent to which these labels correlate with the evangelical Protestant and Roman Catholic traditions, as they actually are, is complex.

Western universities or intellectual life, for whatever reasons. When it comes to "theological interpretation of Scripture" as a movement, then, Orthodox scholars have not been significantly engaged to this point.[59] The existence of Orthodox biblical scholarship, however, highlights once again the hermeneutical importance of ecclesiology.

## The "Postmodern" Turn: Themes for Recovering Theological Exegesis

Indeed, much of the contemporary discussion labeled "postmodern" focuses on the role that communities play in interpretation. Postmodern terminology must appear in scare quotes because it is so difficult to define precisely; many resist the idea that accurate, careful definitions are possible.[60] Nevertheless, we can discern influences broadly fitting the category of "postmodern" that operate within the movement seeking theological interpretation of Scripture. We will explore these themes in greater detail in the chapters to follow, tracing an interpretative journey from the early church to our contemporary setting.

59. For a basic understanding of the Orthodox approach, see Theodore G. Stylianopoulos, "Orthodox Biblical Interpretation," *DTIB* 554–58; Thomas Hopko, "The Church, the Bible, and Dogmatic Theology," in Braaten and Jenson, *Reclaiming the Bible for the Church*, 107–18.

60. In my view, there is no such thing as postmodernism; rather, we face many postmodernisms—competing intellectual proposals for how to move past the "modern" age. Yet, in the West we do live in the midst of a transitional cultural condition or dominant mood that can be labeled "postmodernity," in which the adjective "postmodern" is constantly with us, often without the precise definition that the term can have in a context such as architecture. For a handy survey of various Christian approaches to this condition, see Myron B. Penner, ed., *Christianity and Postmodernism: Six Views* (Grand Rapids: Brazos, 2005). For a more advanced collection of essays on postmodernity and theology, see Kevin J. Vanhoozer, ed., *The Cambridge Companion to Postmodern Theology* (Cambridge: Cambridge University Press, 2003). For an example of reading postmodern thinkers more carefully than many Christians do, see Bruce Ellis Benson, *Graven Ideologies: Nietzsche, Derrida and Marion on Modern Idolatry* (Downers Grove, IL: InterVarsity, 2002).

First among "Catalysts and Common Themes" (part 1) is "Recovering the Past: Imitating Precritical Interpretation" (chap. 1). Now under suspicion is the modern idea that newer and bigger always mean better. For a long time, historical criticism of the Bible seemed to involve criticism of everything except itself. Postmodernity extends modern suspicion to include such criticism of critical methods. Realizing that the spiritual practices of precritical readers often nourished the church while biblical criticism sometimes withers it, many seek to recover the best of the past. Critical biblical scholarship offers much help and is here to stay, but perhaps a postcritical approach can incorporate the precritical spirit of interpreting Scripture as well.

Along with the spiritual practices of the ancient church came a commitment to the "Rule of Faith," a trinitarian summary of the structure of the Bible's story that is reflected in creeds such as the Apostles' and the Nicene. Because the doctrine of the Trinity is unbelievable for natural reason apart from divine revelation, it fell into modern disfavor, for the Enlightenment's drive toward universal reason required avoiding the scandalous particularity that accompanies belief in revelation. Thus, for understanding of the Bible to be scientific, one must practice neutral objectivity, supposedly bracketing any creedal commitments out of interpretation, most especially trinitarian creedal commitment, which "rational" people would find incredible. Postmodern critics have highlighted, however, the impossibility of such neutrality; whatever objectivity means, it must include the acknowledgment that our presuppositions are operative. Perhaps, in fact, Christian beliefs can be productive for biblical interpretation, helping us to see what the scriptural texts are really about. If that is the case, then Christian interpreters must discern not only how to read Scripture from a trinitarian perspective but also how other doctrines and broader theological interests might contribute to understanding the text—this is the focus of "Reading within the Rule(s): Interacting with Christian Doctrine" (chap. 2).

If we replace the ideal of neutral objectivity with constructively critical use of interpreters' presuppositions and perspectives, then Scripture study must not be the province of isolated individuals.

None of us can see comprehensively, with the God's-eye point of view that universal reason would require. Admitting this entails not only reading Scripture with Christian doctrine but also "Reading with Others: Listening to the Community of the Spirit" (chap. 3). Acknowledging our situatedness, suggested by various postmodern perspectives and taught by Scripture, allows biblical interpretation to be a spiritual practice, as noted above. The Holy Spirit's work in shaping our Christian communities can then be a factor in how we understand the scriptural texts. Differences exist among advocates of theological exegesis, however, regarding how that works. Hence, we must explore various appeals to virtue—another postmodern philosophical trend—especially in the wake of Alasdair MacIntyre's work.[61] Again people understand its significance for epistemology and ethics in various ways. Those who emphasize listening to the Holy Spirit in community often see Christian virtue as a hermeneutical norm—a criterion that assists us in evaluating possible interpretations. Others, by contrast, view virtue as an aim and an indispensable element of biblical interpretation while restricting the normative role to Scripture itself and the doctrines that emerge from it.[62]

These differences point to "Continuing Challenges" (part 2) faced by the movement toward theological interpretation of Scripture. Chapter 4 explores the nature of "biblical theology" and whether or not it can provide a bridge or serve as an interdisciplinary program between biblical exegesis and systematic theology. Chapter 5 broadens the focus to "general hermeneutics," asking whether or how we should apply theories of interpretation for any text to the special case of understanding Scripture. Chapter 6 recognizes that the recent conversation and emerging movement reflected in this book are overwhelmingly Western and academic. Thus, we

61. See especially Alasdair MacIntyre, *After Virtue: A Study in Moral Theory*, 2nd ed. (Notre Dame, IN: University of Notre Dame Press, 1984).

62. This way of putting the contrast comes from Kevin J. Vanhoozer, "Body-Piercing, the Natural Sense, and the Task of Theological Interpretation: A Hermeneutical Homily on John 19:34," *Ex Auditu* 16 (2000): 1–29. Interest in virtuous aims is "virtue-through-interpretation," with virtue-as-norm named "virtue-in-interpretation," by Stephen E. Fowl, "Virtue," *DTIB* 837–39.

must consider the implications of globalization as well as what it would mean to engage all the social locations in which God's people want to understand the Bible. Finally, the conclusion draws together the threads of our investigation regarding "theological interpretation of Scripture," briefly offering my own attempt at definition. Whatever else it means, theological exegesis deals with the Bible as a word about God and from God, and that makes this movement an exciting project! I hope you will join the quest.

# Part I

# CATALYSTS AND COMMON THEMES

# 1

## Recovering the Past

*Imitating Precritical Interpretation*

An interesting development in American religion since the 1990s has been the recovery of ancient Christian practices. At minimum, an aura of intrigue has developed around spiritual traditions such as the Celtic. Although some people consume these practices as part of have-it-your-way American spirituality, others are returning to the ancient church as a disciplined act of revolt against self-interested religious eclecticism.[1] Occasional Protestant conversions to Roman Catholicism or Eastern Orthodoxy fit within this pattern, as does the recent attraction of many to the movement known as the "emergent" church.[2] As these cultural trends have developed, academic theology has also paid increasing attention to the church fathers, including how these and other classic Christian thinkers interpreted the Bible.

Already such academic interest has trickled down to clergy and laity, with the launch of two commentary series devoted

---

1. See Colleen Carroll, *The New Faithful: Why Young Adults Are Embracing Christian Orthodoxy* (Chicago: Loyola, 2002).

2. For more information and attempts to define this "conversation," see Web sites such as http://www.emergentvillage.com; see also Robert E. Webber, ed., *Listening to the Beliefs of Emerging Churches* (Grand Rapids: Zondervan, 2007).

to patristic biblical exegesis: The Church's Bible (Eerdmans) and the Ancient Christian Commentary on Scripture (InterVarsity). Moreover, the latter will have a companion series on the Protestant Reformation, which is anticipated to be underway soon. Another relevant initiative comes in the Brazos Theological Commentary on the Bible, a projected forty-volume series for a churchly audience in which the commentaries will come from theologians rather than biblical scholars. The series "presupposes that the doctrinal tradition of the church can serve as a living and reliable basis for exegesis." This tradition, more specifically, is that surrounding the Nicene Creed, and the series promotes "intratextual analysis" as its key "method," along with drawing upon "the liturgical practices and spiritual disciplines of the church as a secondary dimension of the canonical context for exegesis of scriptural texts." Such an approach can lead to various senses of Scripture, including "allegorical" readings, and requires that contributors "engage the history of exegesis, not in order to provide readers with a summary of past interpretation, but in order to shape exegetical judgments in conversation with the tradition."[3]

In light of these contemporary developments, the present chapter launches our exploration of themes regarding theological interpretation of Scripture with the beginning of the church's post–New Testament story. For many, recovering the most significant aspects of theological exegesis requires imitation of precritical Christian exegetes. David Steinmetz presents the claim forcefully:

3. From a document introducing the series, which I have received as a contributor. The first volume of the Brazos series is Jaroslav Pelikan, *Acts*, Brazos Theological Commentary on the Bible (Grand Rapids: Brazos, 2005). Exemplifying some of the larger trends pointed out above, Pelikan converted from Lutheranism to Eastern Orthodoxy fairly late in life. For the story of several Protestant theologians who have recently converted to Roman Catholicism, see Jason Byassee, "Going Catholic: Six Journeys to Rome," *Christian Century* 123, no. 17 (August 22, 2006): 18–23. One of these theologians, R. R. Reno, explained his decision in "Out of the Ruins," *First Things* 150 (February 2005): 11–16. Reno is particularly significant here because he is the primary editor of the Brazos commentary series and has written extensively on patristic and theological exegesis (as discussed below).

How was a French parish priest in 1150 to understand Psalm 137, which bemoans captivity in Babylon, makes rude remarks about Edomites, expresses an ineradicable longing for a glimpse of Jerusalem, and pronounces a blessing on anyone who avenges the destruction of the Temple by dashing Babylonian children against a rock? The priest lives in Concale, not Babylon, has no personal quarrel with Edomites, cherishes no ambitions to visit Jerusalem (though he might fancy a holiday in Paris), and is expressly forbidden by Jesus to avenge himself on his enemies. . . . Unless Psalm 137 has more than one possible meaning, it cannot be used as a prayer by the Church and must be rejected as a lament belonging exclusively to the piety of ancient Israel.[4]

In this almost audacious example all the major aspects of the appeal of precritical exegesis surface: (1) reading religiously, (2) with reference to Christ and (3) for certain kinds of application to Christian practice, (4) in light of the canonical story operating as a hermeneutical criterion. For we see connections between Scripture and concern for prayer, between the psalm and Jesus' teaching about love for enemies, as well as between the psalm back then for Israel and what it could mean for proper Christian piety, and these connections result in challenges for reading the Bible as one story, keeping together Israel's Scriptures and the church of Jesus Christ. Yet commitment to one such "Rule of Faith" is not set aside, as we will explore at greater length in the next chapter, on doctrine. In the meantime, the first three dimensions of precritical theological interpretation concern us here.

## Reading as Piety

As we begin, it is important to acknowledge that precritical exegesis was not monolithic. Covering more than a thousand years, the term "precritical" designates a period involving numerous interpreters from various locations, with many differences in

4. David C. Steinmetz, "The Superiority of Pre-Critical Exegesis," in *The Theological Interpretation of Scripture: Classic and Contemporary Readings*, ed. Stephen E. Fowl (Oxford: Blackwell, 1997), 28.

practice and some significant disagreements about interpretative theory. It is also important to recognize that the story of precritical exegesis was not static but rather contained development, some of which resulted in aspects of a more modern, critical approach. Therefore, to use the concept "precritical" reflects our location at a particular stage in the history of the modern West: we are willing to subsume all the premodern variety under this concept because it designates a few features shared by classic interpreters that we sense we lack.

Scholars organize lists of these features along slightly different lines, but common themes surface quickly in a few examples. Brian Daley portrays patristic exegesis as involving (1) conviction of the present reality of God; (2) presumption of a unified narrative (from the Bible and applied to the Bible); (3) the Rule of Faith; (4) Scripture treated as diverse yet a unified whole; (5) scriptural texts treated as having their own "historical" meaning yet "meant for us"; (6) the scriptural text as mystery.[5] According to Robert Louis Wilken, likewise, early Christians read Scripture as "our wisdom," as "a book about Christ" and therefore "a single story." This led to "the inevitability of allegory" and "seeing oneself in what is written."[6] Scott Hahn, another writer whose particular emphasis is the liturgical setting and focus of ancient approaches to Scripture, summarizes those approaches with three terms: "economy," "typology," and "mystagogy" (study of sacramental mysteries). Again, focus lies on the saving acts of God in dealing with creation. This story, centered on Christ, makes possible and even necessary the reading of the Bible as one book by way of figural connections between earlier and later texts, especially Old and New Testament texts. And the point is not simply to learn about the events that connect these passages but rather to be caught up in them: the texts connect us to the saving

5. Brian E. Daley, "Is Patristic Exegesis Still Usable? Reflections on Early Christian Interpretation of the Psalms," *Communio* 29 (Spring 2002): 194–204.

6. Robert Louis Wilken, *The Spirit of Early Christian Thought: Seeking the Face of God* (New Haven: Yale University Press, 2003), chap. 3, "The Face of God for Now," 50–79.

events or "mysteries," in particular through participation in the sacramental life of the church.[7]

Stressing this liturgical dimension helps us once again to see that reading Scripture is traditionally a religious activity, a dimension of piety. As the word "religious" suggests, this is how adherents of various world religions tend to read their sacred texts.[8] But of course the Christian liturgy introduces distinctive elements as well. Daley highlights that "early Christian exegetes often use words that strike us as strangely unscientific when justifying their interpretations of particular texts, arguing that one or another way of interpreting a disputed passage is more 'reverent' (*eusebes*) or more 'appropriate to God' (*theoprepres*) than another—terms which more frequently were associated with doctrinal orthodoxy."[9] Ellen Charry suggests that, in fact, doctrinal orthodoxy itself—regarding the identity of God as revealed in Jesus Christ—developed through the recognition of interpretations that promoted Christian virtue.[10] This primacy of liturgical context and pastoral concerns reflects another reality, noticed by Jaroslav Pelikan:

> During the years 100 to 600, most theologians were bishops; from 600 to 1500 in the West, they were monks; since 1500, they have been university professors. Gregory I, who died in 604, was a bishop who had been a monk; Martin Luther, who died in 1546, was a monk who became a university professor. Each of these life styles has left its mark on the job description of the theologian, but also on

7. Scott Hahn, *Letter and Spirit: From Written Text to Living Word in the Liturgy* (New York: Doubleday, 2005), chap. 2, "Defining Terms," 13–32.

8. See Paul J. Griffiths, *Religious Reading: The Place of Reading in the Practice of Religion* (Oxford: Oxford University Press, 1999). Note, however, his cautions regarding the term "religion" in Paul J. Griffiths, "Religion," *DTIB* 672–75.

9. Daley, "Is Patristic Exegesis Still Usable?" 202.

10. Ellen T. Charry, *By the Renewing of Your Minds: The Pastoral Function of Christian Doctrine* (Oxford: Oxford University Press, 1997). See the summary of her argument on this point in Daniel J. Treier, "Let the Dead Heal Us," *Books & Culture* 7, no. 6 (November–December 2001): 26–27.

the way doctrine has continued to develop back and forth between believing, teaching, and confessing.[11]

It is important to remember that, due to factors such as illiteracy and (at times) clericalism, religious reading of the Bible as Scripture mostly involved church leaders, not the common layperson.

Nevertheless, the criteria for judging interpretations were not what we know today as "critical," because the assumptions and goals of the theological enterprise were very different. Modern biblical interpretation is, according to John J. O'Keefe and R. R. Reno, dominated by "a referential theory of meaning," which "encourage[s] us to read out of the text and toward the true subject matter to which it seeks to refer."[12] Our gaze moves away from the signs and words of the Bible itself. By contrast, however, Scripture did not direct the church fathers elsewhere but rather absorbed their attention. And this leads to an interesting aspect of their approach that Reno has called "intensive" reading, "a broad category that ranges from philological analysis that is indistinguishable from aspects of modern biblical study to word associations that are utterly alien to the critical sensibilities of contemporary readers . . . an almost sensual attempt to engage the words of scripture."[13] For intensive readers, "Exegesis was a spiritual discipline, a journey through the literality of scripture in which one is not only to dwell in the clear teachings of Jesus or the great theological pronouncements of Paul but by the very ambition of a total reading of scripture one is led through the thickets and brambles of seeming contradiction, blank oceans and dry deserts of obscure and uncertain material."[14]

11. Jaroslav Pelikan, *The Christian Tradition: A History of the Development of Doctrine*, vol. 1, *The Emergence of the Catholic Tradition (100–600)* (Chicago: University of Chicago Press, 1971), 5.

12. John J. O'Keefe and R. R. Reno, *Sanctified Vision: An Introduction to Early Christian Interpretation of the Bible* (Baltimore: Johns Hopkins University Press, 2005), 9.

13. O'Keefe and Reno, *Sanctified Vision*, 19. For Reno's early thoughts on this concept, see Russell Reno, "'You Who Were Far Off Have Been Brought Near': Reflections on Theological Exegesis," *Ex Auditu* 16 (2000): 169–82.

14. O'Keefe and Reno, *Sanctified Vision*, 44.

Sometimes the resulting word associations might seem playful, but they reflect the belief that God has structured Scripture in order to be endlessly profound and spiritually challenging as well. The process of encountering the depths in the text is transformative in and of itself, before one even secures the content of one or more interpretations, any number of which might be accepted in certain circumstances. Precritical readers hypothesized theologically about potential readings, and these readings passed the test if they showed how orthodoxy illuminated the mysteries of the biblical text and the God to whom it points. The concern was not so much to defend theological reading strategies as to deploy them and see how well they worked.[15] Regarding the associative dimension of the precritical, religious approach in particular, "By and large, modern readers distrust the ways in which words are easily connected simply on the basis of verbal echoes and patterns,"[16] yet this simply points us toward assessment of the typological and allegorical approaches by which classic interpreters found Christ throughout the Bible.

## Reading about Christ

It is a widely held consensus that "typological interpretation is rightly viewed as the most important interpretive strategy for early Christianity. Without typology it is difficult to imagine patristic theology and the concept of Christian orthodoxy it defined and supported as existing at all."[17] A "type" deals with figures or patterns, and in Scripture it is a person, institution, or event prefiguring a later fulfillment in God's plan. The most familiar examples are New Testament patterns of connecting something from the Old Testament with fulfillment in Jesus and the church, such as elements of Israel's story in 1 Corinthians 10 as a type for sacraments versus idolatry, or the Noahic flood as a type for

15. See, e.g., O'Keefe and Reno, *Sanctified Vision*, 60–61.
16. O'Keefe and Reno, *Sanctified Vision*, 63.
17. O'Keefe and Reno, *Sanctified Vision*, 69.

baptism in 1 Peter 3.[18] These New Testament examples built upon Old Testament instances of innerbiblical exegesis and upon Israel's convictions about their God acting consistently in directing history to accomplish a redemptive purpose. These examples also became precedents for early Christian interpretation of Scripture.

Irenaeus and other orthodox fathers soon had to resist gnostic forms of dualism that, in addition to privileging the immaterial or spiritual over the material realm, rejected the Old Testament and even portions of the New Testament. Patristic interpreters appealed to a "Rule of Faith" that held together the Testaments: the story of Israel's God found its extension and fulfillment in the revelation of Jesus Christ. Origen, a complex and important figure, sought to maintain the importance of the literal, historical sense throughout the Bible. However, influenced by aspects of Greek dualism and literary theory as well as religious priorities, he freely pursued a "spiritual" sense in the text by means of allegorical interpretation. Others continued in this practice, though not always with the same degree or type of allegorizing—notably Augustine, whose *On Christian Teaching* influenced Christian pedagogy, theology, and exegetical practice throughout the Middle Ages.

For a while, debate ensued between the Alexandrian school, influenced by Origen, and theologians from Antioch who put more emphasis on the humanity of Jesus relative to the divine Christ, and therefore on the literal sense. The Antiochenes would admit that allegorical terminology appears in the Bible, specifically amid Paul's appeal to Sarah and Hagar in Galatians 4, but they distinguished between allegory and the forms of spiritual reading that they found acceptable, which today are associated with "typology." Origen's form of allegorizing seemed fanciful to the detriment of the historical sense.[19] In the end, though, Augustine and others

---

18. For a brief overview of typology as well as key bibliographical resources, see Daniel J. Treier, "Typology," *DTIB* 823–27.

19. Recent scholarship emphasizes the closeness of Alexandria and Antioch, rejecting the earlier distinctions between them and, as a result, strong distinctions between typology and allegory. Indeed, it is important that Antiochene exegetes still read the biblical text spiritually. But to suggest that there was no distinction

helped to perpetuate a spiritual approach to interpretation that clearly incorporated forms of allegory.

In the later Middle Ages thinkers such as Thomas Aquinas placed increasing emphasis on the literal sense, along with the rise of new grammatical precision through Renaissance humanism. As these trends fed into the Protestant Reformation, controversy over allegorical interpretation revived. The modern university rejected church authority much more thoroughly than the Reformation ever did, and Enlightenment insistence upon a certain ideal of objectivity put spiritual interpretation into further intellectual disfavor. In particular, modern biblical scholarship claims to find fundamental disunity between the Old and New Testaments, and even among the theologies (plural) within them. Thus, many critical scholars reject precritical Christian claims regarding Jesus Christ as the key to all the Scriptures.

Some conservative Christians have reacted to this problem of scriptural unity with apologetics based on direct messianic prophecies from the Old Testament. However much the Old Testament anticipates the Messiah, many of these attempts are unconvincing; in any case, messianic prophecies are insufficient to address the various questions of biblical diversity put forward by contemporary scholars. Meanwhile, certain forms of spiritual interpretation involving "typologies" never completely died out among Protestants, as older devotional commentaries on biblical books such as Joshua demonstrate. Recently, a number of scholars have begun to pursue and defend a more nuanced understanding of typology in order to hold together the Testaments. Conservatives tend to reject allegory while defending typology as a way of respecting salvation history. Others in this group see no real difference between the two ap-

---

seems insulting to the parties involved in the ancient disputes. It appears that the differences lay in the degree rather than the kind of nonliteral interpretation pursued. For further reflections on this point, see Daniel J. Treier, "The Superiority of Pre-Critical Exegesis? *Sic et Non*," *Trinity Journal* 24 (2003): 80–81, 94–97. For a more comprehensive resource on the subject of this chapter, see Charles Kannengiesser, ed., *Handbook of Patristic Exegesis: The Bible in Ancient Christianity* (Leiden: Brill, 2006).

proaches, or they remain open to certain forms of allegory, perhaps as part of a broader category called "figural reading."[20]

We keep circling back to the difficulty of defining these christo-centric reading strategies. It is important to admit that "for all early Christian interpreters, the exegetical arguments are cumulative" rather than necessarily convincing in isolation one by one.[21] Association is key: words of one passage lead to another, supported by another, connected to another, and so forth. The connections are concrete rather than abstract; for example, "The fathers focused the typological reading of Exodus on developing a link, not between Exodus (discrete sequence) and New Life (theological abstraction), but between the Exodus narrative and the practice of baptism."[22] Further, "Allegory and typology are part of the same family of reading strategies, often referred to by the fathers as 'spiritual,' that seek to interpret the scriptures in terms of the divine economy. The difference lies in the amount of work the reader must put into the interpretation."[23] As a consequence, O'Keefe and Reno offer the interesting idea that figuration is a constant feature of daily life in general: we use analogies all the time. Thus, it is not really the figural methodology to which modern people object but rather the divine economy with which the church fathers spiritually connected us.[24]

Allegory stems from the concept of otherness, in which an external symbolic element becomes the key for interpretation. Of course, therefore, allegory often seems to read into or against the text, and this might even be true for typology if we force individual biblical passages into isolation from each other. But if we read the Bible canonically as Scripture, divinely and not just humanly authored, to what extent is it fair to say that teaching from another passage is "external" when we read a biblical text? Instead, typology and allegory actually lie on a continuum, with the issue being

20. Again, for further discussion, see Treier, "Typology."
21. O'Keefe and Reno, *Sanctified Vision*, 76.
22. O'Keefe and Reno, *Sanctified Vision*, 79.
23. O'Keefe and Reno, *Sanctified Vision*, 90.
24. See, e.g., O'Keefe and Reno, *Sanctified Vision*, 109.

what types of external relationships help to interpret a particular passage faithfully.

Sometimes patristic allegory makes spiritual sense out of apparent nonsense, as in approaches from Origen and Augustine to elements of the early chapters in Genesis that concerned them. On other occasions allegory functionally negates the literal sense and turns us toward something else, as perhaps in approaches to Song of Songs or troubling war narratives in Joshua. These types of allegory raise serious questions regarding how to understand the authority of the biblical text along with claims to maintain the integrity of the literal, historical sense. However, many allegorical readings "do not question or doubt the cogency of the literal sense" but instead press it forward "to draw out additional meaning."[25] For Frances Young, then, the real distinction between typology and allegory ought to be reformulated along the lines of "iconic" versus "symbolic" mimesis, which deals with representation of the world considered "real." Antiochene and Protestant objections to allegory concern treating words in biblical texts merely as symbols standing in place of and pointing to something else—a more ultimate reality that seems arbitrarily determined. Yet connections between biblical words and spiritual entities, or between the words of one text and the words of another, can instead be iconic, representing a reality in such a way as to direct our attention toward it for the sake of participation. In this case, there is narrative coherence between type and antitype or between sign and thing.[26] Young seems to recognize that even if Antiochene and Protestant interpreters engaged in spiritual reading, and the lines between typology and allegory are blurry, still there remains some distinction between approaches that import what is alien to the words or treat the historical sense arbitrarily and those that actually extend the literal sense to new reference points.

Such genuine connections may not always be convincing to those without eyes of faith. And, to be sure, Christians will disagree

25. O'Keefe and Reno, *Sanctified Vision*, 92.

26. See Frances M. Young, *Biblical Exegesis and the Formation of Christian Culture* (Cambridge: Cambridge University Press, 1997), especially 2, 162.

among themselves about the narrative coherence of particular figural readings. Without the practice, however, we cannot read Scripture religiously as a unified canon. Moreover, it seems odd to suggest that we can receive the doctrines of the apostles without accepting the legitimacy of the scriptural hermeneutics by which they developed and defended that teaching.[27] How to handle the legitimacy of typological and/or allegorical interpretation becomes a major concern for theological interpretation of Scripture.

Perhaps it would be fitting to close this section with an example. Some once read the number of Abraham's servants—318 (Gen. 14:14)—in such a way that it pointed to Christ.[28] On the arbitrariness of this, we might think, most theological interpreters today could agree. What, then, about Rahab's scarlet cord? Does it point to the blood of Christ, as Clement of Rome suggested, and if so, how?[29] Many critical scholars might assert that there is no connection at all between the two, for the Old Testament writer could not have had the later event in mind. By contrast, many precritical

27. This is, admittedly, a matter of huge debate. A famous advocate of the view that we need not and should not follow the apostolic practices of interpretation is Richard N. Longenecker, *Biblical Exegesis in the Apostolic Period*, 2nd ed. (Grand Rapids: Eerdmans, 1999). This raises the question of how much the apostolic doctrine stemmed from borrowing Jewish and/or Hellenistic exegetical rules (such as *gezerah shawah*, having to do with word association), which we might not want to approve simply on this basis, as opposed to a reading strategy justified by underlying theological premises. In any case, though, without adopting all of the surrounding culture's exegetical approaches, it still seems difficult to ferret out the doctrine from the practice and leave the latter entirely behind. For a collection of prominent essays in biblical studies on this question, see G. K. Beale, ed., *The Right Doctrine from the Wrong Texts? Essays on the Use of the Old Testament in the New* (Grand Rapids: Baker Academic, 1994).

28. *Epistle of Barnabas* 9:8 (see *Apostolic Fathers*, trans. Kirsopp Lake, vol. 1, Loeb Classical Library [Cambridge, MA: Harvard University Press, 1998], 373). See also Ambrose in Mark Sheridan, ed., *Genesis 12–50*, Ancient Christian Commentary on Scripture, Old Testament 2 (Downers Grove, IL: InterVarsity, 2002), 23.

29. See *1 Clement* 12:7: "And they proceeded to give her a sign, that she should hang out a scarlet thread from her house, foreshowing that all who believe and hope in God shall have redemption through the blood of the Lord" (in Lake, *Apostolic Fathers*, 29).

interpreters would find such an association clearly willed by the divine Author. Is the color of the cord really ingredient to the story in such a way that we should connect it to Christ? If a mental association based on scarlet is arbitrary, merely symbolic in itself, does that mean that we cannot read the text in a way that prefigures Christ? Or might it point us toward a deeper narrative connection, coherence that is more inherent within the story? In that case, we might consider how the divinely appointed object served as the sign and means of God's deliverance, typifying how God rescues people and brings them into promised blessing.

### Reading for Christian Practice: The Fourfold Sense of Scripture

Such a reading could offer spiritual nourishment without simply being a creation of our own cleverness or heroic piety. This Christ-centered dimension of classical theological interpretation, though, was only one aspect of the "fourfold sense" that developed from Augustine, Gregory, and others. Steinmetz suggests that the three nonliteral senses correlate with the three theological virtues: "The allegorical sense taught about the Church and what it should believe, and so it corresponded to the virtue of faith. The tropological sense taught about individuals and what they should do, and so it corresponded to the virtue of love. The anagogical sense pointed to the future and wakened expectation, and so it corresponded to the virtue of hope."[30] For Augustine, the special focus is charity: the double love of God and neighbor serves as the criterion of proper theological understanding. We should seek the verbal sense of the text, but charity is the ultimate goal, and if we reach such an understanding without the ideal historical interpretation of the words, there is no ultimate harm.[31] As we have just seen, these virtues are, of course, centered on Christ as the key to Scripture. In his classic

30. Steinmetz, "Superiority of Pre-Critical Exegesis," 29.

31. In particular, see Augustine, *On Christian Teaching*, trans. R. P. H. Green (Oxford: Oxford University Press, 1997), I.86–88, III.54 (for a critical edition, see *De doctrina Christiana*, ed. J. Martin, Corpus Christianorum: Series latina 32 [Turnhout: Brepols, 1982]). For further reflections on hermeneutics of charity,

and winsome portrayal of precritical exegesis, Henri de Lubac shows that "the allegorical sense is in any case for everyone *the Christian sense of Scripture*," tied to the miracle of conversion.[32] From John 2 comes a favorite image: in Christ, the water of the letter is changed into the wine of the Spirit.[33]

Even so, precritical interpreters did not approach the Bible without various limits. For the most part, they insisted that spiritual readings must be consistent with the literal sense. In the next chapter we will examine another form of constraint—the Rule of Faith—as well as the contribution of Christian doctrine more broadly. Historical perspective reminds us further that Thomas Aquinas and others in the later Middle Ages placed greater emphasis on the verbal sense, maintaining ever more carefully that the spiritual senses had to convey truth taught literally somewhere else in Scripture, and that one could derive doctrine only from the literal.[34] While everyone supported the monastic practice of *lectio divina* (contemplative, prayerful "divine reading") to some degree, the growing medieval emphasis on the moral sense and the development of a kind of monastic "spiritual hothouse culture" did not please all. Heroes such as Bernard seemed to "follow the Spirit" far beyond the text, and such a spiritual aristocracy may not have been entirely healthy.[35] Precritical interpreters would never have conceded that grammatical and historical matters exhaust interpretation, but neither did they show any tendency to reject out of hand the general hermeneutical tools of their day; instead, they critically appropriated them.

---

see Alan Jacobs, *A Theology of Reading: The Hermeneutics of Love* (Boulder, CO: Westview, 2001); "Love," *DTIB* 465–67.

32. Henri de Lubac, *Medieval Exegesis: The Four Senses of Scripture*, vol. 2, trans. E. M. Macierowski (Grand Rapids: Eerdmans, 2000), 123–24.

33. de Lubac, *Medieval Exegesis*, 2:253.

34. See Thomas Aquinas, *Summa Theologica* 1a.1.10, ad. 1. For secondary literature on Thomas and theological exegesis, see Thomas G. Weinandy, Daniel A. Keating, and John P. Yocum, eds., *Aquinas on Scripture: An Introduction to His Biblical Commentaries* (London: T&T Clark International, 2005). In particular, see the introduction by Nicholas M. Healy.

35. On this, see especially de Lubac, *Medieval Exegesis*, 2:150–53, 176.

Therefore, in light of these nuances, one might think of the fourfold sense of Scripture as a theological effort to guide or even restrain "application" of the Bible more than the contemporary "one interpretation, many applications" paradigm can do. When we assess the significance of premodern exegesis for today, we must of course consider not only the patristic and medieval periods but also the extent to which the Protestant Reformers, even with their formal rejection of allegorical interpretation, qualify as precritical. John Calvin's approach, for example, can be seen as parallel to the fourfold sense in some ways,[36] although he "did not devote much, if any, attention to the traditional distinction between letter and spirit."[37] Martin Luther similarly rejected allegorizing in theory but read spiritually in practice. Elements of the Reformation surely fit into the flow of history toward modernity, but it would be unwise to characterize early Protestant exegesis simply as protomodern.

In any case, we must furthermore reflect upon the ways in which we cannot and should not seek to turn back the clock. Literary and historical tools should not be spurned but rather used—to illuminate rather than to speculate.[38] Christian commitment to

36. According to Richard Muller, "the 'literal' meaning of the text, for Calvin, held a message concerning what Christians ought to believe, what Christians ought to do, and what Christians ought to hope for. This paradigm seems suspiciously familiar . . . *credenda*, *agenda*, and *speranda*" ("Biblical Interpretation in the Era of the Reformation: The View from the Middle Ages," in *Biblical Interpretation in the Era of the Reformation*, ed. Richard A. Muller and John L. Thompson [Grand Rapids: Eerdmans, 1996], 11). Calvin seems to function as the ideal precritical reader, paradigmatic of sophisticated "figural reading," in the eyes of Hans W. Frei, *The Eclipse of Biblical Narrative: A Study in Eighteenth and Nineteenth Century Hermeneutics* (New Haven: Yale University Press, 1974).

37. David C. Steinmetz, "John Calvin as an Interpreter of the Bible," in *Calvin and the Bible*, ed. Donald K. McKim (Cambridge: Cambridge University Press, 2006), 283.

38. This is consistent with the practice of precritical interpreters relative to their day, as noted by Richard A. Muller and John L. Thompson, "The Significance of Precritical Exegesis: Retrospect and Prospect," in Muller and Thompson, *Biblical Interpretation in the Era of the Reformation*, 345. It should also be noted that premodern interpretation often revolved around the Latin Vulgate rather than texts in the original Greek and Hebrew. This affected the grammatical considerations with which many could operate.

the divine economy narrated in the Rule of Faith should not be confused with a somewhat Platonic orientation regarding signs and things; earthly realities have their own dignity and integrity rather than simply serving as pointers to the heavenly or something more ultimate.[39] As a result, to speak more practically, many premodern challenges that were handled with interpretations once seen as "allegorical" can today fit under categories such as "metaphor" or "figurative" language.[40] Moreover, the kind of spiritual reading that was possible only for an elite few with various forms of theological leadership in the premodern church ought not simplistically become democratized for each and every contemporary Bible reader. We must ponder the implications of this for both American and non-Western contexts.

Once those qualifications have been made, however, we should not ignore the virtues of precritical biblical interpretation. From the ancient masters we can recover a way of integrating Scripture study with piety that has been virtually lost in much of late modern Western culture.[41] We can also learn to read the Bible as Christ-centered in a way that makes possible spiritual participation in the realities of which Scripture speaks. Moreover, we can imitate reading for application with theological, not just narrowly exegetical, guidance and restraint. As George Lindbeck notes, "Traditionally expressed, one could perhaps say that typological tropology or tropological typology was the chief interpretative

39. On the other hand, opposition between "figural" and "literal" should not be overdone, since the figural classically involved the extension of the literal sense to the canonical level. Seeing the two as opposites occurred newly in the modern period, as noted by Frei, *Eclipse*, 7.

40. William Tyndale is an important figure in the shift toward such a broadening of the "literal sense" to include figurative language, according to G. R. Evans, *The Language and Logic of the Bible: The Road to Reformation* (Cambridge: Cambridge University Press, 1985), 49. Thomas had a similarly broad definition of "literal," however, according to Healy, introduction to Weinandy, Keating, and Yocum, *Aquinas on Scripture*, 16.

41. See Griffiths, *Religious Reading*; Eugene H. Peterson, "Eat This Book: The Holy Community at Table with the Holy Scripture," *Theology Today* 56, no. 1 (1999): 5–17; Robert W. Jenson, "The Religious Power of Scripture," *Scottish Journal of Theology* 52, no. 1 (1999): 89–105.

strategy for making the Bible contemporary, for absorbing one's own world into the world of the text."[42] Relearning such an approach, instead of making analogical applications between the Bible and today at the whim of extrabiblical principles, seems vital for ecumenical endeavors and authentically biblical spirituality.[43] Clearly, not all precritical exegesis is exemplary, but the ancients do have much to teach us about reading the Bible ultimately as one book from one Author. They remind us that critically oriented interpretation, however important, is not the primary context within which people encounter the Bible. So we must heed Daley's call for "a more positive perception of early Christian exegesis . . . as not merely 'pre-critical' but as thoroughly and—in many cases, at least—successfully *theological*."[44] If nothing else, earlier Christian exegetes demonstrate the treasures that await those who know Scripture deeply[45] and who do not make the modern assumption that "misunderstanding and alienation constitute the normal state of affairs in hermeneutics."[46] Historical distance can sometimes be a problem, yet spiritual participation in the divine realities of the biblical text can turn historical development into an opportunity for creatively faithful understanding on the part of the church over time.

42. George A. Lindbeck, "Postcritical Canonical Interpretation: Three Modes of Retrieval," in *Theological Exegesis: Essays in Honor of Brevard S. Childs*, ed. Christopher Seitz and Kathryn Greene-McCreight (Grand Rapids: Eerdmans, 1998), 31.

43. Lindbeck, "Postcritical Canonical Interpretation," 38–39.

44. Daley, "Is Patristic Exegesis Still Usable?" 214 (italics in original).

45. As O'Keefe and Reno note, "The fathers have a great deal of the Bible memorized" (*Sanctified Vision*, 122).

46. Roger Lundin, "Interpreting Orphans: Hermeneutics in the Cartesian Tradition," in *The Promise of Hermeneutics*, ed. Roger Lundin, Clarence Walhout, and Anthony C. Thiselton (Grand Rapids: Eerdmans, 1999), 41.

# 2

# Reading within the Rule(s)

*Interacting with Christian Doctrine*

The preceding chapter outlined "precritical exegesis" as one of the ways in which theological interpretation departs from business as usual in biblical studies. Among the themes that surfaced in defining a precritical approach is the Rule of Faith, a basic summary of the biblical story centered on identifying God to be triune—Father, Son, and Holy Spirit. As we explore in this chapter, the *Regula Fidei* took tangible shape in the ecumenical creeds and directed the church's interpretation of Scripture for centuries. A return to such a Rule may involve not only accepting its explicit boundaries but also approaching the Bible with a wider set of doctrinal interests and commitments.

## The Patristic Consensus: Identifying the God of the Bible

The Rule of Faith refers, in the writings of Irenaeus, Tertullian, and other ante-Nicene fathers, to "the sum content of apostolic teaching," formulated as "a confession of faith for public use in worship, in particular for use in baptism."[1] Probably it grew out of the shortest baptismal formula from early Christianity, "Jesus is Lord," which we see in the New Testament itself (Rom. 10:9–10; 1 Cor. 12:3). The Rule generally "was not written down, other than . . . for the purpose of its defense, and was not revealed until baptism."[2] Thus the wording often differs when it comes to particulars, but the basic content of the Rule can be seen in the Nicene Creed or the Apostles' Creed, the latter reading,

> I believe in God the Father Almighty, Maker of heaven and earth,
> And in Jesus Christ his only Son our Lord; who was conceived by the Holy Ghost, born of the Virgin Mary, suffered under Pontius Pilate, was crucified, dead, and buried; he descended into hell; the third day he rose again from the dead; he ascended into heaven, and sitteth on the right hand of God the Father Almighty; from thence he shall come to judge the quick and the dead.
> I believe in the Holy Ghost; the holy catholic Church; the communion of saints; the forgiveness of sins; the resurrection of the body; and the life everlasting. Amen.[3]

### Classic Figures

Irenaeus provides the classic illustration of the Rule's function: imagine a mosaic with tiles that can be assembled to picture a king or a dog. Such a mosaic, in antiquity, required a key—Greek, *hypothesis*—to indicate how the tiles should be arranged upon receipt. According to Irenaeus, the Rule of Faith serves as the *hypothesis* for Christian reading of Scripture. Heretics such as the gnostics would arrange the verses of the Bible in a manner that set the New Testament against the Old Testament, and the God revealed in Jesus Christ against the God of Israel, thus, by analogy, making the mosaic resemble a dog or fox. Orthodox readers,

---

1. Kathryn Greene-McCreight, "Rule of Faith," *DTIB* 703. See also Paul M. Blowers, "The *Regula Fidei* and the Narrative Character of Early Christian Faith," *Pro Ecclesia* 6, no. 2 (Spring 1997): 199–228.

2. Greene-McCreight, "Rule of Faith," 703.

3. Office of the General Assembly, *The Book of Confessions* (Louisville: Presbyterian Publishing Company, 2002), 7.

rather than taking apart the Bible's bits and pieces according to whim, would follow the church's *hypothesis* in such a way that Scripture tells one story. The true mosaic thus pictures the king, Jesus Christ.[4]

Church fathers acknowledged that various readings of the Bible were possible to some degree. Even today we have to address the inevitable plurality that ensues, especially as some contemporary scholars trumpet anew the early "gnostic" viewpoints and our culture magnifies fascination with them through works such as *The Da Vinci Code*.[5] The Rule of Faith enabled the church to identify, preserve, and pass on a coherent doctrine of God in the face of competing accounts of Christian identity. The tradition embodied in the Rule of Faith came ultimately from the apostles, who handed down a basic approach to the Scriptures from Jesus to their successors.

Yet the plurality of potential interpretations did not entail the equal legitimacy of all the various claims, as if the church simply appealed to tradition because the Bible was defenseless. Instead, the early Christians saw the Rule of Faith as a form of moral restraint, against human tendencies to twist the Scriptures in self-interested ways. Furthermore, the Rule not only defines and defends parameters for proper interpretation but also derives from Scripture itself. While the "literal sense" of the Bible is not simply or completely transparent, the words of the text restrain and guide the churchly reader, ultimately telling the story of the Triune God.

### Current Followers

Among "postliberal" theologians, portraits of doctrine have begun to appear from the perspective of the Rule of Faith, with the creed(s) as an organizing principle.[6] Meanwhile, in terms of

4. See Irenaeus, *Against Heresies* I.8.1 (for a critical edition, see *Libros Quinque Adversus Haereses*, ed. W. W. Harvey, 2 vols. [Cambridge: Academy, 1857]).

5. For an overview of gnosticism and its significance for theological interpretation of Scripture, see Nicholas Perrin, "Gnosticism," *DTIB* 256–58.

6. See, e.g., Ephraim Radner and George Sumner, eds., *The Rule of Faith: Scripture, Canon, and Creed in a Critical Age* (Harrisburg, PA: Morehouse, 1998);

the Rule's hermeneutical application, Kathryn Greene-McCreight has provided one of the most significant recent studies. Examining how Augustine, Calvin, and Barth read Genesis 1–3, she demonstrates that their pursuit of the text's "plain sense" did not imply belief in "single meaning" according to the modern sense of that concept: "One cannot conclude that the plain sense of scripture is an objective, static 'given' to be mined from the text like a diamond from the river bed."[7] In Barth, for example, "verbal sense" and "Ruled reading," though conceptually distinct, are impossible to pull apart. Far from leading to undue constraint, then, reading with the Rule of Faith elicits creative interpretation— within limits.[8] These limits stem in part from the fact that divine authorship must have some relationship to the verbal features and even human intentionality of the biblical text. Thus verbal sense and Ruled reading tend to "exert a counter-pressure" in relation to each other.[9]

A contemporary example supporting such Ruled reading, widely cited among theologians, comes from David Yeago. Using Philippians 2:6–11 as a test case, he contends that "the ancient theologians were right to hold that the Nicene *homoousion* [the Son is "of one being" with the Father] is neither imposed *on* the New Testament texts, nor distantly deduced *from* the texts, but, rather, describes a pattern of judgments present *in* the texts, in the texture of scriptural discourse concerning Jesus and the God of Israel." Yeago seeks to discern the New Testament doctrine of God from its primary reference points: "the distinctive practices of Christian worship, and the scriptures of Israel."[10] These two

---

Christopher R. Seitz, ed., *Nicene Christianity: The Future for a New Ecumenism* (Grand Rapids: Brazos, 2001).

7. Kathryn Greene-McCreight, *Ad Litteram: How Augustine, Calvin, and Barth Read the "Plain Sense" of Genesis 1–3*, Issues in Systematic Theology (New York: Peter Lang, 1999), 243.

8. Greene-McCreight, *Ad Litteram*, 244.

9. Greene-McCreight, *Ad Litteram*, 245.

10. David S. Yeago, "The New Testament and the Nicene Dogma: A Contribution to the Recovery of Theological Exegesis," in *The Theological Interpretation of Scripture: Classic and Contemporary Readings*, ed. Stephen E. Fowl (Oxford: Blackwell, 1997), 88.

realities intersect in Philippians 2, which refers to the exaltation of Jesus Christ and may even do so in the context of an early Christian hymn.

Meanwhile, much of Yeago's burden in his essay is to explore how Paul speaks of this exaltation using Isaiah 45:21–24, one of the strongest monotheistic passages in the Old Testament:

> The text from Philippians *identifies* the prophesied turning of all the earth to YHWH as the only God with the universal acclamation of Jesus as Lord; that Jesus is acclaimed as *kurios* "to the glory of God the Father" implies that YHWH comes to his rightful, exclusive sovereignty over the whole creation, proclaimed in Isaiah, precisely *through* creation's acknowledgement of the lordship of the particular person Jesus. Within the thought-world of Israel's scriptures, no stronger affirmation of the bond between the risen Jesus and the God of Israel is possible.[11]

How can such an affirmation be consistent with worship of YHWH as the one true God? It cannot be that now there are two gods, or that the identity of YHWH has suddenly changed. If Paul is in fact claiming that Isaiah supports his teaching, then he could not have pulled enough wool over Philippian eyes to get away with such a rejection of Israel's basic monotheistic understanding. Therefore Philippians 2 must include the Son eternally in the identity of Israel's God, the one unchanging Creator of everything else. And, in the larger context of Isaiah 45, there must be anticipation of further revelation concerning YHWH's identity.[12]

Why, then, have many scholars refused to find a "high Christology" in the New Testament, except perhaps in the Gospel of John? James Dunn is Yeago's illustration of one who refuses to connect the "incarnational" Christology of John 1 with passages

11. Yeago, "The New Testament and the Nicene Dogma," 90.

12. For further discussion of Isaiah 40–55 in connection with Philippians 2, showing how Paul's reading coheres with the identity of YHWH in relation to the suffering Servant, see Richard Bauckham, *God Crucified: Monotheism and Christology in the New Testament* (Grand Rapids: Eerdmans, 1999).

61

such as Philippians 2. Dunn bases this refusal on a historical reconstruction of the concept behind the passage, arguing that Paul's language reflects an "Adam Christology" focused on the humanity of Christ without the Son's eternal "preexistence" as God. Yeago responds by pointing out that an "Adam Christology" is a scholarly construct and should not be used to reject "the way the words go"—that is, what the text actually says. Furthermore, Dunn confuses concepts with doctrinal judgments. Concepts, the particular ways that words convey ideas and refer to objects, are for the sake of communicating judgments about truth.[13] Simply because different concepts are used in John 1 and Philippians 2 does not require the conclusion that the texts differ to the point of contradiction; Philippians 2 can teach that the Son is eternally one with the Father even if the concept "incarnation" does not appear.

This points to a further implication of Yeago's argument: these New Testament passages together can teach the same judgment that we find in the Nicene Creed even if they do not contain the Greek philosophical language developed later.[14] Much of the widespread opposition to "dogmatics" within biblical studies, therefore, ignores the speculative character of historical reconstruction as well as the need for a sophisticated understanding of how language relates to doctrine. Yeago makes use of historical research, but he sees it ultimately as a servant rather than master of "the real theological-exegetical task":

> If "biblical theology" is anything coherent at all, it is just "theology,"
> an engagement with the biblical texts no different in principle

13. Yeago, "The New Testament and the Nicene Dogma," 95–96. See also Daniel J. Treier, "Concept," *DTIB* 129–30.

14. Much contemporary scholarship suggests that it was not the orthodox fathers whom Greek philosophy held captive; rather, to some degree, heretical parties such as the Arians were more captive, or at least committed, to deploying fully certain Greek assumptions (see the work of figures such as Thomas Weinandy and Paul Gavrilyuk). The creeds use philosophical concepts to preserve biblical teaching about the God of Israel, fully revealed in Jesus Christ. For an illustration of this, see Books VI–VII of Augustine's *De Trinitate*, which is discussed below.

from that undertaken in the theological exegesis of St Athanasius, St Basil, St Thomas, Martin Luther, and Karl Barth, and it will not fare well if it is not pursued by the means proper to theological reflection. Those means are chiefly those of close reading and conceptual analysis, attention (in St Athanasius's terms) to the *skopos* and *akolouthia*, the tenor and coherence of the judgements rendered in the texts.[15]

As we have seen, in many sectors of modern biblical scholarship it is controversial enough to read the New and Old Testaments as part of a coherent whole—ultimately one "book" and accordingly Scripture—let alone to see consistency between their portrayals of God and the trinitarian doctrine of the later creeds. Perhaps, though, in addition to affirming such consistency, we can proceed even further. Might we find basically the same theological commitments throughout the church fathers, however various the verbal expressions might be? That has been the claim of Thomas Oden and many others involved with the Ancient Christian Commentary Series. Such a belief seems to appear as well in the series preface to the Brazos Theological Commentary on the Bible, where, for example, R. R. Reno writes of "the Nicene tradition" that "the Rule of faith cannot be limited to a specific set of words, sentences, and creeds. It is instead a pervasive habit of thought, the animating culture of the church in its intellectual aspect."[16] If this approach is correct, then interpretation according to the Rule of Faith does not simply involve coming to exegetical conclusions that cohere with trinitarian orthodoxy; rather, it means stretching ourselves to explore imaginatively the classic Christian consensus about God, suspecting that the tradition can illuminate far more in the Scriptures than simply the doctrine of the Trinity or incarnational Christology, narrowly conceived. Beyond merely setting boundaries, the Rule of Faith grants us true freedom by guiding us to pursue particular directions of interpretation.

15. Yeago, "The New Testament and the Nicene Dogma," 97.
16. R. R. Reno, series preface in Jaroslav Pelikan, *Acts*, Brazos Theological Commentary on the Bible (Grand Rapids: Brazos, 2005), 14.

## Contemporary Theological Hermeneutics: Interpreting with and for Doctrine

The natural follow-up question concerns the broader use of Christian doctrine in biblical interpretation. If truly "Christian" understanding of Scripture occurs within the boundaries of the Rule of Faith and even receives helpful guidance from Nicene orthodoxy, then what about those teachings on which various Christians disagree? Can or should particular theological traditions inform interpretation? And in what way ought the church's current concerns intersect with the reading of Scripture? These questions highlight our need to assess how the contemporary contexts of Christian doctrine might influence biblical interpretation.

### Doctrinal Contexts

Another crucial author galvanizing the recovery of theological hermeneutics is Francis Watson. In 1994 his *Text, Church and World: Biblical Interpretation in Theological Perspective* brought together the three concerns of his title: biblical interpretation involves attention to the canonical text in the context of the church and in relation to the world. Some of Watson's inspiration was "postmodern," yet his appropriation of such theories was critical as well as constructive. Watson's work is worth exploring further not only because of his historical influence over many regarding theological hermeneutics but also because his proposals continue to represent a way in which biblical scholars might approach theological interpretation, especially contemporary discussions of Christian doctrine, sympathetically.

Regarding the "text," Watson recognized the insight of thinkers such as Hans Frei. Frei highlighted the importance of the early modern shift toward "historical consciousness" for how interpreters moved from the Gospels to teaching about Jesus Christ. Critics no longer accepted the assumption that the story told by the biblical texts was unified or accurate. Once the Bible was seen as a collection of stories that did not fit together and were assumed to be fictional because they made claims about the miraculous, the identity of Jesus Christ became newly flexible. German scholars

especially tended to reinterpret the meaning of the Bible's christological claims for the sake of preserving their truthfulness. Thus,
for instance, Jesus became a great human exemplar or teacher
of the morality universally held by philosophers. Likewise, the
resurrection narratives pointed symbolically to hope or newness
of life. Accordingly, conservative scholars focused on defending
the Gospels' reference to historical reality instead of unfolding the
way their narratives portray Jesus' identity.[17]

Frei led Watson to emphasize that "the reality of Jesus is only accessible to us through the mediation of an irreducible textuality,"[18]
which became Watson's focus in part 1, "The Autonomous Text."
We come to know Jesus as presented in the Bible and not apart from
it, not merely by recourse to historical investigation "behind" the
text. Alongside this emphasis, however, Watson also highlighted
the reality of Jesus. What the text mediates are not fictional stories
but rather narrative claims about God's action in Christ. Watson
held that thinkers following Frei, and appreciating his emphasis
on unfolding the narrative world of the Bible, needed to be clearer
on that point.

The concerns of the contemporary "church" and "world" arose
more clearly in Watson's next two sections, "Theology and Postmodernism" and "Holy Scripture and Feminist Critique," yet the
strategy remained similar. Watson accepted aspects of contemporary theories while also seeking to criticize them constructively.
A distinctive feature of the work is the frequency of biblical case
studies. Watson addresses hermeneutical issues and appropriates
Christian doctrines as a biblical scholar, in the midst of exegesis.
For an illustration, consider the so-called patriarchal texts of terror
in the Bible that are highlighted by feminist scholars. Whatever
one's ideological stance on these matters, Scripture does indeed
contain some disturbing stories, such as the account of Jephthah's
daughter in Judges 11. In response, Watson's hypothesis involved

17. See Hans W. Frei, *The Eclipse of Biblical Narrative: A Study in Eighteenth and Nineteenth Century Hermeneutics* (New Haven: Yale University
Press, 1974).

18. Francis Watson, *Text, Church and World: Biblical Interpretation in Theological Perspective* (Grand Rapids: Eerdmans, 1994), 3.

intracanonical criticism of injustice: "Criticism would then be not an extraneous imposition but an interpretation of the text's own capacity for *self*-criticism."[19] To accomplish this, Watson pointed to "the Pauline law/gospel antithesis," suggesting that *"since theological interpretation must distinguish the law from the gospel within the biblical text, the decision to work with the canonical form does not render the text immune from criticism."*[20] Christians must even anticipate external prompting toward such canonical criticism. Accordingly, *"Insights originating in the secular world outside the Christian community can have a positive role in assisting the community's understanding of holy scripture."*[21]

Watson discussed Luther's significance for law/gospel hermeneutics fairly briefly. In general, he interacted with theological issues and contemporary hermeneutics while interpreting Scripture, but in the 1994 book he did not heavily appropriate doctrinal traditions for the sake of gaining insight into biblical texts. We should also note that Watson's appropriation of contemporary theories such as "feminism," even if they can criticize church teaching only indirectly by illuminating fresh understandings of Scripture's internal checks and balances, may run afoul of Frei's concern for "intratextuality." This is because these theories seem to function as issues or frameworks outside the text that are then brought to the text, eclipsing its internal frames of reference and reflecting Watson's relative inattention to the older doctrinal tradition. For those, on the other hand, who find Frei's hermeneutical approach to be too biblically self-contained, Watson's may provide an appealing alternative.

Watson's next book, *Text and Truth: Redefining Biblical Theology*, from 1997, continued to sound earlier themes while adding a bit more interaction with theological tradition. There Watson engages key figures in the history of modern Old Testament scholarship at a number of points, in addition to theologians such as Jürgen Moltmann and patristic interpreters. Although he does

19. Watson, *Text, Church and World*, 190 (italics in original).
20. Watson, *Text, Church and World*, 231 (italics in original).
21. Watson, *Text, Church and World*, 236 (italics in original).

not provide sustained examples of using tradition deeply within biblical exegesis, he does begin to offer theological hermeneutics a doctrine-friendly proposal:

> All Christian theology must be "biblical theology"—not in the sense that it should consist in nothing but biblical exegesis but in the sense that the particular truth attested in the biblical texts must constitute its centre and foundation. If—as I shall argue—a specialized "biblical theology" is needed that is not coextensive with Christian theology as a whole, this necessity can only be a pragmatic one.[22]

Some division of labor is necessary between biblical studies and systematic theology, but the distinction is functional, not normative.[23] The modern academic division between the two probably has stemmed in part from Protestantism gone wrong: "When one has the Bible, what need is there for the subtleties and sophistries of theology?" And the result can be the driving of theologians away from Scripture: "At home with Irenaeus, Schleiermacher and Barth, one is in danger of trespassing if one engages too freely in the interpretation of Isaiah, Paul or John. The biblical writings are no longer the intellectual property of the theologian."[24] Recognizing the connection between this Bible-versus-theology division and the separation of Old and New Testament studies is what leads Watson to focus on christological interpretation of the Old Testament, along with a defense of canonical "biblical theology" against the attacks of James Barr and others.

Overall, Watson's work has served as a clarion call for doctrine to illuminate the meaning of biblical texts via three contexts. First, all Scripture requires interpretation with the reality of Jesus Christ as the center of its narrative world, whether one is reading the Gospels or even the Old Testament. Second, the reality of life in Christian community shapes our reading of biblical texts (as we

22. Francis Watson, *Text and Truth: Redefining Biblical Theology* (Grand Rapids: Eerdmans, 1997), 2.
23. Watson, *Text and Truth*, 3.
24. Watson, *Text and Truth*, 4.

will explore in the next chapter). This raises the need for insight from current Christian teaching as well as posing fresh questions for the tradition to ponder. Third, the contemporary context outside the church likewise evokes theological reflection on the meaning of biblical texts and can contribute fresh insight as well as important criticisms of existing Christian understanding. Watson does not exemplify the full range of possibilities for using doctrine to guide biblical interpretation, but he does illustrate how biblical scholars can begin to pursue theological interests, and he articulates why we must find a way beyond the current fragmentation of theological disciplines.

### Doctrinal Commentary

As noted earlier, one of the new efforts to transcend such fragmentation involves the writing of theological commentaries. In addition to the Brazos Theological Commentary on the Bible, a series written largely by systematic and historical theologians, publication has begun on the Two Horizons series from Eerdmans. These commentaries seek to "span" New Testament studies and systematic theology; some volumes will be coauthored by a scholar from each discipline, whereas others take a single-author approach.[25] Only time will tell what the full range of contemporary possibilities for theological commentary will look like.

The most doctrinally oriented early example, though, comes from the volume on the book of Acts in the Brazos series by historical theologian Jaroslav Pelikan. Although the volume's table of contents broadly follows the outline of Acts, its structure is distinctive. In some places, after a verse is printed and Pelikan comments on it, a title appears in bold, followed by text in bold. These sections address themes that recur throughout the book of Acts, collecting Pelikan's reflection on them in particular places. Along the way, in regular text, verses appear in parentheses with

25. For a collection of essays that serves as a programmatic introduction to the series, see Joel B. Green and Max Turner, eds., *Between Two Horizons: Spanning New Testament Studies and Systematic Theology* (Grand Rapids: Eerdmans, 1999).

arrows—for example: (→ 7:22). This device signals the reader to look at the commentary on 7:22 for one of the bold thematic sections, a *locus communis*:

> Because this commentary is intended to be primarily theological rather than philological, the discussion of an individual theological issue or *locus communis*, which is printed in bold type, has been concentrated at one or another particular passage of the book of Acts where that issue and doctrine are prominent, with consideration of other passages in Acts related to this discussion; and the headings of these discussions often include quotations from or references to the tradition of creeds, councils, and liturgies, as well as to the biblical text. For example, there are numerous references to the angels scattered throughout most of Acts, all the way from 1:10 to 23:8, so that discussing the doctrine in full at each location would have been cumbersome and repetitive, while discussing the peculiar angelology of any single passage in isolation from the doctrine as a whole would have been fragmentary and disconnected. Bringing together in its heading a quotation from the Niceno-Constantinopolitan Creed (art. 1) and one from the Epistle to the Hebrews (1:14), the consideration of the doctrine of angels, therefore, is concentrated at 12:7.[26]

Using *loci* as an approach stems especially from the Protestant Reformers, who used them to treat subjects that were helpful to reading Scripture but were one step removed from the actual text. The *loci* were kept outside the main flow of their commentaries, later being bound separately and serving as the basis for their "systematic theologies." Here, though, Pelikan places the *loci* clearly within the commentary.

Pelikan, a convert to Eastern Orthodox Christianity from Lutheranism, sought to pay attention to the church's traditional use of Acts, yet unfortunately the book has not enjoyed a prominent place in the church's liturgical life. Thus, he had to focus more upon bringing patristic commentaries and broader examples of theological reflection to bear on the text.[27] Ecclesiastical commit-

26. Pelikan, *Acts*, 29.
27. Pelikan, *Acts*, 26.

ment also led Pelikan to study the various manuscript versions of Acts that we possess, and to value the so-called Western Text more highly than do most biblical scholars. Furthermore, Pelikan uses the Septuagint, a Greek translation, rather than the Hebrew versions that we have, as the basis of his Old Testament references, following the apparent practice of Luke.[28]

Pelikan's work and the idea behind this series are controversial, especially concerning whether such theological commentaries adequately focus upon the biblical text itself.[29] Yet from this example we can see that doctrine shapes both the questions we ask of biblical texts and the ways we communicate our answers. As reflected long ago in Augustine's hermeneutical treatise *On Christian Teaching*, these are in fact inseparable. Our need to communicate the Word of God shapes our priorities in discovering the meaning of the text; sometimes excessive critical scrupulousness (e.g., over minor details regarding the original wording of a text) must give way to a focus on its larger theological message. And treating a passage in relation to others may be standard practice within a given biblical book, yet the *loci* model facilitates not only recognition of themes and connections but also engagement with the wider array of texts in Scripture—truly canonical reading. Moreover, it requires exploring the relationships between various concepts that we use to communicate. This makes engagement with both past and present understandings of Christian teaching inescapable and fruitful.

## A Case Study: Imaging God

Throughout this book so far, and especially this chapter, we have encountered various examples with respect to theological interpretation of Scripture. Perhaps, however, these examples seem to be

28. Pelikan, *Acts*, 33–35.
29. For a critical review by a person generally sympathetic to theological exegesis, see Joel B. Green, review of *Acts*, by Jaroslav Pelikan, *Journal of the Evangelical Theological Society* 49, no. 4 (December 2006): 852–53. See also the book symposium in *Pro Ecclesia* 16, no. 1 (Winter 2007): 14–32.

one step removed from the actual texts of the Bible, hanging a bit in mid-air. So it is appropriate to undertake a case study regarding a classic Christian doctrine that spans both Testaments without appearing directly in the Nicene Creed. One such candidate, which appears in Watson's work, concerns the *imago Dei*, the nature of human being(s) as the image of God.

Of course, a comprehensive study is far beyond this volume, requiring at least a book of its own. But perhaps the doctrine is manageable for the sake of illustration at several points in the chapters that follow. Right here I seek to tie together threads from chapters 1 and 2 by examining Augustine's various treatments of the *imago Dei*, as a patristic example of theological interpretation of Scripture.

Previously, I suggested that precritical exegesis involved reading as an act of piety, reading the text as being about Christ, and reading for the sake of Christian practice. The developed fourfold sense of Scripture, and its incorporation of allegorical interpretation, served these ends. We can readily observe such features in Augustine's writings on the *imago Dei*. His great work *De Trinitate* (*The Trinity*), in which he uses the image of God as an incentive to contemplate God's triune life, ends with prayer and contains numerous side comments reflecting his piety. Furthermore, scholars generally agree that Book VIII serves as a hinge between Books I–VII and Books IX–XV. Book VII concludes with a scriptural quote in VII.12: "Unless you believe, you will not understand" (Isa. 7:9 [in the Old Latin rendering]).[30] Book VIII then begins with a prayer for understanding, as the focus shifts from direct scriptural engagement (Books I–IV) and exposition of the church's consensus (Books V–VII) to more speculative efforts in the second half of the work. Even this sanctified speculation remains saturated in prayer and, toward the end, in Scripture; the entire work is an act of piety, and its goal is to promote our transformation into the image of God in Christ, as Edmund Hill notes:

30. Augustine, *The Trinity*, trans. Edmund Hill, ed. John E. Rotelle (New York: New City Press, 1991), 232 (for a critical edition, see *De Trinitate*, ed. W. J. Mountain, Corpus Christianorum: Series latina 50 [Turnhout: Brepols, 1970]).

71

It is to be noted that from the first the idea of image is linked with the idea of imitation. The link between the two ideas, illustrated by their etymological relationship, was a commonplace for the Latin writers in the Church of all ages. But it means, what is sometimes perhaps overlooked, that the doctrine of the image is a practical doctrine. Man's being in the image of God is not just a theological fact to be observed and interpreted as throwing light on the nature of the Trinity; it is also an imperative, a program to be carried out in order to discover the mystery of the Trinity by achieving its likeness in oneself.[31]

The link between reading as piety and reading for the sake of Christian practice, in this case certainly, is reading about Christ. We can see this by examining Augustine's approach to Genesis more concretely.

At first, Augustine apparently took the view that we are conformed simply to the image of Jesus Christ. Eventually, however, he concluded that we become the image of the entire Trinity in and through our conformity to Jesus as the Son, the true image of God. Augustine comes to this interpretation because of the plural pronoun "our" that precedes "image and likeness" in Genesis 1:26–27.[32] All three Persons of the Godhead must be involved rather than just the Father making the Son, and thereby humanity, conform to his image.[33]

Along the way, as he worked on Genesis, Augustine was unafraid of allegory. For example, he connected the divine image to the later mystery of Christ's dominion over the church as a parallel to human rule over the animals.[34] Yet he was also scrupulous about the

31. Edmund Hill, in Augustine, *The Trinity*, 233–34n23.

32. Augustine, *Unfinished Literal Commentary on Genesis*, in *On Genesis*, trans. Edmund Hill, ed. John E. Rotelle (New York: New City Press, 2002), 150 (§61) (for a critical edition, see *De Genesi ad litteram imperfectus liber*, Corpus scriptorum ecclesiasticorum latinorum 28.1 [Vienna, 1866–]).

33. Augustine, *Unfinished Literal Commentary*, 151 (§61).

34. Augustine, *On Genesis: A Refutation of the Manichees*, in *On Genesis*, trans. Edmund Hill, ed. John E. Rotelle (New York: New City Press, 2002), 65 (I.40) (for a critical edition, see *De Genesi adversus Manicheos*, Corpus scriptorum ecclesiasticorum latinorum 91 [Vienna, 1866–]).

literal sense of the clause "male and female," so that an apparent contradiction between Genesis 1:26–27, in which woman is clearly image of God, and 1 Corinthians 11:7, in which the man is image of God while woman reflects the man, must be addressed. This challenge Augustine undertakes with a complex and unsatisfying spiritual interpretation,[35] but it is noteworthy that he tackles the problem.

As for the actual nature of the *imago Dei*, Augustine interprets it "with reference to the interior man, where reason is to be found and intelligence." Most contemporary biblical scholars do not take this "metaphysical" or "substantive" view of the image and accuse classic interpreters of doing so due to Greek philosophical influence. However, as noted above, this accusation is now coming under fire from some patristics scholars. And it is interesting that Augustine argues his case by pointing to elements in the biblical text, suggesting that human reason is what gives us authority over the animals, as the next phrases of Genesis 1 seem to indicate. In other words, Augustine includes the "functional" emphasis of recent scholarship within his rationale for the rational view: when it comes to human stewardship over the rest of creation, reason is "the power by which he [humanity] surpasses all cattle, all animals."[36]

To be sure, Augustine interprets the passage from the standpoint of some cultural premises. His focus on humans as "rational animals," as some have put it, leads him to believe that "even our body is so constructed that it indicates how we are better than the beasts and therefore more like God."[37] For we stand upright, and this hints that we are able to set our minds on things above in a way other creatures are not, as Colossians 3:2 exhorts.[38] Yet even

35. Augustine, *The Trinity*, Book XII.
36. Augustine, *On Genesis: A Refutation*, 57 (I.28).
37. Augustine, *On Genesis: A Refutation*, 57 (I.28).
38. Augustine, *Unfinished Literal Commentary*, 149 (§60); *The Literal Meaning of Genesis*, in *On Genesis*, trans. Edmund Hill, ed. John E. Rotelle (New York: New City Press, 2002), 314 (VI.22) (for a critical edition of the latter, see *De Genesi ad litteram imperfectus liber*, Corpus scriptorum ecclesiasticorum latinorum 28.1 [Vienna, 1866–]).

here Augustine claims textual support; he finds a difference between God creating others via the words "Let it be made" and creating humans via the more active phrase "Let us make," which, in addition, hints at the plurality or relationality by which all Persons of the Trinity participate in this act.[39]

Christological interpretation means that Augustine cannot interpret the Genesis passage in isolation from other biblical references to the image of God, many of which, in the New Testament, relate the concept distinctively to Jesus Christ. He concludes that we are made in the image of God, but not all images are like each other or exactly like what they mirror. The term "likeness" therefore appears to refer ultimately to the Son, or Word, of God, who is distinctively like God in a way that we could never be.[40] In fact, everything in the universe is like God to some degree because God is the Creator; yet "not all of them, however, [are] such as to be made to the likeness itself, but only those of a rational nature [humans]. Thus all things through the likeness [Christ, the Logos], but not all to the likeness."[41] Distinctions between "image" and "likeness" are common in classic exegesis, with the latter usually taken christologically and morally in some fashion, dealing with what we ought to become.[42] By contrast, modern biblical scholars usually take the terms to be relatively similar in theological import, appearing for the sake of stylistic variation or slight differences in nuance.[43]

Of course, contemporary biblical scholarship generally refuses to take seriously christological interpretation of such a passage. Understanding the image with respect to Christ directs us to consider his distinctiveness as the bearer of wisdom and truth, the light by which the Spirit enlightens us (can you hear the echoes of John 1?). When we take into account all of canonical Scripture, we

39. Augustine, *Unfinished Literal Commentary*, 147 (§56).

40. Augustine, *Unfinished Literal Commentary*, 147–48 (§§57–58).

41. Augustine, *Unfinished Literal Commentary*, 149 (§59).

42. See Irenaeus, *Against Heresies*, V.16.2. At least this apparent distinction between image and likeness remains significant to Eastern Orthodox theology.

43. See, e.g., Victor P. Hamilton, *The Book of Genesis, Chapters 1–17*, NICOT (Grand Rapids: Eerdmans, 1990), 135–37.

realize that "human nature too is intellectual like that light, and that is why being made is the same thing for it as recognizing the Word of God by whom it is being made."[44] On this basis Augustine proceeds with his speculative effort, in *De Trinitate*, to discover "vestiges" of the Trinity in creation, specifically in humanity's rational nature. It is there that he seeks trinitarian images, for which he settles finally on the unity of our memory, understanding, and will when we engage in self-reflection and divine contemplation (though even this is heavily qualified).[45] Memory has an originating role in recalling something to us and hence is appropriately associated with the Father. The understanding (or Logos?) itself naturally relates to the Son. The will by which we love what we truly know must receive this charity by the Holy Spirit. Augustine is very clear that this is only an image—a fuzzy one at that—given how mysteriously beyond our knowing God really is.[46] Indeed, regarding humans as the image of God, he urges us to "note how great the dissimilarity is in whatever similarity there may be."[47]

The kinds of associations by which Augustine relates Genesis 1 to other biblical texts are partly verbal and partly doctrinal. We have seen that Christology and trinitarian theology play their parts, sending Augustine to passages such as John 1. In terms of verbal associations, Augustine ranges not only to verses that explicitly mention the *imago Dei* but also to passages that are conceptually parallel to such verses. For instance, beyond Ephesians 4, Colossians 3, and other such candidates, he sees 1 Corinthians 13:12 to be crucial, with its reference to a mirror. Since mirrors involve images, the verse becomes relevant to our consideration of what the image must mean and how it addresses our conformity to Christ.[48] Whatever we make of Augustine's *imago Dei* doctrine overall,

44. Augustine, *Literal Meaning of Genesis*, 235 (§31).

45. See especially Book XIV of *De Trinitate*.

46. He makes such affirmations particularly in his final book of *De Trinitate* (Book XV), but they are scattered throughout the work. See also his *Confessions*, Book XIII (for a critical edition, see *Confessionum libri XIII*, ed. L. Verheijen, Corpus Christianorum: Series latina 27 [Turnhout: Brepols, 1981]).

47. Augustine, *The Trinity*, 426 (XV.39).

48. Augustine, *The Trinity*, Book XV.

these examples demonstrate the exegetical help that theology can provide. John 1 surely is a parallel to Genesis 1 in various ways, not least given its placement in the canonical structure of its book and even its inauguration of the gospel in its Testament, along with the vocabulary of "beginning," "light" and "darkness," plus the focus on creation. If we take the unity of Scripture seriously, then the Christ-centered, sanctification-focused New Testament *imago Dei* passages must cohere in some respects with the message of Genesis 1, even if we conclude that "on its own terms" Genesis 1:26–27 is explicitly about neither Christ nor sanctification, and that the later passages may address more than we find there. The conceptual parallels by which Augustine brings other texts, such as 1 Corinthians 13:12, into play seem suggestive. They are at least as relevant for unfolding the theological message and implications of Genesis 1 as are ancient Near Eastern parallels.

We must continue to evaluate the adequacy of Augustine's particular approach, and the classic view generally, in succeeding chapters. The ancient Near Eastern parallels, the message of Genesis 1:26–27 "in its own right," and the other biblical passages, even in the New Testament (e.g., James 3:9–12), that do not interpret the *imago Dei* christocentrically—all these need further consideration. Here, though, I have tried to show that Augustine and other classic interpreters addressed challenging questions and discovered conceptual richness within a given passage, as well as finding other relevant biblical material, by approaching Scripture with doctrinal interests and commitments. If time later tells that some of those commitments reflect a theologian's cultural lenses—and inevitably they do—nevertheless elements of such interpretations stand the test of time as well.

Since the Nicene era, of course, formal confessions and less formal theologies have proliferated. Advocates for theological interpretation of Scripture probably credit some doctrinal statements with less authority than the Rule of Faith itself, and with varying degrees of authority depending on particular traditions. At minimum, though, such extensions of the Rule beyond explicitly christological and trinitarian boundaries can and should play a ministerial role in biblical exegesis. For Catholic and Orthodox

Christians, later dogma even exercises magisterial authority. Once again, ecclesiology gives density to theological hermeneutics. Beyond our particulars and our differences, though, lies the broader principle of this chapter: far from regulating biblical interpretation arbitrarily, doctrinal frameworks challenge new generations to recognize their own cultural assumptions and to revise them in light of how the church has understood Scripture as a whole.

# 3

## Reading with Others

*Listening to the Community of the Spirit*

The importance of doctrine for interpreting Scripture puts a spotlight on the church. Recovery of this premodern theme entails reading the Bible not only within the Rule of Faith but also with Christian piety at heart. Yet classic spiritual formation is not private. At its best, precritical exegesis was not individualistic. Not all laypeople could access the Scriptures, but those who could do so were seeking to orient their spiritual lives around participating in the divine liturgy and teaching others.

When we consider how to emulate this classic pattern for ourselves, we must reflect on the promises and pitfalls of a democratic environment.[1] Today there are greater opportunities for lay participation in Scripture reading and theological discernment than in the premodern period. However, the temptation is also very real to pursue individualistic and idiosyncratic interpretation, imitating the isolated moments when the medieval tradition of spiritual

---

1. Somewhat famously on this theme, see Stanley Hauerwas, *Unleashing the Scripture: Freeing the Bible from Captivity to America* (Nashville: Abingdon, 1993).

Piety = devotion or spirituality

Liturgy = worship done according to a particular Tradition

reading was at its worst.[2] Thus we need to discern how the Holy Spirit leads members of the Christian community to discover the meaning of Scripture, and in particular how different parts of the body of Christ connect with each other in that process.

## Setting the Context for Emphasizing Community: "Postliberalism"

Probably the most influential contemporary thinker on the issue of community and interpretation is Stephen Fowl. Accordingly, this chapter examines his viewpoint in particular. Before that, though, the context for some of Fowl's key themes needs attention: George Lindbeck's understanding of doctrine and Stanley Hauerwas's emphasis on character are among the key factors that prepared recent discussion for an orientation to community.

### George Lindbeck on Doctrine

In 1984 Lindbeck published *The Nature of Doctrine: Religion and Theology in a Postliberal Age*,[3] which became one of theology's most widely discussed books for a couple of decades and began to popularize the term "postliberal." The book contrasts three basic understandings of what doctrine is: (1) "cognitive-propositional" (the early modern position of classic conservatives); (2) "experiential-expressivist" (the later modern, liberal position); (3) "cultural-linguistic" (Lindbeck's own approach). According to Lindbeck, we should not think of doctrines directly as truth claims about reality (the conservative approach) or simply as expressions of human religious experience (the liberal tendency, with classic Christian doctrines reinterpreted in light of contemporary thought and often in the absence of belief in the supernatural). Lindbeck's rejection of these former approaches lies in concern for the unity of the church. His participation in the ecumenical

2. Henri de Lubac, *Medieval Exegesis: The Four Senses of Scripture*, vol. 2, trans. E. M. Macierowski (Grand Rapids: Eerdmans, 2000), 150–53, 176.
3. George A. Lindbeck, *The Nature of Doctrine: Religion and Theology in a Postliberal Age* (Philadelphia: Westminster, 1984).

Ecumenical = worldwide (universal) applicability relating to the christian church.

movement led him to seek an understanding of doctrine that could explain how to reach agreement among different theological traditions. Against strict propositional views, doctrines could change in their wording over time and could mean roughly the same thing in different words. Thus different traditions could work toward agreement while retaining the integrity of the concerns that inspired them in the first place. Yet such agreement need not entail ignoring the pursuit of truth: against purely expressivist views, doctrines deal with God, not just with various, relativistic ways of talking about human experience.

*The Nature of Doctrine* generated controversy, especially because in using generalizations about other views, Lindbeck inevitably oversimplified them and treated them somewhat unfairly. Yet most people also recognized his insight and, for our purposes here, it is his cultural-linguistic approach that matters. In this view, the Christian religion is like a culture that operates with a system of signs. This language shapes our religious experience because we operate with these symbols as we reflect and speak about God. For instance, eating bread and drinking wine with others means something specific for Christians and helps us to understand the reference in John 6 to eating Jesus' flesh and drinking his blood. By contrast, rumors about such talk and practices outside the Christian community early on fostered accusations of cannibalism. When it comes to doctrine, though it is for communal insiders first and foremost, it is not "first-order" religious speech, such as prayer or praise. Doctrine instead provides the "second-order" rules for speaking, like grammar. Doctrine helps Christians to inhabit the faith of the church as a culture and to pass on the meaning of its signs and symbols with integrity.

The general effect of *The Nature of Doctrine* on theological interpretation of Scripture involves this focus on Christian community as a culture. Late modern or mildly postmodern thinking owes much to Wittgenstein's concept of "language games," with a focus on how words have meaning only as they are used in particular contexts. Just as swinging a wooden bat is a good activity in baseball yet possibly criminal elsewhere, so too the biblical claim "Christ is Lord" can ring false in the context of a Crusader yelling it while splitting open an infidel's skull. This theme of focusing on language use means that we must pay attention not only to the original contexts of the Bible's composition but also to the historical and contemporary contexts of its reading.

More specifically, Lindbeck also advocates "intratextuality," in which the biblical text "absorbs the world" rather than vice versa. Paying attention to the contemporary context of the church's Scripture reading does not mean that today's culture determines the meaning of the texts. This is the error of liberalism, according to Lindbeck: an "extratextual" approach thinks that there are public, universal categories from philosophy or somewhere else with which we must correlate biblical meanings. By contrast, Lindbeck's intratextual approach to theology consists in trying to have Scripture's language and story-shaped worlds provide the categories through which we interpret our experience and even contemporary culture.[4] Of course, we need to use extrabiblical language to communicate biblical truth. But imagine two sermons on Nehemiah, one centering on "successful leadership" while the other emphasizes the text's vocabulary of "servanthood": the former could be extratextual in an unhealthy way, since the connotations of success cannot help but reflect aspects of contemporary culture, and these might not be questioned. The latter would be more intratextual, with the result that the narrative of Nehemiah might begin to inculcate a countercultural understanding of courageous leadership in the sermon's hearers. Similarly, Christian doctrine ought to promote a more biblical imagination in the lives of Christians.

### Stanley Hauerwas on Character

Thus, an important theme for Lindbeck, and for his Yale colleague Hans Frei as well, is biblical narrative, which prompts the question of what story will provide the lens through which we understand our lives. The majority of Scripture comes in narrative form, and the rest of the Bible still involves a narrative dimension

---

4. See Lindbeck, *Nature of Doctrine*, 113–24. Also relevant is Hans W. Frei, *The Eclipse of Biblical Narrative: A Study in Eighteenth and Nineteenth Century Hermeneutics* (New Haven: Yale University Press, 1974).

Inculcate = to teach and impress by frequent repetition or admonition.

in reading it, as we discern "figural" relationships between the world of the text and our own. For all the complexity involved in trying to figure out what "narrative theology" means, at least we can highlight an added focus on the Gospel narratives about Jesus. Frei showed that with the rise of modernity, liberals tended to change their meaning into something else besides portraying the divine identity of Jesus, whereas conservatives reacted by trying to prove their supernatural claims using ordinary historical arguments. For instance, on the one hand, the resurrection narratives might point to hope or new life; on the other hand, they might provide apologetic proof for the truth of Christian faith. In both cases the theological priority of the narrative portrayal of Jesus is eclipsed.

This narrative of Jesus concerns not only who God is but also who we are to become, which is the focus of Stanley Hauerwas. Hauerwas was deeply influenced by his colleague in philosophy Alasdair MacIntyre, who challenged the Enlightenment project and called for recovering classic concepts of virtue tied to tradition.[5] The story that shapes a community's self-understanding should shape the character of its members. Moreover, the Mennonite theologian John Howard Yoder impressed upon Hauerwas the nature and importance of "Christian non-violence" as "the politics of Jesus."[6]

Hauerwas is a prolific writer, calling the church to be "a community of character."[7] Whether or not we learn the virtues of

5. See especially Alasdair MacIntyre, *After Virtue: A Study in Moral Theory*, 2nd ed. (Notre Dame, IN: University of Notre Dame Press, 1984).

6. John Howard Yoder, *The Politics of Jesus* (Grand Rapids: Eerdmans, 1972).

7. Stanley Hauerwas, *A Community of Character: Toward a Constructive Christian Social Ethic* (Notre Dame, IN: University of Notre Dame Press, 1981). For what is perhaps the most coherent expression of Hauerwas's thought, which also traces some of its background, see *With the Grain of the Universe: The Church's Witness and Natural Theology* (Grand Rapids: Brazos, 2001). For an example of Hauerwas as a theological interpreter, see *Cross-Shattered Christ: Meditations on the Seven Last Words* (Grand Rapids: Brazos, 2004). He has also recently authored a volume in the Brazos theological commentary: *Matthew*, Brazos Theological Commentary on the Bible (Grand Rapids: Brazos, 2006).

Jesus will determine our faithfulness in reading Scripture, and, of course, how we read Scripture shapes in return the way we imitate Jesus. Fowl's early hermeneutical work, coauthored with L. Gregory Jones, contains an endorsement from Hauerwas on the front cover. The book, *Reading in Communion: Scripture and Ethics in Christian Life*,[8] urges Christians to embody Scripture in living faithfully before God, and to do so communally. Only in this way can we develop the judgment necessary to discern how the Bible deals with difficult ethical issues. Fowl and Jones exhort us to characterize interpretative disputes charitably and to listen to outsiders who can challenge us. In other words, they focus on who readers are (as embodied Christian communities, not just ethereal individuals) rather than what methods we use, and in so doing they criticize excessive preoccupation with professional biblical studies and ethics. Their final chapter portrays Dietrich Bonhoeffer, long a favorite Hauerwas subject, as a "performer of Scripture" whom we ought, in many ways, to emulate.

Bonhoeffer's writings often pursue an understanding of Christian community,[9] and several of these have become classic texts on discipleship, even at the popular level.[10] While lauding Bonhoeffer's emphasis on community in works such as *Life Together*, Fowl and Jones are unafraid to criticize his involvement with a plot to assassinate Hitler. Bonhoeffer's difficulties at that time and later in prison show him "searching for an adequate understanding both of Scripture and the world in a context of extremity."[11] So these difficulties "suggest that we are less likely to read Scripture

8. Stephen E. Fowl and L. Gregory Jones, *Reading in Communion: Scripture and Ethics in Christian Life* (Grand Rapids: Eerdmans, 1991).

9. An early and theoretical work is Dietrich Bonhoeffer, *Sanctorum Communio: A Theological Study of the Sociology of the Church*, trans. Reinhard Krauss and Nancy Lukens, ed. Clifford J. Green, Dietrich Bonhoeffer Works 1 (Minneapolis: Fortress, 1998).

10. See especially Dietrich Bonhoeffer, *Life Together and Prayerbook of the Bible*, trans. Daniel W. Bloesch and James H. Burtness, ed. Geffrey B. Kelly, Dietrich Bonhoeffer Works 5 (Minneapolis: Fortress, 1996); *Discipleship*, trans. Barbara Green and Reinhard Krauss, ed. Geffrey B. Kelly and John D. Godsey, Dietrich Bonhoeffer Works 4 (Minneapolis: Fortress, 2001).

11. Fowl and Jones, *Reading in Communion*, 157.

wisely when we do so outside the context of Christian community." For Fowl and Jones, "the continuing existence of a Christian community like that described in *Life Together* and *The Cost of Discipleship* might have made a significant difference."[12] In the next section, then, we explore Fowl's subsequent discussions of such Christian community affecting biblical interpretation.

## Emphasizing the Church as Scripture's Interpretative Community: Stephen Fowl

The crucial work is *Engaging Scripture*, from 1998.[13] Here, according to Fowl, interpretation "needs to involve a complex interaction in which Christian convictions, practices, and concerns are brought to bear on scriptural interpretation in ways that both shape that interpretation and are shaped by it. Moreover, Christians need to manifest a certain form of common life if this interaction is to serve faithful life and worship."[14] As Fowl writes in a later context, "The argument in a nutshell is that theology and ecclesiology should drive scriptural hermeneutics, not the other way around."[15]

Fowl sets forth three possible views of how the church ought to understand biblical interpretation: "determinate," "antideterminate," and "underdetermined." Determinate interpretation is the approach of theologically interested biblical scholars such as Brevard Childs and Francis Watson.[16] Antideterminate interpretation

12. Fowl and Jones, *Reading in Communion*, 158.

13. Stephen E. Fowl, *Engaging Scripture: A Model for Theological Interpretation*, Challenges in Contemporary Theology (Oxford: Blackwell, 1998).

14. Fowl, *Engaging Scripture*, 8.

15. Stephen E. Fowl, "The Importance of a Multivoiced Literal Sense of Scripture: The Example of Thomas Aquinas," in *Reading Scripture with the Church: Toward a Hermeneutic for Theological Interpretation*, A. K. M. Adam, Stephen E. Fowl, Kevin J. Vanhoozer, and Francis Watson (Grand Rapids: Baker Academic, 2006), 37.

16. For more on Childs, see, in the present volume, chap. 4; for discussion of Watson, see chap. 2. Also associated with determinate interpretation is Werner Jeanrond, who works with theological hermeneutics from a fairly philosophical

is the polar opposite, associated with strongly relativist "postmodern" thinkers who, for example, apply deconstruction as their major paradigm for interpreting the Bible.[17] The implication seems to be that antideterminate interpretation arises as an overreaction to the problems of determinate interpretation, which Fowl characterizes as follows:[18]

1. The aim of determinate interpretation is to "render biblical interpretation redundant."[19]
2. "Determinate interpretation views the biblical text as a problem to be mastered."[20]
3. "Determinate interpretation sees the biblical text as a relatively stable element in which an author inserts, hides, or dissolves (choose your metaphor) meaning."
4. Determinate interpretation assumes "that matters of doctrine and practice are straightforwardly determined by biblical interpretation and never the other way around."[21]
5. Determinate interpreters "trump others" by demonstrating that "opponents have allowed theological concerns, prejudices, or preferences to determine their interpretation, rather than rigorously mining the text for its meaning and then letting that meaning shape their theology."[22]

---

standpoint and believes that theological interpretation of Scripture ought to be accountable for interaction with general hermeneutics (on which, see chap. 5).

17. Associated especially with Jacques Derrida, deconstruction examines texts carefully for places or ways in which meaning unravels due to the flow of history. This flow leads to instabilities in the contexts of authorship and slippages in the system of language as texts cross various contexts of reading. For Derrida, it may not be that there is no meaning, but rather that meaning can never be fixed with certainty or comprehensiveness. For a basic introduction to deconstruction with examples of its relevance for biblical interpretation, see Craig G. Bartholomew, "Deconstruction," *DTIB* 163–65.

18. I first collected these quotations in Daniel J. Treier, "Theological Hermeneutics, Contemporary," *DTIB* 791. See also Daniel J. Treier, *Virtue and the Voice of God: Toward Theology as Wisdom* (Grand Rapids: Eerdmans, 2006), chap. 4.

19. Fowl, *Engaging Scripture*, 32.

20. Fowl, *Engaging Scripture*, 32.

21. Fowl, *Engaging Scripture*, 34.

22. Fowl, *Engaging Scripture*, 35.

6. Determinate interpretation goes with "method,"[23] which determines in advance how all interactions between reader and text ought to operate and thereby takes the Bible away from lay Christians, handing it over to professionals.[24]

7. Determinate interpretation thus goes with "various forms of historical criticism."[25]

8. Finally, determinate interpretation always ends in "question-begging" to support its theory of meaning.[26]

Rather than trying to insert theological concerns into the nooks and crannies of critical biblical scholarship, Fowl favors acknowledging that, for the church, biblical interpretation is theoretically underdetermined. No general theory of meaning is necessary or even possible, so that biblical criticism must be used carefully, on an ad hoc basis only.[27] The lack of theoretical determination and the situation-specific way of using professional biblical scholarship point to the church's need for practical reason, or *phronēsis*. Such practical reason makes the reading of Scripture a pneumatological practice, a work of the Holy Spirit.[28]

To unpack this first requires an understanding of a "practice."[29] The aforementioned Alasdair MacIntyre defined a "practice" in the context of ancient virtues as

> any coherent and complex form of socially established cooperative human activity through which goods internal to that form of activity are realized in the course of trying to achieve those standards

---

23. E.g., Fowl, *Engaging Scripture*, 60, 74.

24. Fowl, *Engaging Scripture*, 47.

25. Fowl, *Engaging Scripture*, 183.

26. Fowl, *Engaging Scripture*, 35.

27. See Fowl, *Engaging Scripture*, 8, 33, 40–56, 179.

28. Fowl and Jones, *Reading in Communion*, 90.

29. For essays that apply this type of approach to practices, see James J. Buckley and David S. Yeago, eds., *Knowing the Triune God: The Work of the Spirit in the Practices of the Church* (Grand Rapids: Eerdmans, 2001). For caution about this, see Nicholas M. Healy, "Practices and the New Ecclesiology: Misplaced Concreteness?" *International Journal of Systematic Theology* 5, no. 3 (2003): 287–308.

of excellence which are appropriate to, and partially definitive of, that form of activity, with the result that human powers to achieve excellence, and human conceptions of the ends and goods involved, are systematically extended.[30]

Two points about this definition are worth highlighting. First, practices are social. Therefore the reading of Scripture is not a private matter for Christian individuals but rather a public activity of the church, of which personal Bible study is an extension. Accordingly, we need to discuss the meaning of the texts together rather than simply deciding on our own. Second, practices are sometimes essential rather than optional for reaching a goal. We often think instrumentally, in terms of various means (or instruments) being available to achieve an end. I can drive to work via Naperville Road or President Street, largely depending on my mood. By contrast, though, I cannot pick and choose among optional approaches to godliness, as if prayer works for me but Scripture reading does not. Certain aspects of godliness are God's gift in and through those activities, not apart from them. This means that what defines faithful Scripture reading is not some generic standard (Does it make me feel good? Does it satisfy scholarly standards?) but rather that inherent excellence for which God gives the practice to the church. "Practices" might be another way to describe "means of grace"—those ways through which God has committed characteristically to transform the people in the church.

What, then, is the good end for which God gives Scripture? Early on Fowl speaks of Christians' interpreting Scripture "as part of their ongoing struggles to live and worship faithfully before the triune God in ways that bring them into ever deeper communion with God and others."[31] Because these ongoing struggles are part of a "journey," Christians "will need to bring an ever-changing set of interests and concerns to bear on scripture."[32] This points

30. MacIntyre, *After Virtue*, 186–87.
31. Fowl, *Engaging Scripture*, 3.
32. Fowl, *Engaging Scripture*, 7.

again to the nature of practical reason.[33] For Aristotle, *phronēsis* was the aspect of wisdom that connected contemplation of ultimate, unchanging reality with the flux of social life in the world. How could one take an understanding of the good life and recognize concrete opportunities for living it? Practical reason was the virtue of good judgment that regulated how the other virtues could work together and take shape in the specific situations of a well-lived life. These concrete decisions might also help a person to understand reality better.

We learn such virtuous judgment, in part, by imitating others to whom we are apprentices. For Fowl, contemporary Christians need to pay attention to ancient Christian interpreters: "I am particularly concerned that Christians learn from the best interpretive habits and practices of those who both clearly understood the purposes for which Christians interpret scripture, and were relatively adept at keeping convictions, practices, and scriptural interpretation together as part of a single, complex practice called theology."[34] Theological interpretation of Scripture, therefore, does not treat doctrine as a rationalist enterprise of determining rigidly what is true from the Bible and how to prove that; instead, it focuses on the arduous but rewarding journey of communing more faithfully with God and others in concrete circumstances.[35] Understanding Scripture is a means to that end, not the end in itself; but it is an essential means to that end, not simply a matter of "theory" waiting to be applied. The ways we read Scripture are themselves part of the journey and shape our character.

Having set forth his understanding of Scripture in an introductory chapter, and his understanding of three approaches to its interpretation (chap. 2, "Stories of Interpretation"), Fowl fills out *Engaging Scripture* with several chapters of case studies before

33. Fowl's treatment of this subject has appeared in several works. Most recently it has significance for his theological commentary on Philippians, where the vocabulary appears ten times: Stephen E. Fowl, *Philippians*, Two Horizons New Testament Commentary (Grand Rapids: Eerdmans, 2005), especially 6, 28–29.

34. Fowl, *Engaging Scripture*, 9.

35. Consider in this regard the final section of Fowl's Philippians commentary, which contains a thematic treatment of friendship.

concluding with a chapter on "Practical Wisdom, Christian Formation, and Ecclesial Authority." The case studies embody his emphasis on practical wisdom by discussing theoretical points in the context of concrete examples.[36] Moreover, these examples emphasize the need for Christian communities to listen to narratives of the Spirit's work in human lives in order to discern the connections between them and the biblical story. Fowl does not believe that interpretative anarchy or even violence requires theoretically determined hermeneutics or the dominance of professional critical scholarship. Instead, Christian communities need to become vigilant about fostering virtues in their readers.[37]

As an illustration, Fowl's study of Ephesians 4:25–5:2 suggests "that Christians' abilities to speak truthfully with each other, to offer edifying and gracious words, to be angry without sinning, and so forth, are directly connected to issues about how they acquire and hold wealth."[38] Such practices of paying careful attention to words, which relate so obviously to how well the church interprets Scripture together, connect to other patterns or problems of communal life. Another illustration is undoubtedly more controversial, as one should expect in light of the disagreements in several mainline Protestant churches: from Acts 10–15, in which the Jerusalem church welcomes Gentiles into fellowship, Fowl finds a possible analogy for the full inclusion in contemporary churches of those who engage in homosexual behavior. On this reading, the force of biblical law must sometimes be set aside in light of the Holy Spirit's present work, as Fowl believes it was in the case of the Gentiles, and this might serve as a pattern for setting aside certain

---

36. This seems to be a tendency of the "theological interpretation of Scripture" movement more generally, as illustrated by the works of Francis Watson and Kevin Vanhoozer, plus Craig Bartholomew's "Scripture and Hermeneutics" symposia, among other examples. For a symposium organized around wisdom as a theme, see David F. Ford and Graham Stanton, eds., *Reading Texts, Seeking Wisdom: Scripture and Theology* (Grand Rapids: Eerdmans, 2004).

37. Note the title of chap. 3: "Vigilant Communities and Virtuous Readers."

38. Fowl, *Engaging Scripture*, 174. This is part of chap. 5, "Making Stealing Possible: Criminal Thoughts on Building an Ecclesial Common Life."

proscriptions regarding homosexual acts—if through friendship the church hears narratives of the Spirit's activity in the lives of persons who engage in that behavior. Although Fowl's discussion of this controversial analogy is tentative,[39] it apparently manifests the extent of his hermeneutical focus on the Spirit and community relative to the direct content of biblical texts. Regarding such divisive issues, Fowl acknowledges that our hermeneutical thoughts are preliminary and inconclusive. Nevertheless, he asserts that "when the church divides over Scripture, it is not so much an issue of scriptural interpretation as it is the result of a separation of scriptural interpretation from a variety of other ecclesial practices. . . . All church division is fundamentally a failure of love."[40] Such is the vigilance he enjoins regarding interpretative virtue.

Like his reading of Acts 10–15 and his view of church division, Fowl's characterizations of determinate interpretation are questionable. Regarding such biblical scholarship, arguably he describes a worst-case scenario and then treats it as normal. Other objections to Fowl's work are possible as well, yet ultimately he confronts the church with quite a necessary challenge. He suggests that the academy has been much more successful at serving as a community of formation—at socializing its members into its practices of biblical interpretation—than the church has.[41] Whereas, for example, many biblical scholars inherently exclude Christian readings of the Old Testament from the outset, simply out of habit or instinct, churchly readers struggle to discuss Scripture together at all. It is perhaps ironic, if this is true, that a community defined around assumptions about neutrality, objectivity rather than subjectivity, and so forth could shape the commitments of its members in such strong but often unhealthy ways. Regardless, though not everyone who advocates "theological interpretation of Scripture" agrees with all the particulars of Fowl's view, they all affirm the need for

39. For Fowl's discussion and the broader literature he references, see *Engaging Scripture*, 113–26.

40. Stephen E. Fowl, "Further Thoughts on Theological Interpretation," in Adam et al., *Reading Scripture with the Church*, 128.

41. Fowl, *Engaging Scripture*, 179.

the church to improve the theological formation of its members and thus of their engagement with the Bible.

## Making Practice (Closer to) Perfect: Becoming Virtuous Readers

Discussion of communal practice also comes from another, complementary angle: the way biblical interpretation relates to virtue. As noted above, Fowl and others focus on the different habits of mind and heart fostered in the academy and the church. These communally shaped character traits influence our practices of interpretation considerably. From a Christian perspective, we can proceed beyond this descriptive point to a normative one: these dispositions are both a result and then a component of the Spirit's "means of grace" for understanding Scripture. Thus virtue has become a vital way in which to frame how the character of the interpreter(s) influences biblical interpretation, with particular relevance to the church and its aim of formation in the fruit of the Spirit. Advocates of theological exegesis agree that the formation of Christian virtue is a crucial aspect of interpretative practice, perhaps even the most appropriate way of stating its central aim.

Virtues deal with the dispositions to act in certain ways, and to do so reliably—characteristically—over time. A courageous person is not someone who makes a tough choice occasionally, in a few isolated instances, while often taking the easy way out; rather, a courageous person is someone who consistently, even if not perfectly, embodies that character trait over the course of a lifetime. In the words of Fowl, virtues are "those habits of seeing, feeling, thinking, and acting that, when exercised in the right ways and at the right times, will enhance one's prospects of both recognizing, moving toward, and attaining one's proper end."[42]

Christians understand virtue in some ways that are distinct from its classic definitions by the Greeks. First, ancient virtues were the moderate means between two extremes: a generous person, for example, neither gives away everything nor gives away nothing. At one level this is true enough, but such moderation is also connected

---

42. Stephen E. Fowl, "Virtue," *DTIB* 838.

to the male- and warrior-dominated context of ancient thinking about virtue. Virtues were not really for everyone, but rather were for the elite men who would run society. By contrast, of course, Christian faith sees the virtues as expectations for all of us who are graciously called and enabled to imitate Christ.

Such divine enablement points, second, to the way we acquire virtues. Ancient virtue involved an apparent paradox: one had to be virtuous in order to learn virtue, and to learn virtue in order to be virtuous. How could this process start? Which is the chicken, and which is the egg? Again, Christians affirm that there is divine action breaking into the immanent human sphere in Christ, calling and enabling us to pursue virtue. This unique answer regarding our path into the formation of virtue also gives rise to distinctly "theological virtues" of faith, hope, and charity. These are distinct from other ancient virtues not only in their acquisition from God but also in their definition of the virtuous life. Charity, for instance, operates in antielitist fashion, both in who its objects are and in who may attain it. Ultimately, of course, these virtues define the good human life as centered in Jesus.

As mentioned briefly in chapter 1, Ellen Charry has shown that classic theologians, from the apostle Paul to Thomas Aquinas, from Athanasius to John Calvin, had "sapiential" (wisdom-oriented), "aretegenic" (virtue-producing) aims in what they wrote. It is not simply that they wanted to apply doctrinal "theory" to practice in a one-way, linear move; rather, their purpose statements containing "so that . . ." or "in order that . . ." indicate that part of the criteria by which they recognized true doctrine involved whether or not a particular formulation would promote Christian virtue.[43] In a manner consistent with this focus on virtue, Christology often proved to be crucial, as, for example, when Athanasius fought so hard against heretical Arian Christology for aretegenic reasons: he resisted its removal of God's love from the cross.[44]

43. Ellen T. Charry, *By the Renewing of Your Minds: The Pastoral Function of Christian Doctrine* (Oxford: Oxford University Press, 1997).
44. On this point, see C. Fitzsimmons Allison, *The Cruelty of Heresy: An Affirmation of Christian Orthodoxy* (Harrisburg, PA: Morehouse, 1994), 81–94.

Augustine provides a good illustration of this classic orientation applied to hermeneutics, with his criterion of "double" love for God and neighbor:

> So anyone who thinks that he has understood the divine scriptures or any part of them, but cannot by his understanding build up this double love of God and neighbour, has not yet succeeded in understanding them. Anyone who derives from them an idea which is useful for supporting this love but fails to say what the writer demonstrably meant in the passage has not made a fatal error, and is certainly not a liar. In a liar there is a desire to say what is false, and that is why we find many who want to lie but nobody who wants to be misled. . . . Anyone with an interpretation of the scriptures that differs from that of the writer is misled, but not because the scriptures are lying. If, as I began by saying, he is misled by an idea of the kind that builds up love, which is the end of the commandment, he is misled in the same way as a walker who leaves his path by mistake but reaches the destination to which the road leads by going through a field. But he must be put right and be shown how it is more useful not to leave the path, in case the habit of deviating should force him to go astray or even adrift.[45]

Though not dismissive of the biblical text itself, Augustine clearly prioritizes the virtue of charity in interpretative decisions. In fact, Fowl asserts that "perhaps the clearest statement of the relationship between scriptural interpretation and the formation of virtue is found in Augustine's *On Christian Doctrine*."[46]

Referencing Augustine reminds us that accounts of virtue formation vary between Christians, and these variations have hermeneutical implications. On the one hand, many pentecostal Christians would have a very different and more supernaturally oriented account of the Holy Spirit's role in leading the community than

45. Augustine, *On Christian Teaching*, trans. R. P. H. Green (Oxford: Oxford University Press, 1997), 27 (I.86–88). For a substantial recent reflection on the significance of this work, see Alan Jacobs, *A Theology of Reading: The Hermeneutics of Love* (Boulder, CO: Westview, 2001).

46. Fowl, "Virtue," 838.

do Fowl and many other Protestants. Our discussion of global Christianity in chapter 6 will illustrate this further. Meanwhile, on the other hand, Augustine's account of virtue formation makes a sacramental context very explicit. Robert Dodaro shows that for Augustine, "the relationship between examples and sacraments parallels the relationship between knowledge (*scientia*) and wisdom (*sapientia*)."[47] Simply reading the Bible for moral examples—even Jesus—does not make a person virtuous the way that sacramental grace does, which operates analogously "to the transformation of Christ's human nature through its union with his divine nature"[48] (although, of course, sacraments may not lead automatically to virtue either). Like Augustine, more recent Catholic thinkers, including those mentioned earlier in the introduction, put much more direct emphasis on the sacraments than does Fowl's account of virtue.[49]

Not only do we have various accounts of virtue, but as Fowl acknowledges, we actually find not just one, but "two basic ways

47. Robert Dodaro, *Christ and the Just Society in the Thought of Augustine* (Cambridge: Cambridge University Press, 2004), 117.

48. Dodaro, *Christ and the Just Society*, 147.

49. For Henri de Lubac, it can even be said that "the principles of spiritual exegesis provide an intellectual framework for understanding how the Eucharist is at one and the same time the historical body of Christ, the sacramental body, and the ecclesial body," according to Susan K. Wood, *Spiritual Exegesis and the Church in the Theology of Henri de Lubac* (Grand Rapids: Eerdmans, 1998), 26. "In other words, de Lubac perceives the relationship of the sign and that which is signified in sacramentality to be analogous to that between type and antitype within spiritual exegesis" (Wood, *Spiritual Exegesis and the Church*, 107). The point is that, from this perspective, the church is not simply the accumulation of separate individuals who come together for (among other things) discussing Scripture. The church brings people into participation in the body of Christ, a historical entity that mysteriously transcends the sum of its members and their human activities. The various senses of Scripture are not simply constructed by readers or reading communities but instead are discerned as God leads the church into greater unity through maturing participation in Christ. Scripture reading is an aspect of that participation and is also shaped by other aspects, such as the sacraments. On the Eucharist and reading Scripture, see also R. W. L. Moberly, *The Bible, Theology, and Faith: A Study of Abraham and Jesus*, Cambridge Studies in Christian Doctrine (Cambridge: Cambridge University Press, 2000), chap. 2, "Christ as the Key to Scripture: The Journey to Emmaus."

of thinking about the relationship between virtue and theological interpretation of Scripture": "The first has to do with the ways in which theological interpretation aids in the cultivation of virtue. The second has to do with the ways in which virtue aids in the practice of theological interpretation. I will call the former virtue-through-interpretation and the latter virtue-in-interpretation."[50] About "virtue-through-interpretation," or what Kevin Vanhoozer calls virtue as an "aim" of theological interpretation,[51] there is widespread agreement. Yet, when it comes to "virtue-in-interpretation," or the possibility of virtue acting as a criterion or "norm" for theological interpretation, various thinkers differ.

To what extent, in other words, should we move beyond pursuing virtue as an aim of biblical exegesis to applying it as a theological criterion within interpretative practice? This question is complicated at multiple levels. At one level, the question involves the definition of virtue: who decides what counts as a virtue, or good interpretive fruit, and how do they decide? How does the material in one passage relate to other passages, to the teaching of Scripture as a whole, and to traditional interpretations of all these? Once again this requires an account of the biblical canon and the church, discerning the nature of their interaction—about which, as we have seen, Christians disagree and traditions vary. It is important, at least, to acknowledge that the ways in which we should use virtue as a theological norm for biblical interpretation are perhaps not as self-evident as either Fowl or his detractors might claim. At another level, we come to the end of major agreements about "theological interpretation of Scripture" and move toward the continuing challenges of self-definition that the movement faces. Before beginning to chronicle such challenges in part 2, I return to our case study.

50. Fowl, "Virtue," *DTIB* 837.
51. Kevin J. Vanhoozer, "Body-Piercing, the Natural Sense, and the Task of Theological Interpretation: A Hermeneutical Homily on John 19:34," *Ex Auditu* 16 (2000): 1–29.

## Extending the Example: Community as the Image of God?

The remaining task for this chapter is to relate its focus on community with our extended illustration concerning the image of God. Two connections emerge rather quickly. First, many theologians in the past few decades have adopted a "relational" understanding of the *imago Dei*, so that being made for community is a significant aspect of what constitutes humans as the divine image. In other words, is the content of the *imago Dei* communal? Second, since most Old Testament scholars reject this view, favoring other interpretations of Genesis 1:26–27, theologians are adopting it based on other criteria besides professional biblical scholarship concerning this particular passage. This raises the question, What are the hermeneutical implications of the communal approach as a case study?

The relational understanding rose to prominence in the writing of Karl Barth. Regarding the Genesis text, Barth sees "in our image" as the decisive phrase because it is "repeated twice"; "in our likeness" deals with our being made in the pattern of the divine image. Nonhuman creation is distinct from God, but is not a "counterpart" like humanity is.[52] The phrase "he created them male and female . . . is the interpretation immediately given to the sentence 'God created man.'"[53] The *imago Dei* consists not in a set of qualities but rather in the "I-Thou" relation of humans to God, in being created as God's counterpart.[54] Barth acknowledges that humans share being created male and female with animals, yet animals have other forms of differentiation (such as species), whereas gender is the only form of "differentiation and relationship" among humans relevant to the *imago Dei* in this biblical text.[55] Human rationality and rule over the animals are both subordinate under God and require divine blessing; in this way Barth

52. Karl Barth, *Church Dogmatics*, vol. III/1, *The Doctrine of Creation*, trans. J. W. Edwards, O. Bussey, and H. Knight, ed. G. W. Bromiley and T. F. Torrance (Edinburgh: T&T Clark, 1958), 183–84.

53. Barth, *Church Dogmatics*, III/1:184.

54. Barth, *Church Dogmatics*, III/1:184–85.

55. Barth, *Church Dogmatics*, III/1:185–86.

ties together creation and redemption.[56] The *imago Dei* ultimately points to Jesus Christ.[57]

In one of his renowned small-print sections Barth refers the divine plural of Genesis 1:26, "Let us," to "a genuine plurality in the divine essence," discussing various alternatives from critical scholarship that he finds unsatisfactory and borrowing significantly from Bonhoeffer.[58] For Barth, the text itself contains the necessary interpretative clue; the phrases after the initial reference to the image explain it.[59] The original or prototype according to which we are created is "the relationship and differentiation between the I and the Thou in God Himself."[60] This is not lost through the fall.[61] The New Testament focus, meanwhile, is not on us but rather on the prototype Jesus Christ.[62] Moreover, a parallel with Genesis 1 having Adam and his wife in view suggests that the church as the bride of Christ is ultimately in view along with him: in an important sense, this Christology is inclusive of ecclesiology and anthropology.[63]

Probably few people accept Barth's interpretation today as it stands. Among other reasons for this, few today agree with Barth's doctrine of the Trinity, given its tendency to emphasize divine oneness. Yet Barth surely helped to popularize a relational approach in which I-Thou relationships among humans are analogous to the I-Thou relations within God's triune life as Father, Son, and Holy Spirit. In this broader approach, God is communal, and so are we.

This type of approach serves noble causes, such as criticizing the individualism of modern Western society or calling for a more egalitarian, democratic notion of social order.[64] If the relational

---

56. Barth, *Church Dogmatics*, III/1:188–89.
57. Barth, *Church Dogmatics*, III/1:190–91.
58. Barth, *Church Dogmatics*, III/1:191–96.
59. Barth, *Church Dogmatics*, III/1:195.
60. Barth, *Church Dogmatics*, III/1:198.
61. Barth, *Church Dogmatics*, III/1:200.
62. Barth, *Church Dogmatics*, III/1:201.
63. Barth, *Church Dogmatics*, III/1:203.
64. For select examples of such an approach, see J. Richard Middleton, *The Liberating Image: The* Imago Dei *in Genesis 1* (Grand Rapids: Brazos, 2005), 23–24n28. Within theological hermeneutics literature, see the application of a

interpretation of the *imago Dei* helps people to rediscover the importance of the church and to commit themselves afresh to imitating Jesus' love and pursuing Christian community, then what should be our response when most critical biblical scholarship rejects it? Should we apply the principle "By their fruits you will know them" to potential interpretations of Scripture? If so, then should we adopt the relational *imago Dei* on those grounds in spite of the scholarly arguments against it? Do Augustine's words, cited in chapter 1, about reaching an interpretation that promotes charity—whether or not we take an improper shortcut—apply here?

To what extent, accordingly, should what Christopher Seitz calls "matters in front of the text"—"virtues, habits, community ethos and the like"[65]—influence or even determine our decisions about how to read the texts? Should we in fact favor such considerations because there is a relational character to our being the image of God, which must play out in how we pursue biblical interpretation—namely, engaging Scripture in the community the Holy Spirit is conforming to Jesus Christ? My goal is not to convince you that an approach such as Fowl's is correct but instead to give it a hearing. Nor is it my goal to have you reach your own conclusions about our case study yet. Furthermore, Barth and others might argue theologically for a relational anthropology even if they were to concede its absence in Genesis 1, since we have a variety of interpretative aims besides historical-critical repetition of an original author's view and since doctrinal decisions rarely hinge on exegetical choices in any one text. For the moment, my purpose is only illustrative; soon we will examine both these hermeneutical questions and the associated case study in more detail.

---

relational view in Francis Watson, *Text, Church and World: Biblical Interpretation in Theological Perspective* (Grand Rapids: Eerdmans, 1994), especially chaps. 6, 8. In a way, however, Watson retracts this in *Text and Truth: Redefining Biblical Theology* (Grand Rapids: Eerdmans, 1997), 304n26.

65. Christopher R. Seitz, "Christological Interpretation of Texts and Trinitarian Claims to Truth: An Engagement with Francis Watson's *Text and Truth*," *Scottish Journal of Theology* 52, no. 2 (1999): 210.

Indeed, at this point we find ourselves face-to-face with crucial challenges of definition. About the manner in which theological exegetes ought to interact with extratextual frameworks—biblical scholarship, especially the discipline of "biblical theology"; hermeneutical approaches for texts in general, besides the Bible; and the variety of global culture(s)—there is a lack of agreement within the movement. Thus, part 2 of this book involves outlining these challenges and the various differences within theological hermeneutics concerning how to address them.

# Continuing
# Challenges

# 4

# "Plundering the Egyptians" or Walking Like Them?

*Engaging Biblical Theology*

Among the crucial beliefs animating "theological interpretation of Scripture," as detailed in part 1, an underlying implication was the movement's critique of modern biblical scholarship. However, the extent and precise focus of that critique vary among the movement's participants. Such disagreements and ongoing challenges regarding definition will now be the focus of part 2. The starting point, chapter 4, concerns a particular mode in which the academic discipline of biblical studies has previously engaged theology. It should be noted, however, that engagement is an ambiguous metaphor, having connotations serviceable for either romance or warfare. Is biblical theology then an attempt by biblical studies to interact with theology or, rather, to tyrannize it? In any event, "biblical theology" in the modern sense has a complicated history of creation by eighteenth-century German scholars, apparent maturity in the middle of the twentieth century, and then a fall out of scholarly favor shortly thereafter.

After sketching that history, this chapter examines various proposals for the redemption of biblical theology: some see it as a bridge between Scripture and theology and therefore between biblical studies and theology as academic disciplines. In that case it could overlap a great deal with theological interpretation of Scripture. Yet others think that its decline was necessary to make space for the church to interpret the Bible as Scripture once again, and therefore they treat theological exegesis ultimately as a replacement for biblical theology.

The title of this chapter signals that tension. Early Christians spoke of interacting with pagan learning as "plundering the Egyptians."[1] In a reading of the exodus story, they saw a parallel between Israel's receiving gold from the Egyptians before their journey (Exod. 3:22) and Christians using truth discovered by non-Christians for other purposes. The potential application to biblical scholarship (this chapter) and the use of hermeneutical theories (next chapter) should be obvious. But to what extent and in what ways can the church learn from scholarship that is undertaken on the Bible without treating it as Scripture? Furthermore, to what extent can or should the church's scholars adopt, as part of engagement with Scripture, the modern historical methods that dominate such "biblical theology"? Consideration of the possible answers to that question requires a review of some history.

### The Modern Development of Biblical Theology as a Discipline

In a broad sense, biblical theology stems from the earliest days of Christian faith, as the church fathers and even the apostles struggled to make sense of Jesus Christ in relation to the Old Testament Scriptures. Developing and deploying the Rule of Faith against false "gnostic" dichotomies between the God of Israel and the God revealed in Jesus Christ was an enterprise seeking the unified teaching of the Bible. Later on, while the Protestant Reformers applied humanist resources to interpreting the Bible,

1. See, e.g., Augustine, *On Christian Teaching*, trans. R. P. H. Green (Oxford: Oxford University Press, 1997), II.144.

they still read it very much as a coherent whole—as Scripture. Thus Charles Scobie describes biblical theology in this more classical sense as "integrated."

In another sense, though, "biblical theology" names a modern endeavor, striving to apply historical methods in a "scientific" way for the sake of describing the religious ideas found to lie behind the scriptural texts. Though not without antecedents, J. P. Gabler provides a convenient starting point for discussing this version of biblical theology, which Scobie labels "independent." Gabler gave an address in 1787 entitled "An Oration on the Proper Distinction between Biblical and Dogmatic Theology and the Specific Objectives of Each."[2] Gabler and others worried that dogmatic theology often obscured the meaning of the Bible with human doctrinal constructions. Moreover, the contingent, situation-specific elements of biblical religion needed separation from the universal, rational elements of dogmatics.[3] Historical understanding of the biblical texts on their own terms could prevent such errors. This distinction between historical description and normative appropriation of the Bible came to characterize the discipline of biblical studies, usually with an antitheological edge. A famous expression of the distinction with respect to biblical theology came from Krister Stendahl in 1962 in *The Interpreter's Dictionary of the Bible*: biblical theology deals first with what the text "meant"—descriptively—separate from "what it means."[4]

A key theological problem with such independent biblical theology is fragmentation. The Old Testament and the New Testament become very difficult to integrate, which creates apologetic

2. See Charles H. H. Scobie, *The Ways of Our God: An Approach to Biblical Theology* (Grand Rapids: Eerdmans, 2003), 5. For the actual text, see John Sandys-Wunsch and Laurence Eldredge, "J. P. Gabler and the Distinction between Biblical and Dogmatic Theology: Translation, Commentary, and Discussion of His Originality," *Scottish Journal of Theology* 33 (1980): 133–58, especially 133–44.

3. Craig G. Bartholomew, "Biblical Theology," *DTIB* 85.

4. Krister Stendahl, "Biblical Theology, Contemporary," in *Interpreter's Dictionary of the Bible*, ed. G. A. Buttrick, vol. 1 (New York: Abingdon, 1962), 418–32.

problems for Christians who seek to defend the viability of their faith as a fulfillment of Israel's Scriptures. Certain biblical books start to fall apart into sections that come from different sources and contain different perspectives. The academy and the church separate further, since biblical scholarship tends to focus on describing historical origins and tracing the development of distinct concepts, while the church finds meaning in relating the texts to each other and to contemporary situations.

In the middle of the twentieth century came the most sustained attempt to pursue biblical theology in a more theologically interested, holistic manner: the "Biblical Theology Movement" (hereafter BTM). From roughly the 1940s until severe critiques in the 1960s, the BTM sought to retain historical-critical methods while also recovering the Bible as God's address to humanity. Some biblical theologians found Karl Barth's approach to divine revelation appealing, and they developed a focus on God's self-revelation via mighty acts in history. The Bible records such acts vis-à-vis the interpretation of their meaning for faith and can therefore be a vehicle through which the contemporary church receives the divine self-revelation.

Yet this movement never proved to be decisive for the American church life that it sought to address. Strong objections especially came from Langdon Gilkey and James Barr. As Craig Bartholomew notes, "Gilkey argues that the BTM got caught between being half liberal and modern, and half biblical and orthodox: 'Its world view or cosmology is modern, while its theological language is biblical and orthodox.'"[5] The BTM seemed to believe in divine self-revelation without holding that very many or even any of the mighty acts recorded in Scripture actually happened as such. The language of the religious experiences reflected in the Bible appeared to be "univocal"— that is, speaking directly or in one clear voice about reality. On Gilkey's view, modern people, however, could no longer believe that human language reflects the divine in any strong sense, because we "have *not* repudiated the liberal insistence

5. Bartholomew, "Biblical Theology," 87.

on the causal continuum of space-time experience."[6] The use of language raised Barr's chief problem with the movement as well. Barr criticized the BTM's use of word studies to trace the meaning of biblical concepts. He claimed that scholars wrongly committed "illegitimate totality transfer," assuming that biblical words inherently accumulated multiple meanings from their various uses and carried those meanings with them as developed theological ideas.[7]

Along with churchly ineffectiveness, these critiques apparently devastated the BTM. Yet a biblical scholar at Yale, Brevard Childs, responded to some of these problems and continued certain themes in a new key, a "canonical approach." Francis Watson later retained aspects of the BTM as well, defending it against Barr's criticisms in particular.[8] The next section of this chapter explores their proposals, along with others, for the future of biblical theology.

Meanwhile, what are the issues that such proposals must address? First, considerable debate rages over the scope of biblical theology, whether it approaches each author or text or community in isolation, or can also integrate them into larger sections—maybe seeking Old or New Testament theology or even whole-Bible theology. Most writing under the heading of "biblical theology" does not address the whole Bible but rather only one Testament or the other at most. That Childs's *Biblical Theology of the Old and New Testaments* and Scobie's *The Ways of Our God* stand virtually alone as exceptions helps to prove this. Even scholars who agree on the need for theological interpretation of Scripture differ about whether or not to interpret the Old Testament "on its

6. Langdon Gilkey, "Cosmology, Ontology, and the Travail of Biblical Language," *Concordia Theological Monthly* 33 (1962): 143–54, quotation at p. 144 (italics in original; reprinted from *Journal of Religion* [July 1961]: 194–205).

7. See the summary and sources in Bartholomew, "Biblical Theology," 87–88. Of special significance is James Barr, *The Semantics of Biblical Language* (London: Oxford University Press, 1961).

8. Francis Watson, *Text and Truth: Redefining Biblical Theology* (Grand Rapids: Eerdmans, 1997), 18–26.

own terms" before or in addition to interpreting it with reference to Jesus Christ.[9]

Second, how should one organize biblical theology? Some pursue one overarching theme or "center," such as promise or covenant or kingdom of God; others borrow categories from systematic theology, such as the doctrines of God, Christ, Spirit, and sin; still others use multiple biblical themes, as Scobie does with God's order, God's servant, God's people, and God's way. Those are *material* approaches, seeking to organize around theological content that appears across a range of texts and can hold them together. Frequently, though, scholars use more *formal* approaches to organization instead. One way to organize without a direct focus on content is to use historical development as a structuring principle and then trace a particular theme or an author's thought across time. There may or may not be aspirations of finding agreement with this author or occurrences of this theme in the rest of the Bible. Other scholars organize their work around the forms of the texts themselves in terms of literary genre or a corpus such as Wisdom literature. In any case, it can seem very difficult using purely historical or literary criteria in isolation to discover a comprehensive, organic unity within the biblical texts.

Third, then, what are the methods by which biblical theology defines itself, and how does it relate to other theological disciplines? Again, are its methods primarily historical or literary: should the focus be on discovering the historical origins of the theological ideas behind the biblical texts or on studying the literary relationships between these ideas and their expressions as the sources of contemporary meaning? Can these approaches work together, or must one choose a dominant approach? To what extent does biblical theology involve philosophical methods of conceptual analysis? Does the "theology" in its name come from using such analytical methods as it interacts with the biblical texts, or is biblical

9. See Christopher R. Seitz, "Christological Interpretation of Texts and Trinitarian Claims to Truth: An Engagement with Francis Watson's *Text and Truth*," *Scottish Journal of Theology* 52, no. 2 (1999): 209–26; Francis Watson, "The Old Testament as Christian Scripture: A Response to Professor Seitz," *Scottish Journal of Theology* 52, no. 2 (1999): 227–32.

theology really just a matter of imaginative reconstruction and historical description regarding the ideas in the Bible—in which case "theology" simply deals with the nature of the content that biblical scholars examine but not what they do?

After his critique of the BTM, Barr seems to represent the operative ideas of many biblical scholars. According to him, we usually define biblical theology in distinction from other fields with which it interacts and with which it may even share similar aspects. Thus it overlaps with, but is not the same as, biblical exegesis, the history of religions, systematic theology, and so forth. The key point is that biblical theology is descriptive, not normative. Its particular descriptive task is reconstructing historically the religious ideas that generated or came to expression in the biblical texts. Barr and many other scholars think that large portions of the Bible do not contain "theology" in any direct sense, because, for them, theology involves formal ideas and abstract concepts. For Barr, then, Stendahl's framing of the distinction between what the text "meant" (back then) and "what it means" (for today) should be more precise: biblical theology deals not with what the text "meant" (the task of exegesis) but rather with what the theology behind or of the text "was" (descriptively).[10] Often, since the text is not directly theological, getting to biblical theology requires imaginative reconstruction of latent ideas "behind" the text that gave rise to what was written. Meanwhile, normative meaning remains the province of systematic or dogmatic theology, in interaction with philosophy. Thus, biblical theology is essentially historical theology done on the Bible, reading it to discover a theology (or theologies) the same way that historians read Martin Luther to reconstruct his theology.[11]

Accordingly, from an intellectual perspective, Christians are permitted to read the Bible only in ways that historians allow. Reading the Old Testament and the New Testament together as

10. See Stendahl, "Biblical Theology, Contemporary."
11. James Barr, *The Concept of Biblical Theology: An Old Testament Perspective* (Minneapolis: Fortress, 1999), 203–5.

coherent Scripture is entirely an act of faith.[12] If biblical theology is thoroughly historical in the manner that Barr's representation suggests, then that is why Stephen Fowl rejects it: he views such an approach as standard in scholarly circles, and he does not believe that it permits the church to read the entire Bible as Scripture bearing witness to the Triune God.[13]

Hence, one option, as we have just seen, is to treat biblical theology and theological interpretation of Scripture as rivals—pure and simple. In that case, you must pick one or the other: the interpretative interests and methods of either the academy or the church are paramount. History demonstrates that we must take this possibility seriously, since much biblical scholarship has been antiecclesiastical in its effects and even its aims. Yet that is not the only side of the story. Responses to Barr and alternative versions of biblical theology have developed in recent decades.

## Proposals for the Theological Future of "Biblical Theology"

Of course, the following survey of recent proposals for biblical theology cannot be comprehensive or detailed enough to cover all the variety and nuance on the issue. Nevertheless, it is helpful to survey, roughly in chronological order, three major options for seeking to rejuvenate biblical theology in service to the church.

### Progressive Revelation: Revising Biblical Theology's Historical Results

The first approach took off with the rise of substantial evangelical scholarship in the second half of the twentieth century.[14]

---

12. Barr, *Concept of Biblical Theology*, 104.

13. Stephen E. Fowl, "The Conceptual Structure of New Testament Theology," in *Biblical Theology: Retrospect and Prospect*, ed. Scott J. Hafemann (Downers Grove, IL: InterVarsity, 2002), 225–36; *Engaging Scripture: A Model for Theological Interpretation*, Challenges in Contemporary Theology (Oxford: Blackwell, 1998), 36, 126n59.

14. See Mark A. Noll, *Between Faith and Criticism: Evangelicals, Scholarship, and the Bible in America* (New York: Harper & Row, 1986). See also the introduction to the present volume.

Its emphasis is the historical integrity and coherence of the Bible. Differences between the Old and New Testaments, or within the Testaments and among various books, can often be explained in terms of development over time. Revelation progresses as God gives it throughout the biblical history. Other differences may involve, rather than conflicting perspectives, complementary angles on commonly held truths.

Scholars in this tradition for a long time called their practice "grammatical-historical exegesis." Despite their recent adoption of some literary methods to complement the grammatical focus, the way they structure biblical theology still remains largely historical. Frequently this structure is called "redemptive-historical" in order to emphasize that the progress of revelation occurs alongside the progress of redemption as part of God's one unfolding story of salvation. The chief difference between this tradition and Barr, therefore, lies not in method but rather in assumptions and results. This is evident in the work of D. A. Carson, perhaps the most articulate defender of an approach tied to progressive revelation.[15]

Admitting the vast problems of definition, Carson still proceeds to stipulate that "by *biblical theology* I refer to that branch of theology whose concern it is to study each corpus of Scripture in its own right, especially with respect to its place in the history of God's unfolding revelation."[16] In supporting that definition, Carson defends the unity of Scripture against the fragmentation alleged by James Dunn and others. It is clear that his concern also involves the actuality of the historical events to which the Bible witnesses and the integrity of Scripture's historical portrayal of its own composition. In fact, historical concern extends even further, beyond both the unity of the ideas and the reality of events, to

---

15. "Progressive revelation" is susceptible to many definitions, and some of them are incompatible with the evangelical project, as noted by D. A. Carson, "Unity and Diversity in the New Testament: The Possibility of Systematic Theology," in *Scripture and Truth*, ed. D. A. Carson and John D. Woodbridge (Grand Rapids: Baker Academic, 1992), 82. Carefully used, however, the phrase still seems to capture the heartbeat of the tradition that I am sketching here.

16. Carson, "Unity and Diversity," 69.

embrace the goal of replicating those ideas and representing those events in our own understanding. In Carson's summation, "As I read the evidence, I perceive great diversity in emphasis, formulation, application, genre of literature, and forms of ecclesiastical administration. But I also perceive that there is a unity of teaching that makes systematic theology not only possible but necessary, and that modern theology at variance with this stance is both methodologically and doctrinally deficient."[17]

As for moving from Scripture to theology, then, Carson admits that the hermeneutical process is nonlinear and even messy. Yet the line of authority still moves in one direction, from the Bible to the contemporary world.[18] Therefore exegesis has a certain kind of principial privilege—to be followed by biblical theology, historical theology, and so forth—tied to the respective degrees of closeness between each of these disciplines and Scripture itself. The virtues of this tradition thus include its robust acknowledgment of the Bible's authority and its demonstration that many "scholarly" objections to Scripture's trustworthiness are not assured or self-evident. Such historical-critical objections to scriptural unity or accuracy often stem from a set of assumptions, and these presuppositions may be similar in strength and character to the faith commitments supporting more traditional views. Biblical diversity is real, but it does not necessarily threaten the possibility of developing a kind of coherent theology from these texts.

Among the potential problems for this tradition are occasions when biblical diversity seems to go farther than complementary variety, and sometimes evangelical scholars appear to be defensive or excessively interested in apologetic responses to critical viewpoints. Giving up scriptural unity is not necessarily a good solution in these cases either, but it may be that more flexible types of coherence—or

17. Carson, "Unity and Diversity," 94–95.
18. See D. A. Carson, "Systematic Theology and Biblical Theology," in *New Dictionary of Biblical Theology*, ed. T. Desmond Alexander and Brian S. Rosner (Downers Grove, IL: InterVarsity, 2000), 89–104. The differences between the earlier essay and this one may reflect increased literary emphasis on Carson's part.

less "systematic" types of resulting theology—should be sought.[19] A related problem might be that systematic theology in this tradition sometimes appears to be nothing more than a rigorously descriptive biblical theology "contextualized" or translated into contemporary language. Philosophical analysis, engagement with Christian tradition, and other aspects of constructive theology tend to drop out or receive inadequate attention. It is not yet clear whether members of this tradition, on the whole, will adopt or oppose the terminology of "theological interpretation of Scripture"; some may see it as friendly to biblical theology, whereas other biblical scholars may see it as a nonhistorical rival.

Finally, though, there may be a problem regarding the "locus" of biblical theology, or the place where the sought-after theological ideas reside. Do the authoritative biblical concepts come from the texts themselves (which might privilege a literary approach) or from the authors' minds behind the text (which might privilege a historical approach)? The tradition of progressive revelation tends toward author-oriented hermeneutics, for which the concepts in the texts are defined by "authorial intention." While some versions of these hermeneutics are open to considerable challenge, without a clearer answer regarding the locus of biblical theology this tradition must ardently retain a heavy focus on the author(s). That raises hermeneutical challenges discussed in the next chapter, as well as a more immediate one: the more focus placed on the human author(s) as opposed to the text(s), the more potentially problematic diversity one seems to find. Different wording and the like can point to complementary ideas, but moving behind the texts usually generates competing reconstructions of contexts and authors, thereby focusing on the particular factors that make a text or concept unique.

### A Canonical Approach: Reorienting Biblical Theology around "Text"

Another proposal likewise retains historical-critical exegesis instead of opting for postmodern approaches such as reader-response

---

19. See, e.g., the probing questions in Robert H. Gundry, *Jesus the Word According to John the Sectarian* (Grand Rapids: Eerdmans, 2002), 95.

interpretation. However, this canonical approach of Brevard Childs seeks to derive its biblical theology from the text(s) rather than from the author(s). Study of textual production remains; however, "canonical reading does not seek authorial intent at the level of the text's prehistory, in an alleged source or form, or tied to an historical audience, as these might be reconstructed using various critical tools of retrieval." Rather, this study of textual production is for the sake of theological care regarding history and "can seek to understand the theology of the final-form presentation as a kind of commentary on the text's prehistory."[20] It is not that the newer material always overwrites the old. The final form, though, is what the church recognized as canonical. On that basis theological decisions arise:

> Sometimes earlier traditions will be given literary prominence, while on other occasions a later editorial move will seek to constrain the tradition as received, and seek to coordinate interpretation by an extrinsic link to other texts in the canon. Canonical reading is not therefore an exact science, but a theological decision about what the proper parameters for interpretation are: the final-form presentation and the arrangement and sequencing that it exhibits, over against the simple history of the text's development as this is critically reconstructed.[21]

In terms of broader theological decisions, a canonical approach is "catholic/ecclesial," and therefore its orientation to the church requires openness to selective use of precritical exegesis. Its submission to the Rule of Faith is not an argument based on the virtue of the church community but instead an appeal to objective canonical unity based on God's use of the scriptural texts to bear witness to Christ.[22] At the same time, of course, there is indeed an implied ecclesiology: presumably, those forms of the text that bear the

20. Christopher Seitz, "Canonical Approach," *DTIB* 100.
21. Seitz, "Canonical Approach," 101. I focus on Seitz here because he provides not only a student's restatement but also a defense of Childs.
22. Seitz, "Canonical Approach," 102.

most faithful and fruitful witness to God's activity are what the church preserves "finally" over time.

The virtues of such an approach for the kind of theologically interested Scripture reading that we seek in this book probably are self-evident. A canonical approach is church-centered, somewhat hermeneutically and methodologically flexible, and creedally orthodox. As with the other options, though, we may notice a couple of potential weaknesses. Methodological flexibility can easily extend to incoherence.[23] On the one hand, the canonical approach is less determined by historical results than is the evangelical emphasis on progressive revelation. It appears more open to literary methods; it is more text- than author-centered. However, on the other hand, the canonical approach sometimes seems tailored to make room for certain historical-critical results. The documentary hypothesis regarding several sources for the Pentateuch, multiple authorship of the book of Isaiah, and other such critical viewpoints seem to be taken for granted. By what standard do canonical readings assume particular critical results while rejecting others?

An illustration of this tension is the problem of the "disappearing redactor": the way to discover various stages or sources behind a text is to see different parts that do not quite fit together seamlessly, yet if the final editor appears too skillful, according to the reconstructions of scholars, then the text is so smooth that evidence of stages or sources is erased.[24] Somewhat more generally, the effort to investigate how various oral and written traditions led to the texts' final form threatens to give back a possible theological gain. The focus on text can help the church to be less dependent

23. Regarding the canonical approach, Seitz notes that "'weaknesses' are often deemed to be such by those holding diametrically opposing views," while they "point up disagreements which plague the discipline *in any event*" (Christopher R. Seitz, "The Canonical Approach and Theological Interpretation," in *Canon and Biblical Interpretation*, ed. Craig G. Bartholomew et al., Scripture and Hermeneutics 7 [Grand Rapids: Zondervan, 2006], 62).

24. See the discussion and example of this in Seitz, "Canonical Approach and Theological Interpretation," 65.

on the more speculative results of modern biblical scholarship.[25] This motive has led many to call for more literary approaches to interpretation, in an effort to avoid undue historical speculation. Yet sometimes a canonical approach seems to remain dependent on theories of textual origins and historical development, even if the final form is authoritative. In this way it can appear as if the difference from the evangelical emphasis on progressive revelation simply involves another set of assumed historical-critical reconstructions.

Some have suggested that what a canonical approach really needs to be fruitful is a clearer doctrine of biblical inspiration—in other words, a more coherent way of understanding the texts' authority and unity.[26] To be sure, part of the reason for so many objections to the canonical approach is its comprehensive embrace and complex mixture of so many dimensions to interpretation.[27] In any case, like the emphasis on progressive revelation, the canonical approach both is beset by potential problems and offers crucial insights for theological interpretation of Scripture.[28]

### Theological Interpretation of Scripture: Redefining Biblical Theology?

With the relation between evangelical biblical theology and theological exegesis unclear, and with the definition of "theological interpretation of Scripture" unclear from the perspective of

25. On the fact that Childs's concerns are theological and not just literary—along with the fact that he is not just a "formalist" influenced by the literary movement known as "New Criticism"—see Timothy Ward, *Word and Supplement: Speech Acts, Biblical Texts, and the Sufficiency of Scripture* (Oxford: Oxford University Press, 2002), 241.

26. See Paul R. Noble, *The Canonical Approach: A Critical Reconstruction of the Hermeneutics of Brevard S. Childs*, Biblical Interpretation 16 (Leiden: Brill, 1995); Ward, *Word and Supplement*, 252–55.

27. Seitz, "Canonical Approach and Theological Interpretation," 62. This essay is a valiant effort to address many of the objections.

28. For recent reflection from Childs on theological exegesis see Brevard S. Childs, "Toward Recovering Theological Exegesis," *Pro Ecclesia* 6, no. 1 (Winter 1997): 16–26.

a canonical approach to biblical theology,[29] one might think that the water could get no muddier. But it can! Some thinkers seem inclined to use "biblical theology" and "theological interpretation of Scripture" as virtual synonyms, which, of course, requires some redefinition of terms.

Already in prior chapters we have noted Francis Watson's daring effort to bring biblical and systematic theology closer together. He wishes to achieve this by, as in the subtitle of one of his books, "redefining biblical theology."[30] This does not involve ignoring historical study, but it does mean approaching biblical interpretation with all the interests of systematic theology—regarding how the commitments of the church in the contemporary world illuminate the reading of scriptural texts. For Watson, furthermore, it means reading the Old Testament christologically; while taking the textual details seriously, we must admit that we always interpret them after Jesus Christ has filled out the rest of the story. By contrast, Christopher Seitz and advocates of a canonical approach believe that we must read the Old Testament as, from one perspective, a coherent canon in its own right; in a sense, Christ's apostles did so.[31]

More broadly, Watson brings theological interpretation of Scripture and biblical theology closer together by treating the latter as an interdisciplinary program. For him, biblical theology bridges between study of Scripture and systematic theology rather than being a more strictly historical discipline.[32] Brian Rosner similarly advocates a multidisciplinary approach to biblical theology as practicing *"theological interpretation of Scripture in and for the*

29. As noted in Seitz, "Canonical Approach and Theological Interpretation."

30. Watson, *Text and Truth*.

31. See the interchange between Watson and Seitz referenced in n. 9 above.

32. Other voices that seem to speak similarly include Joel B. Green, "Scripture and Theology: Uniting the Two So Long Divided," in *Between Two Horizons: Spanning New Testament Studies and Systematic Theology*, ed. Joel B. Green and Max Turner (Grand Rapids: Eerdmans, 2000), 23–43; "Rethinking History (and Theology)," in Green and Turner, *Between Two Horizons*, 237–42; Steve Motyer, "Two Testaments, One Biblical Theology," in Green and Turner, *Between Two Horizons*, 143–64.

*church*," while comparing this to the integrative nature of civil engineering:

> To make the comparison clear, civil engineering may be defined as the activity which results from the cooperation of various disciplines including metallurgy, physics, mathematics, sociology and town planning with the goal of producing bridges, sewers, roads, canals, etc. It may also be defined as the physical activity of construction in all its vigour and complexity. Similarly, biblical theology may be defined as the cooperation of various disciplines, and with reference to its various processes or methods and its intended product.[33]

Given the emphasis on progressive revelation in the book containing his essay, it may be that he is redefining not only biblical theology but also theological interpretation of Scripture. In other words, to a large degree the latter might be a function of redemptive-historical biblical theology tied to progressive revelation.

That is apparently similar to the approach of Charles Scobie, who puts forth a model of biblical theology as "intermediate": "a bridge discipline, standing in an intermediate position between historical study of the Bible and the use of the Bible as authoritative Scripture by the church."[34] Scobie's magisterial whole-Bible biblical theology does not use doctrinal categories from systematic theology much at all. Instead, its strength lies in proposing an integrative framework that accounts for historical and literary points of unity in the biblical texts themselves. This framework can function like a map, but we must always remember to keep our eyes on the territory itself. The map is only secondary; each different one displays reality in certain ways while distorting it in others.[35]

33. B. S. Rosner, "Biblical Theology," in *New Dictionary of Biblical Theology*, ed. T. Desmond Alexander and Brian S. Rosner (Downers Grove, IL: InterVarsity, 2000), 3–11, quotation at p. 3 (italics in original).

34. Scobie, *Ways of Our God*, 8. For an overview of Scobie's work, see Daniel J. Treier, review of *The Ways of Our God: An Approach to Biblical Theology*, by Charles H. H. Scobie, *Pro Ecclesia* 15, no. 2 (Spring 2006): 249–52.

35. Karl Möller, "The Nature and Genre of Biblical Theology: Some Reflections in the Light of Charles H. H. Scobie's 'Prolegomena to a Biblical Theology,'" in

All of the figures profiled above under these three headings are biblical scholars. They see tremendous value in critical study; the church is not free to ignore it or engage it only on an ad hoc basis. Yet each of these scholars recognizes as well that critical biblical scholars often operate with problematic assumptions. Thus, whether these biblical theologians privilege historical or literary or conceptual analysis, whether they accept or defend against many of the standard critical views concerning the biblical texts' authorship and unity, or whether they see systematic theology as mostly a result or also a component of scriptural interpretation, all of them believe that biblical theology has a future.[36]

## "Image of God": Problems and Possibilities from Biblical Studies

Such an array of voices and methodological arguments is dizzying. So it is time to step back and consider an illustration of how differences over "biblical theology" might matter. For this we return to discussion of the *imago Dei*.

"Image of God" does not appear all that often in the Bible. It seems to be particularly marginal in the Old Testament, from which Christians supposedly derive much of the doctrine of creation, with only three explicit references: Genesis 1:26–27; 5:1; 9:6.[37] Further difficulties involve two views of the *imago Dei* sketched in preceding chapters, which most biblical scholars reject. The "metaphysical" view, in which some structural dimension of human

---

*Out of Egypt: Biblical Theology and Biblical Interpretation*, ed. Craig Bartholomew et al., Scripture and Hermeneutics 5 (Grand Rapids: Zondervan, 2004), 60–62.

36. For a more formal typology and a sketch of my own approach, see Daniel J. Treier, "Biblical Theology and/or Theological Interpretation of Scripture? Defining the Relationship," *Scottish Journal of Theology* 61, no. 1 (2008): 16–31. Small portions of the material in this chapter previously appeared there and are used here with the journal's kind permission.

37. The following summation stems especially from the representative treatment in J. Richard Middleton, *The Liberating Image: The* Imago Dei *in Genesis 1* (Grand Rapids: Brazos, 2005).

beings relates to God, is allegedly associated with Greek thought rather than with Genesis 1:26–27. Since these verses say nothing explicitly about reason or an "immortal soul," how can the image of God be something substantive? Likewise, biblical scholars treat the "relational" view, even though it is tied somewhat to a phrase from the Genesis text, as a foreign import. Since animals too have sexual differentiation, it seems unlikely that "male and female" is an explanatory phrase revealing the nature of the image.

Thus, most biblical scholars today adopt some version of a more "functional" view. Humans' being the image of God consists in ruling on God's behalf over the rest of the created order. Humans therefore are God's representatives, and they display within creation what God is like. This consensus stems from the ancient Near Eastern background and from the near context, with its royal flavor (e.g., the functions mentioned in Gen. 1:26, 28),[38] and its syntax, which connects "let us make" to "let them rule" in such a way that ruling is "the *purpose*, not simply the consequence or result, of the *imago Dei*."[39] Scholars holding this view usually accuse theologians who advocate metaphysical or relational views of, like Humpty Dumpty in conversation with Alice, making the *imago Dei* mean whatever they choose.[40]

Yet what about the "let us" in Genesis 1:26: might it signal divine relationality that humanity images? Against the ancient trinitarian interpretations of the phrase, J. Richard Middleton represents a typical scholarly view when he suggests that "God here addresses the heavenly court or divine council of angels," with parallels in passages such as Isaiah 6 and Psalm 8.[41] What, then, about "male and female he created them": might this third line of the verse help somehow to define the image? As Middleton points out, "the third line in three-line Hebrew poetic units typically does not repeat a previous idea, but more usually serves a progressive function,

38. Middleton, *The Liberating Image*, 25–26.

39. Middleton, *The Liberating Image*, 53 (italics in original).

40. Norman Snaith, "The Image of God," *Expository Times* 86 (1974–75): 24, quoted in Middleton, *The Liberating Image*, 18.

41. Middleton, *The Liberating Image*, 55–59.

introducing a new thought."[42] Moreover, "male and female" are biological rather than social terms in the first instance, so that the phrase might not involve "relationality" even if it were definitive for the *imago Dei*.[43]

It is increasingly common to see in Genesis 1–3 the motif of a cosmic temple: "just as no pagan temple in the ancient Near East could be complete without the installation of the cult image of the deity to whom the temple was dedicated, so creation in Genesis 1 is not complete (or 'very good') until God creates humanity on the sixth day as *imago Dei*, in order to represent and mediate the divine presence on earth." Given the linguistic parallels between Genesis 2:2–3, Proverbs 3:19–20, and Exodus 31, "Bezalel's Spirit-filled craftsmanship, which imitates God's primordial wise design and construction of the cosmos, is functionally equivalent to the *imago Dei*."[44] The unformed and unfilled earth in Genesis 1:2 is reversed by the filling and subduing in Genesis 1:28;[45] thus it makes sense for Adam to have a child in his own image (Gen. 5:1–3), as a necessary part of humanity's vocation.

Unlike at least some Old Testament scholars, Middleton does not see his exploration of the ancient Near Eastern background as absolutely essential:

It is not my intent to claim that knowledge of the historical context of the text is strictly necessary for understanding the meaning of the image. In the field of Old Testament studies, any reconstruction of a text's historical context is largely a matter of hypothesis and plausibility. Reconstructing the historical context of Genesis 1 is particularly difficult, since there is little that could reliably indicate its date or provenance. The meaning of the image, thus, cannot be made to depend on something as tenuous as a particular historical reconstruction. Nevertheless, exploration of the possible historical

42. Middleton, *The Liberating Image*, 49.
43. Middleton, *The Liberating Image*, 50.
44. Middleton, *The Liberating Image*, 87. For extended integration of the temple conceptuality with biblical theology, see Gregory K. Beale, *The Temple and the Church's Mission: A Biblical Theology of the Temple*, New Studies in Biblical Theology 18 (Downers Grove, IL: InterVarsity, 2004).
45. Middleton, *The Liberating Image*, 89.

background and social context of the text may well deepen the understanding of the *imago Dei* that we have arrived at on other grounds.[46]

Despite this disclaimer, Middleton spends many pages—whole chapters, even—on extratextual background. Scholars clearly adopt the functional view due in part to the ancient Near Eastern context, at least as it affects the apparent meaning of the words for "image" and "likeness."

A dilemma surfaces, though, regarding whether to give prominence to the Egyptian or the Mesopotamian context: "while the Egyptian references suggest the image as *representative*, designating the office and status of the king, the Mesopotamian references suggest a *representational* notion of the image," involving behavioral characteristics that Middleton takes to be an addition to the representative notion.[47] He favors Mesopotamian influence, in light of "well-established, widely recognized connections between Mesopotamia and the primeval history"[48] in Genesis 1–11.

Unique to Genesis 1 is the application of such representative and representational concepts beyond the king; it "thus constitutes a genuine democratization of ancient Near Eastern royal ideology."[49] Yet that claim faces a crucial objection from source-critical scholars: according to Claus Westermann, the P source, or Priestly writer, "could not possibly think of a human being as standing in the place of God on earth."[50] This leads scholars such as Middleton into discussions of whether Genesis 1:1–2:3 actually comes from the Priestly source or whether P might be different in character than Westermann and others have thought.[51]

46. Middleton, *The Liberating Image*, 93.
47. Middleton, *The Liberating Image*, 118 (italics in original).
48. Middleton, *The Liberating Image*, 135.
49. Middleton, *The Liberating Image*, 121.
50. Claus Westermann, *Genesis: A Commentary*, trans. John J. Scullion (Minneapolis: Augsburg, 1984), 1.153, quoted in Middleton, *The Liberating Image*, 122.
51. Another illustration of this comes in W. Randall Garr, *In His Own Image and Likeness: Humanity, Divinity, and Monotheism*, Culture and History of the Ancient Near East 15 (Leiden: Brill, 2003), especially 11–12. In dealing with

Biblical theology's interest in close reading as well as historical sources and contexts is evident in these aspects of the illustration. Meanwhile, in Middleton's conclusion regarding Genesis 1–11, we see an example of the biblical-theological effort to interpret particular texts in relation to larger units:

> The Babel narrative of Genesis 11:1–9 thus functions as an appropriate conclusion to the primeval history. Having begun with God's creation of humanity as *imago Dei*, gifted with real power and agency in the world, Genesis 1–11 testifies to the increasing abuse of the power of *imago Dei*, culminating in the impasse of the Babel story, where that violence is substantially more organized (and hidden). This impasse will require a genuinely new departure in the canonical story, namely, the call of Abram (in Genesis 12), to bring blessing to all the families of the earth.
>
> When read against the background of Mesopotamian ideology, Genesis 1–11 discloses a worldview in which humanity is created in God's image and gifted by God with significant agency—able to make history, to affect the outcome of events in the real world, for good or ill. This latter point is important, since the worldview of Genesis 1–11 goes beyond a positive statement of God-granted human historical agency to stress that it is the misuse of precisely this agency that led to human violence in the world. In the end, this misuse leads even to the rise of powerful civilizations like the Assyrian and Babylonian empires, whose own humanly constructed ideology claims that such agency is reserved for its divinely legitimated rulers, while the majority of the human race is disenfranchised of such agency.[52]

---

the divine plurality in Genesis as it might conflict with the assumption of P's strict monotheism, his argument is that P comes from no one person; rather, it designates a source having certain broad characteristics along with a number of separate layers. This also leads to the following proposal: "According to the Priestly writer, humankind is a godlike and God-like creation. Created 'in our image' and 'in the image of God', it represents both levels of divine authority that govern the cosmos. Humankind represents God's community of co-rulers, responsible for performing the justice and enacting the sovereign will of God. It also represents the rule of God himself, at least as he demonstrates it throughout the Priestly cosmogony. A theophany, humankind represents the Enthroned One as well as those surrounding His throne" (Garr, *In His Own Image and Likeness*, 219).

52. Middleton, *The Liberating Image*, 227.

The last two chapters of his book similarly manifest Middleton's theological concerns. He tries to show that Genesis 1, rightly interpreted in relation to the Mesopotamian background, offers us not a violent God but rather a generous God who shares agency with humans.

However, Nathan MacDonald, in a generally appreciative review, doubts whether Middleton can facilitate an interdisciplinary conversation with theologians, as he desires to do:

> The problem is that the representational interpretation derives its principal force from an ancient Near Eastern context that lies *outside* the text of Genesis. Similarly, the theological and ethical implications of this view as Middleton expounds them are not articulated in Genesis but are deduced from the juxtaposition of the biblical text with the Near Eastern parallels. . . . Old Testament scholarship may argue that the ancient Near East is the most appropriate context in which to interpret the biblical text, but this is no longer merely an exegetical argument but also a hermeneutical one!

MacDonald acknowledges that "Middleton is unhappy with merely bringing an ancient Near Eastern royal ideology to bear onto the biblical text. Consequently, he seeks to demonstrate that God is portrayed as a king in Gen 1."[53] Yet, according to MacDonald, this point probably would require ongoing work to attain the necessary level of clarity and confidence.

My goal here has been to illustrate both the various component methods of biblical theology and the tensions that it sometimes raises for theological interpretation of Scripture. Biblical theology can be highly critical of appealing to classic doctrines or even, as in the case of the metaphysical *imago Dei*, believing them. Nor is its criticism limited to what is ancient, as its rejection of the contemporary relational view of the *imago Dei* demonstrates.

53. Nathan MacDonald, review of *The Liberating Image: The* Imago Dei *in Genesis 1*, by J. Richard Middleton, *Review of Biblical Literature* (October 2005): http://www.bookreviews.org/pdf/4737_4887.pdf (italics in original; accessed October 29, 2007).

Biblical scholars sometimes confidently highlight the problems with such views while neglecting their own, as tensions in Genesis 1 connected to the so-called Priestly source might demonstrate. Certainly they prefer to see ancient, original contexts as more hermeneutically decisive than later or contemporary ones. When it comes to the image of God, surely context is key, for the New Testament commonly interprets the *imago Dei* with respect to Jesus Christ. Can these texts indeed be counted as part of the context of Genesis 1:26–27? Clearly they are relevant—according to those who emphasize progressive revelation, take a canonical approach, or equate biblical theology with theological interpretation of Scripture—in various ways.

Apart from these three proposals regarding a theological future for biblical theology, its relation to the interpretative interests of the church would undoubtedly be adversarial. And some tension between biblical studies and theology remains likely in any case. Yet the church often benefits from the challenges of outsiders, since these can elicit fresh efforts to understand its own claims better. A poignant example, with regard to the *imago Dei*, is that both classic and contemporary approaches tend to neglect or exclude the human body. The functional emphasis of biblical scholarship, though, confronts the church with the need to address that reality. Even opposition to Christian doctrine, then, can aid our theological engagement with Scripture. Accordingly, in the next chapter we examine another dimension of the church's encounter with others: the general theories of hermeneutics by which the modern West has tried to understand what it means to interpret texts.

# 5

# Reading the Bible with Other Texts?

*Engaging General Hermeneutics*

In 1860 Benjamin Jowett famously exhorted people to "read Scripture like any other book."[1] Yet this controversial exhortation brings to the surface another challenge for theological interpretation of Scripture with regard to what "plundering the Egyptians" might mean: even if we choose to heed Jowett's call, how should we read books anyway? For it is not as if, when we come to hermeneutics in general, we find widespread agreement.

## The History of Variety in "Hermeneutics"

At its broadest, hermeneutics is an effort to grasp the nature of human understanding.[2] Often, though not necessarily always, this takes the particular form of understanding engagement with texts,

1. Benjamin Jowett, "On the Interpretation of Scripture," in *Essays and Reviews: The 1860 Text and Its Reading*, ed. Victor Shea and William Whitla (Charlottesville and London: University Press of Virginia, 2000), especially 482.
2. Portions of this chapter appeared previously in Daniel J. Treier, "Theological Hermeneutics, Contemporary," *DTIB* 787–93.

or else treating all forms of understanding in terms of "texts"—that is, whether a person, a poem, a play, or a painting is being understood, it is approached *as* a text. Texts have boundaries, or beginnings and endings, they involve signs and symbols in patterns, and they convey meaning(s). In one sense, hermeneutics is at least as old as Plato; ancient interpreters wrestled with textual meaning and sought to develop rules whereby it could be reliably understood. However, in the modern period hermeneutics eventually became a more distinct philosophical project.[3]

### Human Beings in History

The modern age birthed new forms of historical consciousness. Charles Taylor describes the premodern sense of time "as the locus for the recurrent embodiment of archetypes, not themselves temporally placed." For example, in classic art "we feel the incongruity when Mary has the features of a thirteenth-century Tuscan rather than those of a first-century Jew, because to us she is this particular woman, whose placing in history is crucial to what she was. But in a mentality in which there were such, the Mother of God easily gravitates towards an archetype; and as such she is equidistant from, and hence equally belongs to, all ages."[4]

By contrast, the modern preoccupation with historical placement joined with the rise of natural science to promote history as a critical, academic science. This new form of preoccupation with history also connected the meaning(s) of texts more and more with their origins. Because premodern hermeneutical rules so often focused on Scripture or the Christian tradition, they tended to reflect the classic, somewhat timeless status of such texts. To the degree that premodern interpreters read for the literal sense, then, it was not necessarily limited to the historical intentionality

3. For a survey of different uses of the word "hermeneutics" as well as application of its key thinkers to biblical interpretation, see Richard S. Briggs, "What Does Hermeneutics Have to Do with Biblical Interpretation?" *Heythrop Journal* 47 (2006): 55–74.

4. Charles Taylor, *Sources of the Self: The Making of the Modern Identity* (Cambridge, MA: Harvard University Press, 1989), 288.

of the human author. At least with regard to Scripture, God was ultimately the Author of interest.

Modern thinking, however, obligated interpreters of the Bible to focus primarily or even exclusively on the texts' origins. The methods of study became largely historical in the newer critical sense. Moreover, in the new modern universities patterned after the University of Berlin (founded in 1801), the natural sciences became the paradigm for what counts as true knowledge. As the humanities came under threat from this scientific dominance, hermeneutics offered a defense: the sciences would deal with empirical "explanation" according to laws of cause and effect, while the humanities would pursue "understanding" of human beings in relation to their cultural freedom.

The ontological possibility of textual meaning and interpretation via human locatedness in history became a privileged focus after Martin Heidegger's *Being and Time*.[5] According to Heidegger, Western philosophers wrongly studied Being as a general category, as if it had nothing to do with time. They neglected particular beings, especially that being (the human) who could reflect upon the meaning of Being. The relevance of this for hermeneutics lay in Heidegger's preoccupation with language: as the house of being, language is the arena for thinking human possibilities. In Heidegger's thought the distinction between Language and language came to parallel the distinction between Being and being. Discourse is the tangible enactment of his famous concept *Dasein*—that is, the human pursuit of understanding the meaning of B/being. Such a concern arises not due to eternal metaphysical givens (Being as permanent and unchanging, according to the Greeks) but rather due to human "care" in history. We seek to understand the authentic possibilities of meaning for our lives because we find ourselves "thrown" into existence while we are concerned about facing death. Heidegger privileged the language of art and poetry over that of science and analytic philosophy because of his concern for these human existential possibilities. According to Gerald Bruns,

5. Martin Heidegger, *Being and Time: A Translation of "Sein und Zeit,"* trans. Joan Stambaugh (Albany, NY: State University of New York Press, 1996).

Heidegger ties our experience of language to being overwhelmed and "struck dumb" rather than speaking. Thus, "*Listening* is the key word of Heidegger's hermeneutics."[6]

### Hans-Georg Gadamer

Influenced by Heidegger, Hans-Georg Gadamer was probably the most dominant hermeneutical thinker of the twentieth century. Gadamer's *Truth and Method* criticized the modern obsession with methodological clarity and scientific certainty.[7] For Gadamer, truth happens in events of disclosure. We ought not view the interpretation of texts as scientific events in which we "explain" the texts or their origins and determine their meaning on such a basis; instead, to "understand" a text involves existential application in particular contexts. However, contra certain critics, Gadamer is no mere relativist, as a couple of analogies will illustrate.

Reading a text is like playing a game: certain actions become meaningful only within a given context, and one responds within the flow of the play instead of endlessly analyzing every move in isolation. This explains why I am no good at basketball: by the time I have analyzed and figured out whether or not to pass the ball, one of the opposing team's guards has stolen it and sunk a layup at the other end of the court. Similarly, texts act upon us in ways that influence our possibilities for response, and to a degree meaning arises without waiting for our separate activity or initiative as human subjects. We respond within the flow of encountering the text rather than acting upon a neutral object. This kind of textual influence clarifies that an existential focus on application does not mean that *we* can or should do to a text anything we want. There is a form of objectivity that the text exerts upon us.

Reading a text is also like having a conversation: the text "speaks" and we respond, or we ask a question for the text to answer. Negotiation must occur between the "horizons" of the text and the

---

6. Gerald Bruns, *Hermeneutics Ancient and Modern*, Yale Studies in Hermeneutics (New Haven: Yale University Press, 1992), 157.

7. Hans-Georg Gadamer, *Truth and Method*, trans. Joel Weinsheimer and Donald G. Marshall, 2nd ed. (New York: Continuum, 1989).

reader in regard to what the subject matter of the conversation will be. When the negotiation is successful, a "fusion of horizons" results: there is overlap somehow between what the text addresses and what the reader seeks or applies in an existential situation. Again, the text has its say, while there is also a dimension of understanding that is relative to the later context.

Of course, we do not simply leap from our horizon back over the intervening history and into the author's horizon or the text's original context. A text generates a "history of effects" (*Wirkungsgeschichte*) as it is read in various situations over time and across places. These effects accumulate through language and affect subsequent readings—intentionally or unintentionally, for good or ill. This traditioning process provides our linkage back to the text itself and those elements of its context that are carried along with it through history. Hence, for example, one cannot read Romans 4 on "justification by faith" after Martin Luther apart from his influence. Even if a person has never heard of Luther, his interpretation of Paul has shaped the language of Western culture in such ways that translations and linguistic connotations of the words bear its marks. Even a person who rejects a Lutheran interpretation *rejects it* rather than avoiding it altogether.[8]

### Alternatives to Gadamer

Gadamer's recovery of human understanding as responsive agency within the flow of history has been inspirational to a great number of people. In this way he rescued texts and interpretation from certain kinds of historicism and scientism. However, many others have rejected his thought, viewing it as naïvely positive about tradition and entirely too negative about critical methodologies of various kinds. For instance, Jürgen Habermas and others who embrace forms of "critical theory" believe that understanding ideally

---

8. Luther may be an especially appropriate illustration because Bruns finds Gadamer to be a kind of "secular Luther" (see Bruns, *Hermeneutics*, chap. 7). For Luther's hermeneutical influence on others, see also Jens Zimmermann, *Recovering Theological Hermeneutics: An Incarnational-Trinitarian Theory of Interpretation* (Grand Rapids: Baker Academic, 2004), chap. 2, especially 75–77.

involves persuasion using reasons.[9] Striving for anything less than critical objectivity in this sense turns conversation into ideological manipulation and robs people of fully free agency. On the other hand, meanwhile, various "postmodern" thinkers such as Jacques Derrida find Gadamer to be too conservative with respect to textual meaning(s).[10] Emphasis on textual traditions' stability fails to do justice to the slippage that occurs from one context to another and the inevitable plurality of meanings that results. For such thinkers, Gadamer's approach still treats the text as having too much say.

One way to characterize the hermeneutical discussions of the twentieth century is in terms of contrasting traditions: "The first might be called transcendental, and its centerpiece is Edmund Husserl's idea that understanding is of ideal entities called meanings rather than of minds," in which case "interpretation is a working backward rather than a taking forward."[11] This is probably the mind-set that dominates historically oriented biblical scholarship. By contrast, "Opposed to transcendental hermeneutics, at least at first glance, is Heidegger's analysis of understanding as a mode of practical involvement or concern with others and with a world."[12] For the latter, focused with Gadamer on the event of understanding, "The hermeneutical circle in this event is never purely philological, that is, it is not simply an exegetical movement between the parts and the whole of a text that is present before us as an object. Instead, it is an ontological movement between the text and our situation as interpreters of it."[13]

9. See Jürgen Habermas, *The Theory of Communicative Action*, vol. 1, *Reason and the Rationalization of Society*, trans. Thomas McCarthy (Boston: Beacon, 1984); vol. 2, *Lifeworld and System: A Critique of Functionalist Reason*, trans. Thomas McCarthy (Boston: Beacon, 1987).

10. See the survey and bibliography in Craig G. Bartholomew, "Deconstruction," *DTIB* 163–65. There is also Stephen Fowl's treatment of "antideterminate" interpretation, which we noted earlier in chap. 3. A relatively accessible text by Derrida, relevant to biblical hermeneutics because he engages speech-act philosophy, is *Limited Inc*, trans. Jeffrey Mehlman and Samuel Weber, ed. Gerald Graff (Evanston, IL: Northwestern University Press, 1988).

11. Bruns, *Hermeneutics*, 106.

12. Bruns, *Hermeneutics*, 2–3.

13. Bruns, *Hermeneutics*, 4.

Although Paul Ricoeur identifies with the latter view in many ways, his attempt to mediate between various approaches has likewise been influential.[14] Ricoeur speaks of a threefold hermeneutical arc: an initial moment of "understanding" (a first, naïve encounter with the text), a critical moment of "explanation," and then a refigured moment of "application" (a "second naïveté"). The critical moment can involve suspicion, but more fundamental is a "hermeneutic of trust." For Ricoeur, the critical moment involves not merely suspicion about societal power structures and the like but also very careful exegetical study of the text. The goal or regulating principle, though, is not recovery of the original context or author's intention(s) but instead study of the text's "sense" (its semantic features especially—words, grammar, and so on). For example, textual sense involves the ideas of what "The queen of Denmark is dead" means without reference to who the queen of Denmark is, or whether there even is one. Texts have "reference" to reality by projecting a "world" for us to inhabit, in front of the text—a way of living. Notice the relative absence of the historical-critical focus—even the emphasis of much biblical theology—on what is behind the text in its original context. We do not, strictly speaking, recover or reconnect to some world of the author, even if Ricoeur retains a role for critical methodologies and rejects relativism.[15]

14. See the survey and bibliography in Dan R. Stiver, "Method," *DTIB* 510–12; Kevin J. Vanhoozer, "Ricoeur, Paul," *DTIB* 692–95. A comparative source is John B. Thompson, *Critical Hermeneutics: A Study in the Thought of Paul Ricoeur and Jürgen Habermas* (Cambridge: Cambridge University Press, 1981). Most relevant to biblical hermeneutics are Paul Ricoeur, *Essays on Biblical Interpretation*, ed. Lewis S. Mudge (Philadelphia: Fortress, 1980); *Figuring the Sacred: Religion, Narrative, and Imagination*, trans. David Pellauer, ed. Mark I. Wallace (Minneapolis: Fortress, 1995); André Lacocque and Paul Ricoeur, *Thinking Biblically: Exegetical and Hermeneutical Studies*, trans. David Pellauer (Chicago: University of Chicago Press, 1998).

15. Ricoeur's hermeneutics can be viewed more theologically: "Perhaps it is in reading [Walter] Brueggemann that we may get the best idea of what a biblical interpretation informed by Ricoeur's approach might look like" (Briggs, "What Does Hermeneutics Have to Do with Biblical Interpretation?" 69). Brueggemann emphasizes time, narrative, and imagination as he explores the Old Testament

Beyond these well-known thinkers, two additional approaches have especially influenced biblical interpretation. First, E. D. Hirsch's *Validity in Interpretation* has dominated conservative Protestant hermeneutics for several decades.[16] As the title suggests, Hirsch seeks a standard by which to distinguish between valid and invalid interpretations. The only possible standard, he argues, is the author's intention in writing. Readers cannot recover an author's motivations in a psychological sense,[17] but they can begin with a sense of the text's genre before examining its details in light of that and then moving back and forth from part to whole in refining an interpretation. Interpretations cannot achieve total comprehensiveness or certainty, but they can reliably approximate the author's intended meaning. Many conservatives have seen Hirsch's view as a way to preserve the Bible's authority, distinguishing between its objective single meaning, the interpreter's subjective understanding (which seeks that meaning), and the many possible applications that are somewhat relative to the reading context. Hirsch's attack upon Gadamer, published as an appendix in *Validity in Interpretation*, influenced many conservative rejections of that dominant figure as a relativist.[18]

Second, others have taken less author-centered approaches in favor of focusing on the text itself. "Formalist" hermeneutics, associated with the "New Criticism," rejected the pursuit of authorial intention as a Romantic impossibility—trying to "understand the author better than he understood himself" when in fact an author's intentions are inaccessible to us. Instead,

social world(s) and intracanonical disputes (in his view) that expose our contemporary world to prophetic critique.

16. E. D. Hirsch Jr., *Validity in Interpretation* (New Haven: Yale University Press, 1967).

17. Such an aspiration is associated with the "intentional fallacy," about which some believe that Hirsch should be more careful; see Kevin J. Vanhoozer, "Intention/Intentional Fallacy," *DTIB* 327–30.

18. Roger Lundin, *From Nature to Experience: The American Search for Cultural Authority* (Lanham, MD: Rowman & Littlefield, 2005), 158. Hirsch's later works seemed to admit that there might be other interpretive aims besides validity, somewhat weakening his earlier position. However, conservative Protestant admirers of Hirsch have largely ignored this.

somewhat similar to Ricoeur's textual sense interpretation, the literary approach retained objectivity by focusing on a text's formal features such as genre, structure, word repetition, and so forth.

More recently, some biblical scholars are beginning to appropriate "relevance theory" from linguistics.[19] Meaning is not exhausted by semantics; pragmatic factors, in fact, usually dominate our understanding. One needs to have shared background from which to draw mental implications about how to see a statement's relevance. For, most of the time, communicators presume points in common with their audiences; rather than making this background explicit, they leave it implicit and count on the hearers or readers to fill in the necessary mental gaps. Suppose, for example, I say to you, "The meat has been on the counter for seven hours." Do I mean that you should cook it? Throw it away? Come home for dinner in an hour? The meaning might be clear without my saying another word if you know that I let meat thaw a long time before cooking it or, conversely, that I never eat meat thawed in such a fashion.

The obvious question that all these options raise, of course, is whether there should be a definitive context or set of contexts for biblical interpretation, and, if so, what that might be. The history of hermeneutical variety manifests different ways of emphasizing or coordinating the author, the text, and/or the reader. A related hermeneutical triad concerns the historical, literary, and philosophical or theological methodologies mentioned in the previous chapter on biblical theology. Emphasis on the author tends to privilege historical (and grammatical) methods; focus on the text usually fits with prioritizing literary methods. Those who pursue theological interpretation of Scripture must give attention to what should be the proper role of the reader, yet they do not necessarily have to adopt reader-response hermeneutics. For, instead, theological hermeneutics involves thinking about the nature and nurture of interpretation in light of God, whose action puts reader, text,

---

19. Dan Sperber and Deirdre Wilson, *Relevance: Communication and Cognition*, 2nd ed. (Oxford: Blackwell, 1995).

and author in a larger context that decisively alters the character of their interaction.[20]

## Theological Hermeneutics

Thus "theological hermeneutics" is fast becoming a term with its own history, which may designate at least two projects for Christians to undertake. First, Christians may believe that they need to develop an account of text interpretation or even human understanding in interaction with Christian doctrine(s). Second, Christians need to develop an account of how biblical interpretation should shape, and be shaped by, Christian theology. For the first project, the adjective "theological" designates the mode in which we pursue *general* hermeneutics. For the second project, "theological" also designates the material content involved in *special* hermeneutics regarding the Bible. The two projects can occur simultaneously, or distinctly, or even separately, one without the other.

### *Appealing to Precedents*

Thinkers in theological hermeneutics frequently appeal to precedent(s) favoring their work. In particular, as we have seen, advocates for "theological interpretation of Scripture" often find motivation in their admiration for premodern interpreters, resulting in a quest to recover "religious reading" and a unified Bible.

An example of using premodern precedent for general hermeneutics is Paul Griffiths's book *Religious Reading*.[21] Griffiths contrasts the "consumerist" reading carried out in contemporary Western culture, by which we read silently and perhaps do not even "subvocalize" (repeat the words in our minds), with classic approaches to sacred texts. Before current concepts of literacy, people read out loud, and the oral experience of a text was significant. Often

20. See especially Mark Alan Bowald, *Rendering the Word in Theological Hermeneutics: Mapping Divine and Human Agency* (Aldershot, UK: Ashgate, 2007).
21. Paul J. Griffiths, *Religious Reading: The Place of Reading in the Practice of Religion* (Oxford: Oxford University Press, 1999).

the reading was communal, especially since many or most people could not read. Griffiths develops this not only using Christian sources but also by examining adherents of other religions such as Buddhism.

Among the important premodern interpreters and concepts, discussed elsewhere, are the Rule of Faith championed by Irenaeus and Tertullian, Origen's "spiritual sense," and the recoveries of the "literal sense" by Thomas Aquinas, Martin Luther, and John Calvin. Most influential on premodern hermeneutics, however, was Augustine's *De doctrina christiana* (*On Christian Teaching*), which shaped Christian pedagogy and exegetical practice for many centuries.[22] Augustine's twofold focus involves, first, discovery and, second, presentation[23]—already intriguing for modern people, since we often think that the latter does not constitute part of interpretation.

Book I introduces distinctions between signs and things, as well as between their enjoyment (improper, supplanting God with the things in themselves) and their use (proper, for the sake of God, who alone ought to be enjoyed). Having introduced this aim of enjoying God, Augustine addresses signs in Book II, introducing the various distinctions and rules that led many to characterize premodern theological hermeneutics as focused on particular technical points for understanding the Bible. Book III follows with further consideration of how to handle ambiguous signs—whether or not an expression is literal or figurative, and so on. Augustine appeals to Tyconius's book of seven rules for interpreting the Scriptures before, in Book IV, finally arriving at the subject of presentation. Rather than fulfilling his readers' expectations by straightforwardly discussing pagan rhetoric, Augustine focuses on the character of the presenter, exhorting us to wisdom instead of an emphasis on eloquence. As noted earlier, Augustine's interpretative priority involves that which promotes love for God and neighbor.

22. See Edward D. English, ed., *Reading and Wisdom: The "De Doctrina Christiana" in the Middle Ages* (Notre Dame, IN: University of Notre Dame Press, 1995).

23. Augustine, *On Christian Teaching*, trans. R. P. H. Green (Oxford: Oxford University Press, 1997), I.1.

Premodern hermeneutics inevitably elicits different responses. On one side, Werner Jeanrond labels Augustine the father of semiotics (working with signs) and sees the Christian tradition as positively disposed toward interaction with general hermeneutics.[24] He therefore criticizes Karl Barth for his ad hoc approach to historical criticism.[25] Jeanrond notes that both Barth and Rudolf Bultmann "tried to overcome the ideological limitations of historicist interpretation of the Bible," but they opposed each other concerning proper interaction with philosophy.[26] Appreciative of Heidegger, Bultmann distinguished "presuppositions" (which are indispensable) from "prejudice" (which is inappropriate) in studying the New Testament. Famously suggesting the impossibility of believing in miracles now that we use lightbulbs, he defended a program of "demythologization" in which the true theological significance of supernatural claims became the crux of interpretation. Thus would the gospel's claim over modern humans become clear. Bultmann used supposedly historical criteria to separate faith from history, since the latter would, in his version of Lutheranism, constitute reliance upon something besides the Word of God. Being able to know only about the forms of the early church's faith, yet nothing actual about the historical Jesus, sharpens the demand of God for our faith. Bultmann's influence helped to foster the "New Hermeneutic," which was popular for a time due to blending literary formalism with existential emphasis on the Word of God. Against Barth, Jeanrond favors Bultmann, believing that such general hermeneutical engagement is most faithful to Christian tradition.

On the other side from Jeanrond stands Stephen Fowl, who favors the adoption of no general hermeneutical theory. He certainly could point out that for Jeanrond to treat general hermeneutics as foundational—taking first priority preceding any special hermeneutics—is an unlikely oversimplification of Christian tradition. Meanwhile, Fowl appeals even to Thomas Aquinas as an example

24. Werner Jeanrond, *Theological Hermeneutics: Development and Significance* (New York: Crossroad, 1991), 22.

25. For exposition of Barth's approach, see the introduction to the present volume.

26. Jeanrond, *Theological Hermeneutics*, 157.

of someone having a flexible understanding of the literal sense.[27] Given Aquinas's contribution to recovering the literal sense and his interaction with Aristotelian philosophy, one might expect him to follow general hermeneutics carefully. Fowl suggests the contrary. Moreover, Fowl appeals to Jeffrey Stout's argument that any definition of textual meaning is arbitrary.[28] In reality, the concept describes various interpretative interests, and in any given context one should substitute for the word "meaning" an explanation of the particular interest that one pursues.[29]

Still another perspective comes from Jens Zimmermann. Zimmermann argues against Gadamer and others who suggest "that the narrowly defined ground of theological hermeneutics prevented it from articulating universal concepts of understanding."[30] It is not true that premodern Christian hermeneutics consisted entirely of technical rules for the specifics of biblical interpretation. In fact, such hermeneutics embraced universal concerns: "Pre-Enlightenment hermeneutics was all about presuppositions, about psychological and philosophical anthropology, the nature of reality, and ontology."[31] Yet this does not license Jeanrond's pretheological use of general hermeneutics. Instead, Zimmermann claims that theological reflection on the hermeneutical implications of the incarnation counted already as a general theory: true self-knowledge stems from knowledge of God. From that perspective, several contemporary thinkers seek to address general hermeneutics in a specifically Christian manner.

27. Stephen E. Fowl, "The Importance of a Multivoiced Literal Sense of Scripture: The Example of Thomas Aquinas," in *Reading Scripture with the Church: Toward a Hermeneutic for Theological Interpretation*, A. K. M. Adam, Stephen E. Fowl, Kevin J. Vanhoozer, and Francis Watson (Grand Rapids: Baker Academic, 2006), 35–50. See also Eugene F. Rogers Jr., "How the Virtues of an Interpreter Presuppose and Perfect Hermeneutics: The Case of Thomas Aquinas," *Journal of Religion* 76, no. 1 (January 1996): 64–81.

28. Stephen E. Fowl, *Engaging Scripture: A Model for Theological Interpretation*, Challenges in Contemporary Theology (Oxford: Blackwell, 1998), 56–58.

29. Jeffrey Stout, "What Is the Meaning of a Text?" *New Literary History* 14 (1982): 1–11.

30. Zimmermann, *Recovering Theological Hermeneutics*, 18.

31. Zimmermann, *Recovering Theological Hermeneutics*, 24.

### Addressing General Hermeneutics

As noted above, Jeanrond advocates special hermeneutics first following, *then* contributing to, general hermeneutics:

> Our narrative of the history of philosophical hermeneutics began with a theologian, Friedrich Schleiermacher, who discovered that theological interpretation needed a thorough foundation in philosophical hermeneutics. Now the development of philosophical hermeneutics by Ricoeur has revealed the need to include the interpretation of religious texts in an adequate human existential reflection. The symmetry between the theological endeavours of Schleiermacher and the philosophical enterprise of Ricoeur is striking![32]

This highlights the pivotal role of Schleiermacher in the development of modern hermeneutics. He "was one of the first major thinkers to wrestle" with the problem of preunderstanding—"If understanding, as it were, presupposes understanding, how can it begin?"[33] Schleiermacher "distinguished between the linguistic or 'grammatical' aspects of hermeneutics and the 'psychological' aspects of the subject,"[34] yet his view that the aim of interpretation is to reproduce the consciousness of the author puts a premium on "self-understanding."[35] Unfortunately, aside from the general problems with such a Romantic "emphasis on feeling and subjective experience," this often plays out in anthropological reductions of Christian doctrine.[36]

The leading chronicler of the hermeneutical tradition after Schleiermacher, in terms of its influence on biblical interpretation, is Anthony Thiselton. His initial work, *The Two Horizons*, bore this descriptive subtitle: *New Testament Hermeneutics and Philosophical Description with Special Reference to Heidegger,*

---

32. Jeanrond, *Theological Hermeneutics*, 77.

33. Anthony C. Thiselton, *The Two Horizons: New Testament Hermeneutics and Philosophical Description* (Grand Rapids: Eerdmans, 1980), 103.

34. Thiselton, *Two Horizons*, 105.

35. Thiselton, *Two Horizons*, 106.

36. Thiselton, *Two Horizons*, 107.

*Bultmann, Gadamer, and Wittgenstein.* Critically appreciative of philosophers such as Gadamer and Ricoeur, Thiselton has maintained the possibility of scholarly exegesis alongside personal and theological engagement with the scriptural texts.[37] He has addressed a wide range of subjects, from a significant commentary on 1 Corinthians to a hermeneutical recovery of human "selfhood."[38] Thiselton also links us to additional strands of theological conversation about hermeneutics.

First, Thiselton collaborated with literary scholars on two books, and this collaboration points to another group of Christian hermeneutical endeavors. These scholars offer theologically informed assessments of modern literary hermeneutics' cultural history and seek to recover the best of Christian humanism in the West.[39] Such

37. For his magisterial survey of hermeneutical options with some assessment of their usefulness, see Anthony C. Thiselton, *New Horizons in Hermeneutics: The Theory and Practice of Transforming Biblical Reading* (Grand Rapids: Zondervan, 1992).

38. Anthony C. Thiselton, *The First Epistle to the Corinthians*, New International Greek Testament Commentary (Grand Rapids: Eerdmans, 2000); *Interpreting God and the Postmodern Self: On Meaning, Manipulation and Promise* (Grand Rapids: Eerdmans, 1995).

39. See Roger Lundin, Anthony C. Thiselton, and Clarence Walhout, *The Responsibility of Hermeneutics* (Grand Rapids: Eerdmans, 1985); *The Promise of Hermeneutics* (Grand Rapids: Eerdmans, 1999); Roger Lundin, *The Culture of Interpretation: Christian Faith and the Postmodern World* (Grand Rapids: Eerdmans, 1993); Roger Lundin, ed., *Disciplining Hermeneutics: Interpretation in Christian Perspective* (Grand Rapids: Eerdmans, 1997); Lundin, *From Nature to Experience*; David L. Jeffrey, *People of the Book: Christian Identity and Literary Culture* (Grand Rapids: Eerdmans, 1996); *Houses of the Interpreter: Reading Scripture, Reading Culture* (Waco, TX: Baylor University Press, 2003). For cautions against Christians misreading Derrida and deconstruction too harshly, see the more optimistic approach of James K. A. Smith, "Limited Inc/arnation: Revisiting the Searle/Derrida Debate in Christian Context," in *Hermeneutics at the Crossroads*, ed. Kevin J. Vanhoozer, James K. A. Smith, and Bruce Ellis Benson, Indiana Series in the Philosophy of Religion (Bloomington: Indiana University Press, 2006), 112–29. Unfolding hermeneutics of charity recalling Augustine, Alan Jacobs appeals to Mikhail Bakhtin as a resource for exploring the "dialogical" nature of interpretation in *A Theology of Reading: The Hermeneutics of Love* (Boulder, CO: Westview, 2001). For a survey and bibliography on Bakhtin, see Susan Felch, "Dialogism," *DTIB* 173–75.

a Christian literary culture must shape, and be shaped by, biblical interpretation, which is never far from these writers' concerns.

According to Bruns, "Gadamer in *Truth and Method* has emphasized the difference between understanding the subject matter of a text (Hegel) and understanding the subjectivity of the text's author (Schleiermacher)."[40] In many ways this contrast is an early form of the distinction between Husserl's (Schleiermacher) and Heidegger's (Hegel) traditions, between transcendental interpretation that moves backward to share an author's mind-set and ontological hermeneutics moving forward to appropriate a text in a new historical moment. Christian literary scholars tend to favor the ontological tradition, though Thiselton cautions that many caricature and wrongly neglect Schleiermacher on the other side.[41] The literary trend can help Christian readers to be cautious about

> a type of theology that wants to adopt only a historical attitude toward religion; it even has an abundance of cognition, though only of a historical kind. This cognition is no concern of ours, for if the cognition were merely historical, we would have to compare such theologians with countinghouse clerks, who keep the ledgers and accounts of other people's wealth, a wealth that passes through their hands without their retaining any of it, clerks who act only for others without acquiring assets of their own.[42]

Meanwhile, a second strand of Thiselton's hermeneutical connections leads to speech-act philosophy. This theory arose in the wake of Ludwig Wittgenstein's later thought, due to the ordinary language philosophy of J. L. Austin and others. Wittgenstein came to focus on the use to which we put language in very particular contexts. Swinging a bat is (usually) a good act in the game of

40. Bruns, *Hermeneutics*, 152.

41. Thiselton, *New Horizons*, 23, 197, 204–36, 267, 558–61.

42. G. W. F. Hegel, *Lectures on the Philosophy of Religion*, vol. 1, *Introduction and the Concept of Religion*, trans. R. F. Brown, ed. Peter C. Hodgson (Berkeley: University of California Press, 1984), 128, quoted in Bruns, *Hermeneutics*, 150.

baseball, whereas it would signify something else in a movie about street gangs. Similarly, the nature of the "language game" is crucial for the meaning of speech or writing. From this focus on meaning as use came considerable attention to language as people ordinarily use it in their everyday lives.

Austin considered "performative utterances" such as "I now pronounce you husband and wife," in which the communication actually alters states of affairs in the world.[43] He came to see that, broadly speaking, all utterances are performative, at least involving some relation or "fit" between their words and the world. When we communicate, we do not simply convey propositional content; what is interesting is the "uptake" of the communication, what we do with our words. Hence we arrive at the basic concept of speech-act theory, the "illocutionary act" done *in* or *by* speaking: asserting something about the world, promising to alter the world in some way, warning someone else not to do something or commanding them to alter the world, and so on.

Thiselton began to draw upon speech-act philosophy with regard to particular biblical texts or problems of interpretation, focusing, for instance, on divine "promising." Some years later the philosopher Nicholas Wolterstorff applied speech-act theory to defend the possibility of "divine discourse" in Scripture and to develop aspects of such a model.[44] He suggested that God appropriates the human speech acts of biblical texts, unless we have good reason to think otherwise (namely, God would only tell the truth and promote love for neighbor). The human discourse "counts as" divine illocutionary activity without God needing direct physical involvement in the world through vocal chords or pens. We therefore ought to approach the Bible with a first hermeneutic (for the human discourse) and then a second (for the divine). Perhaps that double approach illustrates the larger tension with which this chapter wrestles: Wolterstorff almost thoroughly borrowed concepts from

43. J. L. Austin, *How to Do Things with Words* (Oxford: Oxford University Press, 1962).

44. Nicholas Wolterstorff, *Divine Discourse: Philosophical Reflections on the Claim That God Speaks* (Cambridge: Cambridge University Press, 1995).

general hermeneutics for biblical interpretation before addressing its particularities. Wolterstorff's important book did not engage very critically or constructively with general hermeneutics from a theological perspective.

Sharing the interests of Thiselton and Wolterstorff in speech-act philosophy, and of others pursuing a Christian literary culture, is Kevin Vanhoozer, who has variously engaged both general and special hermeneutics. After appropriating speech-act thinking in several essays, Vanhoozer published *Is There a Meaning in This Text? The Bible, the Reader, and the Morality of Literary Knowledge*. This book, often misunderstood as primarily concerned with biblical interpretation in itself, actually defends "the morality of literary knowledge" by way of exploring biblical hermeneutics. In other words, the Bible is a kind of hermeneutical case study for Western culture, and, of course, the most poignant one for Christians. Vanhoozer argues that authors are among the "others" to which readers must do justice. If virtue formation becomes not just the aim of interpretation but even the dominant criterion for recognizing good readings, then, ironically, virtues such as humility could fall by the wayside. We substitute our own thinking about virtue in place of the text's teaching, failing to listen carefully to the virtuous a/Author. According to Vanhoozer, texts do not simply contain, but in a sense *are* (an essential medium of), communicative actions to which we respond—responses for which we are accountable.[45] While the Spirit freely relates textual actions to various contexts and opens up the freedom of interpreters to respond virtuously, trinitarian thinking points us to the Spirit's relation with the Word, who enables stable meaning.

Vanhoozer has subsequently focused more upon special hermeneutics, perhaps responding to worries that *Is There a Meaning in*

45. Wolterstorff criticizes Vanhoozer on this point in "Resuscitating the Author," in Vanhoozer, Smith, and Benson, *Hermeneutics at the Crossroads*, 47–49. For Vanhoozer's response, see "Discourse on Matter: Hermeneutics and the 'Miracle' of Understanding," in Vanhoozer, Smith, and Benson, *Hermeneutics at the Crossroads*, 21–22. The chief issue appears to be whether to use the word "intention" in an ordinary, psychological sense (Wolterstorff) or a more technical sense (Vanhoozer).

*This Text?* neglected specific problems and possibilities involved in reading the Bible as Scripture and responding to the Holy Spirit's particular work accompanying that Word.[46] These worries alert us to criticisms of these projects in theological general hermeneutics and their connections to scriptural interpretation.

### Assessing Criticisms

Stephen Fowl's concerns about submitting the church's interpretative interests concerning Scripture to a general theory of meaning remain somewhat relevant in this context, for Christian thinking about general hermeneutics often doubles back to apply to Scripture. Fowl particularly objects to uses of speech-act philosophy that rejuvenate author-focused hermeneutics after Hirsch. He believes that speech-act philosophy arose not as a global theory of meaning but instead as a more restrained attempt to solve local problems of interpretation.[47]

A related concern comes from Richard Briggs who, along with Fowl, is one of Thiselton's former students. He finds an important distinction between strong speech-acts, such as promising, and weaker ones, such as asserting. The former type, involving distinctively performative utterances, gains illumination from speech-act analysis. Thus Briggs especially analyzes the speech-acts of confession, forgiveness, and teaching.[48] Yet he seems to hold that applying speech-act philosophy across the board, as a comprehensive theory, becomes too general to do much good. Briggs notes that Wolterstorff does not explain very well how to adjudicate between conflicting interpretations of the divine discourse in a given biblical passage. And Vanhoozer's notion of a "canonical illocution"—happening not in any one text but

46. See Kevin J. Vanhoozer, *The Drama of Doctrine: A Canonical-Linguistic Approach to Christian Theology* (Louisville: Westminster/John Knox, 2005).

47. Stephen E. Fowl, "The Role of Authorial Intention in the Theological Interpretation of Scripture," in *Between Two Horizons: Spanning New Testament Studies and Systematic Theology*, ed. Joel B. Green and Max Turner (Grand Rapids: Eerdmans, 2000), 76.

48. Richard S. Briggs, *Words in Action: Speech Act Theory and Biblical Interpretation* (Edinburgh: T&T Clark, 2001).

in terms of the whole Bible, or Scripture serving as the larger context for a particular passage—has not yet offered proof of the pudding in much interpretative eating.[49] Nevertheless, Briggs does draw a larger lesson from speech-act theory: communicative acts require personal investment with public entailments; this "logic of self-involvement" means that communication and interpretation point to beliefs that we hold about truth transforming our lives.

Thus, while Fowl and Briggs offer technical criticisms of general hermeneutics using speech-act philosophy, they also put theological concerns at stake. Another theological worry about the application of general hermeneutics to Scripture comes from John Webster, who believes that secular hermeneutics presumes an underlying anthropology of the isolated self who makes independent judgments. Such an anthropology does not take God's creating and redeeming activity seriously enough, especially given human sinfulness. This concern leads Webster to emphasize the priority of divine action in the scriptural reading situation, so that we are not left with communal and ethical realities all the way down; rather, the church responds to a Word spoken from outside.[50] Even Fowl's approach would be problematic alongside excessive interaction with general hermeneutics, since Fowl appears to treat Scripture reading too immanently, simply as a function of church practice. By contrast, Webster develops a "sacramental" account of Scripture in order to acknowledge the activity of the church while setting it clearly in a divine context: "God's agency is real and effective yet indirect."[51]

It is also important to notice the operation of a certain kind of general hermeneutics beneath the surface of Fowl's thought. He appeals to thinkers such as Jeffrey Stout and Stanley Fish, making it possible to argue that emphasizing the interests of interpretative

49. For these recent applications of Briggs's approach to others in the discussion, see Richard S. Briggs, "Speech-Act Theory," *DTIB* 763–66.

50. John Webster, *Word and Church* (Edinburgh: T&T Clark, 2001).

51. Webster, *Word and Church*, 74. See also John Webster, *Holy Scripture: A Dogmatic Sketch*, Current Issues in Theology (Cambridge: Cambridge University Press, 2003).

communities constitutes a theory, at least to some degree.[52] Of course, Fowl appreciates such a theoretical perspective for theological reasons as well, reasons that include a more "catholic" notion of grace than Webster's; for Fowl, grace operates via the community of the church. Still, if we find antitheory general hermeneutics in play even here, then the larger lesson might be that some hermeneutical interaction is inescapable—try as we may. We can affirm that theology is decisive for the interpretation of the Bible without splitting faith from reason or subordinating reason to faith in such a way that Scripture reading counts as nothing more than personal opinion.[53]

## Attempting to Connect the Special and General

Hesitation about hermeneutics comes not only from those who resist a single theory or set of interpretative procedures but also from biblical scholars who, frequently following Hirsch, favor just such a method. Wary of the understanding shared by premodern interpreters and Gadamer's followers, modern scholars and church people alike become uncomfortable when hermeneutics challenges our sense of control: "Hermeneutics is a loose and baggy monster, or anyhow a less than fully disciplined body of thinking whose inventory of topics spreads out over many different historical, cultural, and intellectual contexts."[54] Bruns avers, "It is true that hermeneutics is not always reputable, and that one should always double one's locks. But a serious hermeneutical lesson that one might draw . . . is that nothing, unfortunately, is meaningless; rather there are more meanings than we know what to do with, and not even texts that resist our efforts of interpretation will save us."[55] Thus, "the argument that anti-relativists have with Gadamer is actually not with Gadamer but rather with the historicality of existence."[56] Ultimately,

52. This appears to be consistent with the assessment of Thiselton, *New Horizons*, 547–48.

53. For a philosophical argument to this effect, see Jorge J. E. Gracia, *How Can We Know What God Means? The Interpretation of Revelation* (New York: Palgrave, 2001).

54. Bruns, *Hermeneutics*, 17 (see also pp. 62–63).

55. Bruns, *Hermeneutics*, 247.

56. Bruns, *Hermeneutics*, 273n27.

"hermeneutics is a name for the desire to know what it is that inspires commentary, or what provokes its desire for what remains undone."[57] In dealing with such desire or even anxiety, as Lundin notes,

> we might find helpful what Joel Weinsheimer says about interpretation in general: "An interpretation as such is different from and yet also the same as what it interprets. Unless it is both, it is not an interpretation." If an interpretation is not in some sense the same as what it interprets, then it is not an interpretation but an entirely new text . . . Yet if an interpretation is not in some sense different from its object, then it "is not an interpretation of the text but a copy of it."[58]

My point is neither that Gadamer or any other thinker is entirely right, nor that I am now rejecting the historical concerns of biblical scholarship addressed in the previous chapter.

However, as James K. A. Smith notes, Christians too often shy away from all forms of interpretative plurality, assuming them to be products of humanity's fall into sin.[59] One gets the idea that we would have no need for interpretation in an ideal world. But in some respects diversity is a creational and pentecostal reality: redemption does not remove interpretation, but rather its traces of violence and tragedy. God made humans as historical creatures, from which legitimate, loving plurality emerges as we understand texts in particular circumstances. Since understanding involves not only aspects of ideal explanation but also concrete embodiment in forms of life, it seems right to affirm the recent use of "performance" as a metaphor for interpretation. What we must now discern is the nature of faithful performances.[60]

57. Bruns, *Hermeneutics*, 14.

58. Joel Weinsheimer, *Philosophical Hermeneutics and Literary Theory* (New Haven: Yale University Press, 1991), 87, quoted in Lundin, *From Nature to Experience*, 139.

59. James K. A. Smith, *The Fall of Interpretation: Philosophical Foundations for a Creational Hermeneutic* (Downers Grove, IL: InterVarsity, 2000).

60. For a survey of the performance metaphor, see Stephen C. Barton, "New Testament Interpretation as Performance," *Scottish Journal of Theology* 52, no. 2 (1999): 179–208. Wolterstorff consistently criticizes "performance interpretation,"

## DRAMA AND SPECIAL HERMENEUTICS

In that light, Vanhoozer's recent *The Drama of Doctrine: A Canonical-Linguistic Approach to Christian Theology* provides the most thorough attempt to appropriate drama for thinking theologically about performance in special hermeneutics. Vanhoozer contrasts two models, rejecting "Performance II," in which "The Interpretative Community Authors and Directs," and promoting "Performance I," in which "The Interpretative Community Responds and Enacts." The biblical canon is the kind of divine performance that elicits the church's performative responses, but these are responses rather than newly creative acts.

Hence, doctrine concerns first and foremost not the linguistic practices of the church but instead those of Scripture itself in its diverse literary forms. In this way Vanhoozer tries to take Lindbeck's cultural-linguistic turn toward focusing on church practice, but without abandoning the priority of Scripture. The biblical story is not simply a narrative or metanarrative; it is a drama.[61]

---

which he understands in opposition to his authorial discourse model; for him, performance involves the reader taking the place of the author in determining what a text means. But some uses of the metaphor in terms of music—such as an orchestra performing a musical score—have been relatively restrained (e.g., Francis Watson, *Text, Church and World: Biblical Interpretation in Theological Perspective* [Grand Rapids: Eerdmans, 1994]; *Text and Truth: Redefining Biblical Theology* [Grand Rapids: Eerdmans, 1997]; Frances M. Young, *Virtuoso Theology: The Bible and Interpretation* [Cleveland: Pilgrim, 1993]). Moreover, using the metaphor in terms of drama inextricably links appropriation of the text with human action in the world, which further ties performances to a reality that requires criteria of interpretation beyond the reader (so Shannon Craigo-Snell, "Command Performance: Rethinking Performance Interpretation in the Context of *Divine Discourse*," *Modern Theology* 16, no. 4 [October 2000]: 475–94).

61. Hans Urs von Balthasar wrote a five-volume theological work around this theme: *Theodrama*. Subsequently, others have used the metaphor suggestively; most notably, N. T. Wright proposed in regard to the Bible's authority that we could think of a five-act play in which now, after Jesus' first advent, we find ourselves in the final act, right at its beginning. The other four acts, recorded in Scripture, give us ways of figuring out how to act in the final stage. See N. T. Wright, "How Can the Bible Be Authoritative?" *Vox Evangelica* 21 (1991): 7–32; *The New Testament and the People of God*, Christian Origins and the Question of God (Minneapolis: Fortress, 1992), chap. 5; *The Last Word: Beyond the Bible*

The gospel is full of entrances and exoduses from the stage, while God's speech and action elicit ours. The ways in which speech *is* action, even within the life of the Triune God, show the propriety of the drama metaphor, in which speech carries the action to a significant degree. Now we engage in communication that carries the action forward by corresponding creatively to the practices of the canonical texts themselves.

Doctrine, then, is direction for how to participate fittingly in the drama of redemption. In this way, doctrine can integrate propositional truths, experience, and narrative (elements that Lindbeck's typology tends to push apart). Moreover, we can recognize that doctrine passes on truth from the past and perpetuates biblical authority in the present, while we must realize that the church will continually face new situations as well. Scripture's authority must then be understood not simply in terms of delivering propositional truth claims but also in terms of directing social action ("practices") by way of normative examples. The various genres of the Bible—ways of relating language to life—deliver these normative patterns of practice. The Spirit works through tradition to help the church apply its criterion for wisdom—Scripture—in the midst of the drama.

Thus, like Fowl, Vanhoozer turns to *phronēsis*, treating it in connection with the theatrical topic of improvisation to deal with the spontaneity of acting in relation to the script.[62] For many theatrical traditions, acting is not simply a matter of method; it deals with becoming a certain kind of person. It is in subjection to Scripture that the church understands the one gospel, played out variously in different contexts; yet Christian persons and communities must still communicate with and learn from each other across time and place.

---

*Wars to a New Understanding of the Authority of Scripture* (San Francisco: HarperSanFrancisco, 2005).

62. On improvisation, see Samuel Wells, *Improvisation: The Drama of Christian Ethics* (Grand Rapids: Brazos, 2004); Bruce Ellis Benson, "The Improvisation of Hermeneutics: Jazz Lessons for Interpreters," in Vanhoozer, Smith, and Benson, *Hermeneutics at the Crossroads*.

## The Incarnation and General Hermeneutics

Whether or not everyone appropriates speech-act philosophy, Vanhoozer's dramatic model offers ecumenical potential for advocates of theological interpretation of Scripture.[63] As the conversation goes forward, we need to maintain the authority and coherence of the biblical texts' presentation of the gospel along with the church's freedom and responsibility to discern its meaning in new and various situations. At the heart of the drama, of course, is God's incarnation in Jesus Christ. Zimmermann sees this event having implications for both theology and general hermeneutics:

> Theology must shed any pretensions to timeless, absolute knowledge and will do itself a great favor by abandoning a scientific model of unmediated, naked truth. Instead theology should embrace a hermeneutical model of self-understanding in which truth is not naked but clothed in the self-giving otherness of God, who offers himself in the incarnation for our contemplation and emulation. The incarnation provides what postmodern ethical philosophy seeks: it embodies radical transcendence in history and time with a human face, and it offers a social subjectivity as persons in relation.[64]

Referring to the "fundamentally ethical nature of theological interpretation," Zimmermann writes, "The central idea that makes ethical transcendence and its communication possible is that in the incarnation, truth is a person rather than a proposition or idea. Theological hermeneutics is conducted on the basis of personal knowledge."[65]

Zimmermann especially defends the Puritan and Pietist inheritance from the Protestant Reformation as providing a way of using

---

63. Use of speech-act philosophy is very clearly restrained in Vanhoozer's *The Drama of Doctrine*, functioning largely as a trope regarding the biblical, covenantal tie between words and deeds (especially God's) rather than as a strong general theory.

64. Zimmermann, *Recovering Theological Hermeneutics*, 318.

65. Zimmermann, *Recovering Theological Hermeneutics*, 318.

critical tools within a spiritual framework,[66] integrating rather than splitting faith and reason via an epistemology of relation to the Triune God.[67] This emphasis on personal knowledge leads once again to *phronēsis* as a way of enacting hermeneutics' ethical turn:

> What a text means, it always means *pro me*, in application to myself. This self, however, stands as a person in relation within a community and the tradition that sustains it. In this way, the incarnation allows us to ground truth ontologically as that which transcends the subject-object divide. Truth is always subjective and relative to cultural-historical context. If it were not *relative* in this sense, it could never be *relevant* either. Yet Gadamer is correct to protest that this in no way implies relativism. Texts, art, objects reveal themselves as they are, even if such revelation involves revealing and concealing.[68]

Such an assertion about revelation precedes Zimmermann's concluding quotation from Dietrich Bonhoeffer concerning Christ as the center from which and toward which history moves.[69] To what extent either the incarnation or *phronēsis* licenses or counts as part of a general theory of understanding remains disputable. And so we return, at long last, to our case study, since many New Testament texts likewise center the *imago Dei* on Jesus Christ.

### Jesus Christ: Interpretation and the Image of God

Among other passages, 2 Corinthians 4:4 and Colossians 1:15; 3:9–10 clearly relate the *imago Dei* to Jesus Christ. In the larger

---

66. See, e.g., Zimmermann, *Recovering Theological Hermeneutics*, 112–13.

67. Zimmermann, *Recovering Theological Hermeneutics*, 88.

68. Zimmermann, *Recovering Theological Hermeneutics*, 321 (italics in original). Throughout his book Zimmermann demonstrates how often modern "secular" hermeneutical thinkers borrow ideas from theological tradition. Zimmermann also addresses a figure whom I have had to neglect here, Emmanuel Levinas, whose Jewish ethical focus criticizes the hermeneutical tradition but also coheres with some of its key themes through the mediation of Christian theology.

69. Zimmermann, *Recovering Theological Hermeneutics*, 322.

context this is consistent with our *phronēsis* corresponding to him. Francis Watson points out the hermeneutical consequences:

> If Jesus Christ is the image of God, and if this expression occupies as it were the same semantic space as its counterpart in Genesis, then a Christian interpretation of the anthropological concept of the image of God will have to take account not only of the Genesis texts but also of their christological transformation. . . . Admittedly, it is initially unclear how the anthropological concept and the christological title are to be related to one another. . . . The anthropological and christological facets of the *imago Dei* must be combined in a way that respects the integrity of the Old Testament text, neither imposing upon it a later, alien christological content nor replacing it with that content.[70]

It will be obvious that many Old Testament scholars would find it impossible to respect the integrity of Genesis 1:26–27 while incorporating Christology within its interpretation. Even many Christians, although they are willing to involve the New Testament christological *imago Dei* texts in an overall theological scheme, resist the idea that these texts are actually interpreting the Genesis passages or have any organic connection to them. If the christological passages made claims about the meaning of the Genesis texts, they would be wrong, since they do not line up with the conclusions of historical-critical exegesis. The key interpretative context, for such scholars, is the ancient Near Eastern royal ideology that supports a functional understanding of the *imago Dei*.

Their overriding concern, no doubt, is to protect the integrity of the Genesis texts so that they can have their say, and this is a noble goal. However, this present chapter demonstrates that Hirsch's author-centered approach is not hermeneutically dominant. Other recent defenses of authorial-discourse interpretation are quite open to contributions from later texts or contexts to our understanding rather than simply assuming that authorial intention in the original context exhausts textual meaning. We do not necessarily violate the original text when we relate it to other canonical passages or

70. Watson, *Text and Truth*, 282–83.

approach it with questions from other contexts, since its subject matter might address those questions, coming newly to light as a result.

To illustrate what this might look like regarding the *imago Dei*: according to Watson, "To claim, with Paul, that Jesus is the image of God is by no means to forget Genesis. The Genesis texts have already influenced the discussion so far by suggesting that the christological image-of-God concept should be understood anthropologically"—that is, in terms of Jesus revealing true humanity rather than just true divinity.[71] Because the Genesis terminology refers to visual representations, "Rather than simply rejecting the postulate of a divine-human likeness, understood in primarily visual terms, an alternative would be a christological interpretation":[72]

> Gen. 1.26–28 is speaking not directly of Jesus but of all humans. All humans may be said to be like God in the sense that they are like Jesus. He shares their human existence, the path they must traverse from birth to death; and they share his human existence. If Jesus is like God, then, in so far as they are like Jesus, all humans are like God. Without this christological reference, the concept of the image and likeness of God should be handed over as quickly as possible to the Platonizers and the spiritualizers, who insist that the image is to be found in the human mind but is absent from the human body. Yet, in Genesis, it is not the mind but the whole human person who is made in the image and likeness of God; and that is the case with Jesus, who mirrors God not only in his mind but also in his bodily action.[73]

Such an approach illustrates that interpretation is broader than simply redescribing the historical author's intentions in an original context; we must engage a passage in light of its potential implications and points of interface with other texts or contexts. Describing the Genesis text's functional *imago Dei* is important

71. Watson, *Text and Truth*, 288.
72. Watson, *Text and Truth*, 290.
73. Watson, *Text and Truth*, 291.

and need not drop out of theological interpretation. But it is not a stopping point, due to theological problems and/or opportunities it presents: Does it mean that God has a body? What is it about humans and our differences from other creatures that coheres with God's decision to create us as image-bearers? What does it mean to represent God in this way? These questions, and others, cause us to look even harder at Genesis 1:26–27 in its immediate historical and literary contexts but also at broader canonical and theological contexts for help that they can provide. In this case, New Testament texts provide the context for God to say more than does the author of Genesis, though not less.

Finally, aside from this illustration, it is worth pondering whether Jesus Christ as the true image of God, in whom all other humans exist and to whom they ought to conform, makes possible connections between general and special hermeneutics. To be sure, we read Scripture with trust that we will encounter God in the truth, goodness, and beauty of Christ as the Word no other book can match. By God's grace the Christian virtues displayed preeminently in Jesus are necessarily conducive to grasping the meaning of biblical Truth in particular. Yet people outside the Christian faith may understand and even obey many divine ordinances due to God's created order and the reaffirmation of this order in Christ's resurrection.[74] Such a possibility is evident in light of the biblical Wisdom literature and its connection to other cultures, as well as the pervasive admiration for Jesus' way of life outside the Christian faith. Although "pagans" may not fear the Lord and therefore do not live out the fullness of God's design, they may have insight into many particular elements, even helping Christians to recognize how beautiful and good patterns of Truth appear in Scripture. Often we will need these insights as well as their criticism when we do not connect our own living with biblical Truth. Non-Christians may become charitable readers to a degree, even of Scripture in certain ways. Although Christian readers receive some distinct privileges from the Holy Spirit, participating in the reality of God's

74. See Oliver O'Donovan, *Resurrection and Moral Order: An Outline for Evangelical Ethics*, 2nd ed. (Grand Rapids: Eerdmans, 1994).

teaching, neither do they yet realize the fullness of what it means to communicate the divine likeness in creation.

If this is so, then general and special hermeneutics may share much overlapping territory, including many scholarly criteria and reading skills. To be sure, biblical interpretation somewhat constitutes a distinct province. Yet, despite its churchly home in the city of God, Christian reading of Scripture may not have to address general hermeneutics either by simply "plundering the Egyptians" or else by defending fearfully against a Trojan horse. Indeed, since its entire realm concerns living virtuously in communion with God according to the image of Christ, all understanding has a theological component. Thus the interpretation of Scripture may have abundant hermeneutical gifts to share, in a developing story of fair trade.[75] And this political metaphor points to the subject of the next chapter: the global surge of Christian faith outside "Western" culture, with the fresh challenges and opportunities that it presents to biblical interpretation.

75. For the larger context of this argument about general and special hermeneutics, see Daniel J. Treier, *Virtue and the Voice of God: Toward Theology as Wisdom* (Grand Rapids: Eerdmans, 2006). Emphasizing *phronēsis* means that I see theory in terms of language for rather low-level discourse about practical rules of thumb, not in terms of an abstract or universal straitjacket that strictly determines procedures.

# 6

# From the "Western" Academy to the Global Church?

*Engaging Social Locations*

A final key challenge of definition for theological interpretation of Scripture concerns the buzzword "globalization." Whereas biblical theology and general hermeneutics—the subjects of the previous two chapters—are frequently addressed at length by advocates of theological exegesis, globalization is not. This chapter, therefore, cannot provide a survey of theological hermeneutics regarding the issue; instead, it introduces the concept of globalization and the broader questions of social location that it raises for biblical interpretation. The hermeneutical significance of globalization might be understood best through examining two phenomena that have arisen in concert with it: postcolonial thought and the rapid growth of pentecostal Christianity in the global South. Initially, though, I offer some basic definitions and descriptions of globalization.

For many, globalization is largely a consequence of consumer capitalism monopolizing and homogenizing culture, and it entails the market's takeover of formerly governmental functions. At the same time, however, it elicits stronger forms of religious funda-mentalism as a backlash and, accordingly, an ever more local focus, to the point of tribalism in some cases.[1] Thus the expansion of American influence makes the world smaller and smaller. Thomas Friedman emphasizes that "globalization is not simply a trend or a fad" but rather an international system with "its own rules and logic that today directly or indirectly influence the politics, envi-ronment, geopolitics and economics of virtually every country in the world."[2] Wilbert R. Shenk notes, "Modernity has produced a powerful culture that has penetrated all aspects of human life and extended itself to every part of the globe. In this respect, globaliza-tion as a process and as a reality is a direct fruit of modernity."[3]

Yet missionary activity has played a significant part in this modern development, as "the single most extensive experiment in intercultural relationships in human history."[4] Thus it is not inappropriate to consider the rise of Christianity in the global South, both in relation to missionary activity and quite apart from it, as an important dimension of globalization. In fact,

> A common misperception of globalization is that it is having such a homogenizing effect throughout the world that diverse cultures are melding into one global culture and that linguistic diversity is disappearing as English gains dominance in the global market economy. This half-truth concerning globalization gives too much credit to economic and technological factors and underestimates the importance of cultural and religious dimensions of human existence.[5]

1. Benjamin R. Barber, *Jihad vs. McWorld*, 2nd ed. (New York: Ballantine, 2001).

2. Thomas L. Friedman, *The Lexus and the Olive Tree: Understanding Glo-balization*, 2nd ed. (New York: Anchor Books, 2001), ix.

3. Wilbert R. Shenk, foreword to *Globalizing Theology: Belief and Practice in an Era of World Christianity*, ed. Craig Ott and Harold A. Netland (Grand Rapids: Baker Academic, 2006), 10.

4. Shenk, foreword to Ott and Netland, *Globalizing Theology*, 11.

5. Darrell L. Whiteman, "Anthropological Reflections on Contextualizing Theology in a Globalizing World," in Ott and Netland, *Globalizing Theology*, 60.

Perhaps we recognize that differences are disappearing, in part, because we recognize difference more than ever. Moreover, "the origins of modernity lie not exclusively in the Western Enlightenment, superficially understood as an atheistic project, but in the complex, historical interplay of European and non-European civilizations beginning in the eighteenth century."[6]

Harold Netland further clarifies that "globalization is more than just the *fact* of worldwide interrelatedness; it also includes our heightened *awareness* of this interconnectivity and the effects of this consciousness on local patterns and identities."[7] Globalization has unfolded in stages: in one sense it could be seen as perennial, but in another sense it moves from Columbus's "discovery" of the New World through the multinational companies of the industrial age to the current postindustrial stage dominated by telecommunications technologies. What is presently unique is the extent of such integration: we have moved from a wall symbolizing the cold war to the interconnectivity of the World Wide Web.[8] Accordingly, "the speed, the scale, the scope, and the complexity of global connections" are unprecedented.[9]

Likewise, unprecedented demographic shifts are taking place. In terms of Christian faith, today about 2 billion of the world's approximately 6 billion people count in some fashion as "Christian"; 560 million are still found in Europe; Latin America has risen to 480 million; Africa, 360 million; Asia, 313 million; North America, 260 million. Yet, if we extrapolate to the year 2025 (without dramatic changes in rates of conversion), 633 million of the 2.6 billion Christians would be African; 640 million, Latin American; 460

6. Vinoth Ramachandra, "Globalization, Nationalism, and Religious Resurgence," in Ott and Netland, *Globalizing Theology*, 223. Ramachandra illustrates this with the modern creation of Hinduism and Buddhism as more singular, text-centered religions in the sense that Westerners could appropriate.

7. Harold A. Netland, introduction to Ott and Netland, *Globalizing Theology*, 19 (italics in original).

8. Netland, introduction to Ott and Netland, *Globalizing Theology*, 20.

9. Whiteman, "Anthropological Reflections," 61. See also the discussion of key literature on globalization and to what extent it differs from the 1900s in Friedman, *The Lexus and the Olive Tree*, xi–xxii.

million, Asian. Meanwhile, Europe would be in third place with 555 million. If we extrapolate still further, "By 2050, only about one-fifth of the world's 3 billion Christians will be non-Hispanic Whites. Soon, the phrase 'a White Christian' may sound like a curious oxymoron, as mildly surprising as 'a Swedish Buddhist.' Such people can exist, but a slight eccentricity is implied."[10] The rate of Christian growth in Africa has seemed particularly extraordinary, from 10 million in 1900 to 360 million by 2000. Western inattentiveness to these phenomena appears in the fact that *Christian History* magazine left the African situation out of its list of the top one hundred events of the twentieth century.[11] Yet today nearly half of all Africans name some form of Christian faith, and in several countries the percentage is well over half.[12]

These important demographic changes extend beyond the issue of adherence to Christian faith and embrace the breadth of political issues as well. For example, the Dalit community that suffers so much persecution in India—even if one takes the lowest possible population estimate—outnumbers the populations of Britain, France, and Italy combined, yet for some reason its plight has not garnered the attention that apartheid did in South Africa.[13] Many of the planet's most desirable "resources" are now located in the hands of religious minorities and in the broader contexts of non-Western poverty, so that religious difference and forms of political conflict often intermingle.[14] A further dimension of the resulting political difficulties concerns the frequent desire of nations in the global South to modernize without Westernizing.[15]

Moreover, issues of poverty and population intermingle in complex ways. The percentage of people living in "advanced" nations continues to fall, having dropped to 29 percent by 1950, 25 per-

10. Philip Jenkins, *The Next Christendom: The Coming of Global Christianity* (New York: Oxford University Press, 2002), 3.

11. Jenkins, *The Next Christendom*, 4.

12. Jenkins, *The Next Christendom*, 44, 56.

13. Jenkins, *The Next Christendom*, 183.

14. E.g., Jenkins, *The Next Christendom*, 188, 216.

15. Meic Pearse, *Why the Rest Hates the West: Understanding the Roots of Global Rage* (Downers Grove, IL: InterVarsity, 2004), especially 35.

cent by 1970, and 18 percent by 2000, while being predicted to lie around 10 or 12 percent by 2050.[16] Whereas in 1900 "Northerners" outnumbered "Southerners" by about 2.5 to 1, that will almost exactly reverse by 2050.[17] Europe's birthrates are falling precipitously, while Africa's populations are growing rapidly as their exceedingly high birthrates outrun even the ravaging effects of AIDS on that continent. Europe is experiencing massive Muslim immigration, allowed in part to provide the necessary population to pay the taxes for its social services. Whether such immigration will be allowed to continue, as well as what its long-term cultural effects will be, is unclear.[18]

Of course, it is impossible to predict what all these facets of globalization will mean in the long term. Imagine the rate of change that we have experienced since the creation of the World Wide Web, much more tremendous than what our parents and grandparents encountered earlier in the twentieth century and counted as dizzying even then, let alone farther back in time. All this change is sufficiently mind-boggling to make predictions futile unless they come from the most certain prophecies! But it is necessary to set the scene in which Christians will pursue biblical interpretation for the foreseeable future. Theological interpretation of Scripture, to the degree that it does not engage these complex phenomena, is a movement that may prove hard to sustain. In the following sections, therefore, I attempt to describe two hermeneutical realities at the intersection of Scripture and globalization: postcolonial thought and pentecostal faith.

16. Jenkins, *The Next Christendom*, 79.
17. Jenkins, *The Next Christendom*, 80.
18. For a discussion of various scenarios, as well as a theological-cultural reading of the causes for Europe's decline, see George Weigel, *The Cube and the Cathedral: Europe, America, and Politics without God* (New York: Basic Books, 2005). Undoubtedly the book bears the marks of Weigel's particular political perspective, but in any case it does contain useful descriptions of the current situation. The matter is further complicated by the fact that "to prevent demographic decline in the long term, only *non*-assimilating immigrants will do," since assimilation into present European cultural patterns presumably would lower the birthrates of the new peoples (Pearse, *Why the Rest Hates the West*, 161; italics in original).

## Postcolonial Thought

Within biblical studies, postcolonial theory is a subset of ideological criticism. Three basic meanings are possible for "ideology": (1) a Marxist view that stresses its falsity, in which it is an enacted description of "how things are"; (2) a view that any "political agenda" at all—any set of political goals and assumptions—counts as ideology; (3) a view that it is a description of all the social interactions ascribing "significance" to our behavior, and thus it is not always false but instead is a condition of possibility for all consciousness.[19] Any of these meanings entails that ideology has pervasive effects even if, from a Christian perspective, tradition can give ideology a positive function in some circumstances.

According to Robin Parry,

> At its most basic, ideological criticism is the task of uncovering the hidden ideologies at work in social practices, structures, and texts. Written texts encode ideology, communicating and reinforcing it in ways usually unperceived. It is often said that every ideology serves the interests of certain people and groups while marginalizing others. This would make every ideology, however liberating for some, a potential source of oppression for others. Unmasking the dynamics of such power-relations is central to the work of the ideological critic. With reference to a written text, the critic will employ a hermeneutic of suspicion, seeking to find whose interests are served by the text.[20]

Moreover, readings themselves are ideological, and so postcolonial theory—like versions of Latin American, Black, feminist, queer, and other "liberation" theologies—suspects not only the biblical texts themselves but also their readers of serving powerful interests.

While according to many of these theologies, "liberating strands" within the Scriptures can help to critique "toxic" texts of "terror," the liberation of one may be the conquest of another,

19. A. K. M. Adam, *What Is Postmodern Biblical Criticism?* Guides to Biblical Scholarship (Minneapolis: Fortress, 1995), 47–48.
20. Robin Parry, "Ideological Criticism," *DTIB* 314.

as the Exodus and Joshua narratives demonstrate regarding the Israelites and the Canaanites.[21] Thus ideological criticism sometimes involves the use of deconstruction or other pluralistic reading strategies to prevent any one ideology from becoming dominant.[22] However, just as liberation theology famously began to speak of God's "preferential option for the poor," so also "postcolonial reading pays primary attention to the voices of the colonized and marginalized in the biblical text."[23]

The contrast between the traditions labeled by "liberationist" and "postcolonial" lies in their origins and, accordingly, in the postcolonialist perception of liberation theology:

> If liberation theology is the product of modernity, postcolonialism is the product of post-modernity. If liberation has its roots in Christian values, postcolonialism's pedigree is in leftist secular humanism. Liberation emerged as a way of dealing with people's suffering and has its base in church communities, whereas postcolonialism arose in anti-colonial struggle and is now located in the academy, seeing its task as to rectify the discursive defamation of the "other." One tries to tend the victims of the past and present

21. Parry, "Ideological Criticism," 314–15. "Texts of terror" is a reference to the famous work of Phyllis Trible, *Texts of Terror: Literary-Feminist Readings of Biblical Narratives*, Overtures to Biblical Theology (Philadelphia: Fortress, 1984). For an overview of liberation theology as it originated in Latin America with the work of Gustavo Gutiérrez (author of *A Theology of Liberation*) and others, see Samuel Escobar, "Liberation Theologies and Hermeneutics," *DTIB* 454–55.

22. It tends, in other words, to be "postmodern"—whatever that means—but only in a broad sense. (R. S. Sugirtharajah contrasts the two in *The Bible and the Third World: Precolonial, Colonial and Postcolonial Encounters* [Cambridge: Cambridge University Press, 2001], 265–66.) For examples of such postmodern readings, often by the most influential theorists, and often with notoriously opaque titles such as "Ecce Homo, Ain't (Ar'n't) I a Woman, and Inappropriate/d Others: The Human in a Post-Humanist Landscape" and "Whom to Give to (Knowing Not to Know)," see David Jobling, Tina Pippin, and Ronald Schleifer, eds., *The Postmodern Bible Reader* (Oxford: Blackwell, 2001). Regarding the exodus and the Canaanites, see Robert Allen Warrior, "Canaanites, Cowboys, and Indians: Deliverance, Conquest, and Liberation Theology Today," in Jobling, Pippin, and Schleifer, *The Postmodern Bible Reader*, 188–94.

23. Moonjang Lee, "Asian Biblical Interpretation," *DTIB* 68–69.

forms of neo-colonialism, whereas the other tries to challenge the colonizers both old and new. One seeks to tell the truth about the powerful to the poor; the other strives to tell truth to power. One attempts to reclaim the monotheistic God as a benevolent God of the poor; the other investigates the colonizing tendencies of this very monotheistic God and seeks to understand the many-layered polytheistic context out of which early Christianity emerged. If the aim of liberation hermeneutics was to understand and interpret and make the text secure, postcolonialism, on the other hand, perceives its task as critiquing, problematizing, and exposing contradictions and inadequacies in both the text and its interpretation.[24]

Earlier editions of the book quoted here contained mostly "liberationist" texts, and so the boundaries between the two movements may be blurrier than this quotation suggests. Colonial struggles in Asia, such as in India, actually preceded liberation theology by a few years, while many of the African independence movements were roughly simultaneous with the rise of the Latin American base communities.[25] (It is for this reason that I use "postcolonial thought" as a section heading to cover a broader set of concerns that slightly predate the recent creation of the narrower theory.) Nevertheless, the above quotation signals that, like the term "postmodern," the term "postcolonial" gains its identity as a contrast term, opposing what are often seen as the legacies of Christian faith and critical scholarship.

For even liberation theology privileges the Bible far too much, in the eyes of many.[26] And, in terms of academic life, Fernando Segovia contrasts three eras within his career as a biblical scholar: historical criticism involved "suppression of the personal voice"; cultural studies elicited the "irruption of the personal voice";

24. R. S. Sugirtharajah, "Introduction: Still at the Margins," in *Voices from the Margin: Interpreting the Bible in the Third World*, ed. R. S. Sugirtharajah, 3rd ed. (Maryknoll, NY: Orbis, 2006), 5.

25. For a poignant travelogue through postcolonial Africa, see Ryszard Kapuściński, *The Shadow of the Sun*, trans. Klara Glowczewska (New York: Vintage International, 2001).

26. See the strongly worded comments of Sugirtharajah, *The Bible and the Third World*, 257–58.

and now, with postcolonial studies, comes the "entrenchment of the personal voice."[27] Furthermore, beyond even these legacies of biblical texts and biblical interpretation, there is yet another issue: "the heavy migration and great movement of people across continents for reasons varying from political persecution to economic advancement."[28] The resulting "concerns and conditions," in postcolonial theoretical terms, include "plurality, hybridity, multiculturalism, nationalism, diaspora, refugees, and asylum seeking."[29]

According to R. S. Sugirtharajah, who is perhaps the most prolific voice of postcolonial theory in biblical studies, "It is important at the very outset to reiterate that while 'postcolonial' indicates an epoch, postcolonial criticism is not limited to such a time frame."[30] Thus the boundaries between eras themselves blur, and of course what counts as postcolonial theory becomes inevitably difficult to define. Even the question of whether or not to hyphenate the term is vexed.[31] Yet the origins of postcolonial theory are reliably associated with the failure of Soviet socialism, the rise of global market capitalism in its current forms, and the loss of "Third World" political momentum. After this, "Utilizing the space offered by the Western academy in the 1980s, diasporic intellectuals of Third World origin returned to the problem of interpreting the understanding of colonialism formulated by both colonialists and nationalists." Edward Said's 1978 book *Orientalism* provided particular impetus.[32] Thereafter "postcolonialism's original incarnation was in the form of imaginative literature, in

27. Fernando F. Segovia, *Decolonizing Biblical Studies: A View from the Margins* (Maryknoll, NY: Orbis, 2000), 147–55.

28. R. S. Sugirtharajah, "Postcolonial Biblical Interpretation," in Sugirtharajah, *Voices from the Margin*, 70.

29. Sugirtharajah, "Postcolonial Biblical Interpretation," 67. "Diaspora" has particular theological potential in light of its biblical overtones, as noted in Kevin J. Vanhoozer, "'One Rule to Rule Them All?' Theological Method in an Era of World Christianity," in Ott and Netland, *Globalizing Theology*, 125.

30. Sugirtharajah, *The Bible and the Third World*, 246.

31. Sugirtharajah, *The Bible and the Third World*, 245.

32. Sugirtharajah, *The Bible and the Third World*, 247–48.

the writings of Indians, Africans and Latin Americans. Theoretical fine-tuning followed later."[33]

Some—even non-Western critics—challenge postcolonial theory for wrongly using the concept of "Orientalism": "Ever since Edward Said transformed the word *Orientalist* into a term of academic abuse, it has been taken for granted that every attempt by Western scholars to understand the non-Western world had as its aim the imperialist subjugation of the other." However, what we frequently forget is that "Orientalism" originally designated Eastern colonization of the Western mind, and that "if European powers justified their imperial conquests with claims of progress and enlightenment, Asian rulers translated those same Promethean claims into brutal nationalist projects, murdering millions of their own countrymen in doing so." Moreover, "Most revolts against Western imperialism, and its local offshoots, borrowed heavily from Western ideas."[34] For this reason, postcolonial theory is distinct from a particular era labeled "postcolonial," as noted above.

The larger point here is that Sugirtharajah and others overtly and unapologetically theorize from a particular set of political perspectives, with certain alternatives excluded as "colonial."[35] Postcolonial theorists claim to engage in "subaltern" studies—that is, describing conditions or advocating perspectives for poor people and marginalized groups. But the identities and experiences of the theorists themselves are indeed hybrid, since frequently they have made it to the Western academy or else they have at least enjoyed enough leisure and privilege to engage in intellectual life wherever they are. To illustrate why this matters, note Sugirtharajah's recent claims regarding the forms of Christian faith that we study in the next section:

33. Sugirtharajah, *The Bible and the Third World*, 272.

34. Ramachandra, "Globalization, Nationalism, and Religious Resurgence," 215.

35. For a recent example of addressing a political theme, see R. S. Sugirtharajah, *The Bible and Empire: Postcolonial Explorations* (Cambridge: Cambridge University Press, 2005).

Among those who celebrate the shifting of Christianity's center of gravity from Western to non-Western countries may be Christians with colonial intentions of expansion and conquest. It is not the numerical power of the Christianity that is emerging, especially in Africa, but rather the type—conservative, politically reactionary, Pentecostal, and charismatic, that gives cause for concern. If in the 1970s theologians in Latin America brought a new lease of life to the Bible and made it relevant to people's needs, in the new millennium a small group of church leaders in Africa are making the same Bible an uncaring, mean-spirited and cruel book by using it uncritically, especially in the vilification of gays and lesbians. The imposition of one's culture on others is plainly unacceptable, whether done by past colonialists or contemporary post-imperialists.[36]

What Sugirtharajah fails to question is his thoroughgoing commitment to a rather Western form of religious pluralism institutionalized in academic culture. Does he not impose it upon others when, apparently, he hopes for people to see the Bible "as an entertaining narrative devoid of its ecclesiastical and dogmatic functions"?[37] Postcolonial theory, as another form of attention to the reader, can be useful for the interpretation of Scripture, helping Christians to recognize elements of human finitude and fallenness in our theological understanding. But such theory will not promote theological interpretation of Scripture if it assumes a normative perspective of religious relativism and the absence of divine revelation. Thus, encountering globalization means accounting for the common witticism that, while intellectuals may have advocated a preferential option for the poor, the poor themselves preferred Pentecostalism.

## "Pentecostal" Faith

Hence, moving beyond theory and more directly to actual practice, we turn to the hermeneutical consequences of the rapid growth

36. R. S. Sugirtharajah, "Afterword: The Future Imperfect," in Sugirtharajah, *Voices from the Margin*, 495.
37. Sugirtharajah, "Afterword: The Future Imperfect," 496.

167

of Christianity in the "global South"—largely Africa, Asia, and Latin America. Of special help in this survey is Philip Jenkins's recent *The New Faces of Christianity: Believing the Bible in the Global South*. His focus is on Africa and Asia, since "in matters of Bible reading and interpretation, many African and Asian societies have a good deal in common, especially in the relative novelty of the faith and its recent emergence from non-Christian backgrounds. In terms of approaches to the Bible, similarities with Latin America certainly exist, but the differences are too marked to make possible any kind of meaningful generalizations."[38]

### Clarifications and Definitions

Another introductory point of clarification concerns Lamin Sanneh's distinction between "global Christianity," imported from the West into the global South, and "world Christianity," which is more indigenous, having arisen or at least flourished at the hands of native, usually poor, inhabitants of these regions.[39]

It is not that all the Christian growth in the global South is pentecostal, at least in the narrow sense of that term.[40] Early Pentecostalism held not only that, based on the book of Acts, the baptism of the Holy Spirit occurs subsequent to conversion, but also that its "initial evidence" included speaking in tongues. By contrast, the second wave of modern charismatic renewal involved Christians who experienced special spiritual gifts within non-Pentecostal, often mainline, churches. This "charismatic movement" affirmed speaking in tongues but did not necessarily require it as initial evidence for the baptism of the Holy Spirit. "Third wave" or Vineyard churches sometimes do not distinguish this baptism from conversion, holding to a more Reformed, progressive understanding of sanctification while still embracing

38. Philip Jenkins, *The New Faces of Christianity: Believing the Bible in the Global South* (New York: Oxford University Press, 2006), ix.

39. Lamin Sanneh, *Whose Religion Is Christianity? The Gospel beyond the West* (Grand Rapids: Eerdmans, 2003), 22.

40. For a survey of various definitions and internal discussions, as well as bibliography, see D. Allen Tennison, "Charismatic Biblical Interpretation," *DTIB* 106–9.

charismatic gifts. This three-stage approach provides fairly standard descriptive categories in the West, but they are breaking down, and the variety of global South Christianity adds even more complexity. Many scholars, perhaps especially those who study these phenomena without adhering to Christian faith or having insider experience, generalize with the label "pentecostal." Yet it appears that phenomena such as healing and exorcism may be more central in the vibrant Christianity of the global South than issues such as speaking in tongues. What holds pentecostal, charismatic, and even Vineyard Christianity in the West together with the faith of the global South, though, is belief in very regular, very supernatural divine intervention. While in a sense this may largely repristinate traditional Christian faith, it emphasizes certain forms of experience uniquely today and involves a different kind of appeal to the Holy Spirit than we saw under the rubric of "community" in chapter 3.

In any case, Jenkins begins his survey with a basic contrast between Western liberals and global South conservatives, especially poignant in the turmoil experienced by the Anglican communion over homosexual practice in 1998 and from 2003 onward. Entitling his first chapter "Shall the Fundamentalists Win?" Jenkins recalls that same question being posed by Harry Emerson Fosdick early in the twentieth century. The terms in which it is now faced, of course, are somewhat different: soon "we will no longer treat the culture-specific interpretations of North Americans and Europeans as 'theology'—that is, as the real thing—while the rest of the world produces its curious provincial variants, of 'African theology,' 'Asian theology,' and so on."[41] Thus, even with the numerical strength of the more conservative, more biblically literalist global South Christians, the hermeneutical struggles within various denominations may not produce simple victories for conservative Westerners. They will face challenging paradigm shifts as well.

It is difficult, no doubt, to generalize fairly: "As in the United States and Europe, global South churches produce a spectrum

41. Jenkins, *The New Faces of Christianity*, 2.

of theologies and interpretations. The North-South difference is rather one of emphasis."[42] This is especially true at the level of lived Christianity, which can involve beliefs and practices quite different from the writings or opinions of academics and church leaders, let alone those elites who are published in the West.[43] Even efforts to interview ordinary believers frequently but unintentionally misrepresent them by steering conversation toward subjects of interest to scholars.[44] The labels that we use, such as "fundamentalist" or "conservative" or "liberal," can mislead as well because they operate relative to the standpoint of the person using them. In all this difficulty, description and extrapolation from present patterns, however imperfect, are more reliable than flat-out prediction: "We can speak with fair confidence about the ethnic composition of the world's Christians in fifty or a hundred years, but we must be on shakier grounds when it comes to predicting attitudes to authority or orthodoxy."[45]

### Cultural Immediacy and the Old Testament

Having introduced some of the issues, Jenkins goes on in chapter 2 of his book to address "Power in the Book." The Bible remains relatively new in much of the global South, and its audiences are not simple hermeneutical victims of Western missionaries but rather are active responders to scriptural themes that resonate more directly with their context than ours. Christianity often has grown in societies with relatively small literacy rates, breaking down elitism in various ways.[46]

This accords with the work of Lamin Sanneh on the "translatability" of Christian faith: even if encountering Hellenism led to inappropriate absolutizing of Greek philosophical culture in "Christendom" for a time, "the very translatability that allowed this transformation to take place also challenged it in the most

---

42. Jenkins, *The New Faces of Christianity*, 6.
43. Jenkins, *The New Faces of Christianity*, 7.
44. Jenkins, *The New Faces of Christianity*, 8.
45. Jenkins, *The New Faces of Christianity*, 15.
46. Jenkins, *The New Faces of Christianity*, 22–23.

radical way."[47] In fact, there has been "significant overlap between indigenous revitalization and the translation enterprise of mission": "Missionary adoption of the vernacular, therefore, was tantamount to adopting indigenous cultural criteria for the message, a piece of radical indigenization far greater than the standard portrayal of mission as Western cultural imperialism."[48] No doubt imperialism occurred, but so also did the inculcation of local leaders who were essential to producing a contextually sensitive Bible translation. Thus, "the instrument that enabled local criticism to take root and flourish was the translation machinery that mission had itself put in place," and "missionaries were effective in their conditioning of the vernacular environment rather than in their making of Christianity a photocopy of its Victorian version."[49] Here is one amusing example of this point:

> Missionaries in one place overeagerly translated Romans 3:23, "We have all sinned and come short of the glory of God," without realizing that in the particular language there was an exclusive as well as an inclusive "we." They had unwittingly adopted the exclusive form with the meaning, "We whites have sinned and come short of the glory of God." The villagers thought this referred to all the wrong things whites had done in their country, something they knew about very well without missionaries coming out to give it biblical reference.[50]

Yet, in a less amusing example, "a similar linguistic clumsiness led missionaries to translate the sentence in the Lord's Prayer, 'Lead us not into temptation but deliver us from evil,' as 'Lord, do not catch us when we sin,' a secret sentiment among the people who were now glad to have explicit biblical authority for it."[51] Such difficulties are not simply due to clumsiness:

47. Lamin Sanneh, *Translating the Message: The Missionary Impact on Culture*, American Society of Missiology 13 (Maryknoll, NY: Orbis, 1989), 1.
48. Sanneh, *Translating the Message*, 2, 3.
49. Sanneh, *Translating the Message*, 4, 5.
50. Sanneh, *Whose Religion Is Christianity?* 124.
51. Sanneh, *Whose Religion Is Christianity?* 124.

To take an obvious problem, there is no point in using the phrase "as white as snow" for people who have never seen snow. Better to speak of "as white as a strand of cotton." Such minor changes can have complex effects. While the Bible has Jesus declare, "I am the true Vine," some African translators prefer to replace vine with fig. This botanical change introduces a whole new theological meaning, since "this African tree represents the ancestors, and is sometimes planted on tombs." Jesus now speaks as the voice of death and resurrection.[52]

Accordingly, as Jenkins puts it, "The use of vernacular Scriptures means that all Christendoms are equidistant from Jerusalem."[53] The challenges of translation have not only required the kind of careful attention to local contexts that helped to foster disciplines such as anthropology in the first place; they have also elicited indigenous leadership.

The liberating immediacy of the Word for global South audiences, not just leaders, is illustrated by one anecdote of a community responding audibly to a Pauline greeting: hearing "My love be with all of you in Christ Jesus," the church responded out loud in unison, "Thank you, Paul."[54] Accordingly, "the passages that work best today are those that most closely recall their origins in oral transmission, the stories and parables, hymns and wisdom literature, psalms and proverbs."[55] The power of scriptural texts extends in and through their influence on sacred music.[56] Prooftexting and prophesying apply Scripture to concrete situations with great immediacy, and this textual power extends even to the point that "the physical object of the Bible itself becomes a locus of spiritual power, which in some circumstances can become superstitious or near-magical."[57]

52. Jenkins, *The Next Christendom*, 113. Of course, "dynamic equivalence" theories of translation, such as this quotation supports, are themselves the subject of considerable debate today.

53. Jenkins, *The New Faces of Christianity*, 25.

54. Jenkins, *The New Faces of Christianity*, 26–27.

55. Jenkins, *The New Faces of Christianity*, 30.

56. Jenkins, *The New Faces of Christianity*, 31–34.

57. Jenkins, *The New Faces of Christianity*, 36.

In chapters 3 through 7 of his book Jenkins proceeds through five distinctive themes or traits of global South encounters with Scripture. "Old and New" highlights the non-Western resonance with the Old Testament as living material for Christians today, followed by "Poor and Rich," "Good and Evil," "Persecution and Vindication," and "Men and Women." In all these areas examples surface in which African, Asian, and/or Latin American Christians share contexts with the original audiences of Scripture that make the texts come distinctively alive. Moreover, global South Christians often face situations in which the biblical content is immediately relevant, whereas Westerners might scratch their heads about how it could apply. For instance,

> Even in relatively small things, African and Asian readers need no gloss to understand Hebrew customs and forms that strike North Americans as archaic and incomprehensible. Was God angry with David for taking a census of the people of Israel? Gikuyu readers instantly appreciate the taboos associated with counting and enumeration. Unlike their Western counterparts, moreover, many African and Asian Christians think it only reasonable that the Bible should include lengthy genealogies for key figures, most obviously Jesus himself: how else does one situate a figure and assert the basis on which he claims authority? . . . Reading a text like Lamentations, meanwhile, a Chinese scholar imbued in traditional culture will automatically turn to the millennia-old tradition of Chinese lamentation literature, which suggests still other dimensions for the Hebrew form.[58]

Other examples proliferate, especially in the African identification with the Old Testament. Prohibitions of idolatry are not just metaphors, as we often take them to be in the West, but apply directly to specific practices in many African or Asian contexts.[59] Global South Christians resonate in particular with Genesis, then Exodus and Isaiah, as well as Ecclesiastes and Proverbs, and with specific portions that we might find puzzling. Matthew is the most

58. Jenkins, *The New Faces of Christianity*, 46.
59. Jenkins, *The New Faces of Christianity*, 51.

beloved Gospel precisely because of its Jewish and Old Testament-oriented focus.[60] Acts, Hebrews, and Revelation are similarly beloved due to their elements that interface with the Old Testament. Cultural elements such as blood sacrifice are not foreign to global South experience and operate at the level of assumptions in their Christian practices.[61] Finally, since it contains elements of wisdom, apocalyptic, Old Testament examples, social activism, a focus on suffering and poverty, and so forth, the book of James is such a favorite that Jenkins prints it as an appendix, in its entirety. In short, one might say that the most popular portions of Scripture in the global South are those usually on the fringe for Western Protestants.[62]

Additional points of biblical content that resonate more directly with non-Western contexts include debt and debt forgiveness; wisdom texts and other teaching on the transience of life; the unreliability of nations and water; and shepherds as leaders.[63] When it comes to differing contexts, the book of Ruth illustrates: "In the American context, the book attracts some interest from feminist scholars, while Ruth's plea to Naomi, 'entreat me not to leave thee,' is included in blessing rites for same-sex couples. In the global South, the book's interest lies in how the various characters faithfully fulfill their obligations to each other and their relatives. The book becomes a model, even a manual, for a situation that could arise all too easily."[64] For Jenkins, such a recovery of the Old Testament is salutary, a gift to the West, although it also may contain a shadowy side if identification with Israel leads to ideas of simply replacing Israel.[65] Moreover, "What the North reads in moral or individualistic terms remains for the South social and communal," with a factor such as tribalism lending extra poignancy to a tale such as the parable of the good Samaritan.[66]

60. Jenkins, *The New Faces of Christianity*, 53.
61. Jenkins, *The New Faces of Christianity*, 54–57.
62. Jenkins, *The New Faces of Christianity*, 61.
63. Jenkins, *The New Faces of Christianity*, 73–78, 146–48.
64. Jenkins, *The New Faces of Christianity*, 79.
65. Jenkins, *The New Faces of Christianity*, 67.
66. Jenkins, *The New Faces of Christianity*, 80–81.

## Complex Encounters

Indeed, Christians in Africa often bump right up against non-Christian religions, especially Islam, while in Asia Christians make up a very marginal percentage of most populations. These realities shape how non-Western Christians interpret the Bible regarding moral issues and matters of eternal destiny for non-Christians.[67] Wisdom texts such as Ecclesiastes or James resonate strikingly with others in interreligious dialogue or encounters.[68] Material on poverty and the transience of life addresses global South contexts in acute ways, where John 10:10—Jesus' mission of bringing abundant life—is a crucial theme and "prosperity gospel" teaching is common.[69] Jenkins cautions Western critics not only to sympathize with the tragic states in which non-Western Christians find themselves but also to recognize that Western churches tend to agree with health and wealth as desirable goals, while merely replacing prayer and godliness with secular means for attaining them.[70]

This highlights the discomfort of many Western Christians, especially less conservative ones, over the supernaturalism of the global South. There, the existence of miracles, angels, demons, and the like is a commonplace assumption, operative in Christian practice.[71] Again, though aware of Western worries and perhaps even sympathetic with them to a point, Jenkins casts global South Christianity in a more favorable light. He sees Christian reinter-

---

67. Jenkins, *The New Faces of Christianity*, 84–85.

68. Jenkins, *The New Faces of Christianity*, 87–90.

69. For an unfavorable portrayal of the inroads of such teaching, see Paul Gifford, "A View of Ghana's New Christianity," in *The Changing Face of Christianity: Africa, the West, and the World*, ed. Lamin Sanneh and Joel A. Carpenter (New York: Oxford University Press, 2005), 81–96. Yet this portrayal is criticized by an important indigenous leader in Kwame Bediako, "Christian Witness in the Public Sphere: Some Lessons and Residual Challenges from the Recent Political History of Ghana," in Sanneh and Carpenter, *The Changing Face of Christianity*, 117–32.

70. Jenkins, *The New Faces of Christianity*, 90–97.

71. Perhaps my favorite story in the book concerns a Western pastor, visiting an African church, who heard the announcement that he, the visitor from America, would be conducting the evening exorcism (see Jenkins, *The New Faces of Christianity*, 105).

pretations of more animistic or traditional religious phenomena and practices as mitigating their negative effects, moving non-Western cultures toward healthy balance.[72] Sanneh notes that, in the context of such encounters, the charge of "syncretism" often comes to Western lips. But he cautions us:

> Syncretism represents the unresolved, unassimilated, and tension-filled mixing of Christian ideas with local custom and ritual, and that scarcely results in the kind of fulfilling change signaled by conversion and church membership. Besides, syncretism is the term we use for the religion of those we don't like. No one calls himself or herself a syncretist! . . . Unless we use the term as a judgment against our own forms of religious practice, I suggest we drop it altogether.[73]

It is troubling that, as more and more Western Christians acknowledge the need for contextualization and indigenous leadership, they have tended to pull not only their missionary leaders out of foreign contexts but also their money.[74] Apparently, we continue to have difficulty in acknowledging our own syncretism and in relinquishing hermeneutical control.

Meanwhile, persecution may make believers living in the global South more attuned to biblical texts on that subject. Beyond such content, however, there is also context. Jenkins provides numerous examples of persecuted Christian leaders who subtly use scriptural narratives or figures, positively or negatively, to criticize unjust leaders or regimes.[75] American Christians need to realize that the United States is sometimes a target of such non-Western prophetic denunciation.[76] In terms of hermeneutical perspectives, the

---

72. E.g., Jenkins, *The New Faces of Christianity*, 125. For an anthropologist's case study on such an issue see Todd M. Vanden Berg, "Culture, Christianity, and Witchcraft in a West African Context," in Sanneh and Carpenter, *The Changing Face of Christianity*, 45–62.

73. Sanneh, *Whose Religion Is Christianity?* 44.

74. See, e.g., Isaac M. T. Mwase, "Shall They Till with Their Own Hoes? Baptists in Zimbabwe and New Patterns of Interdependence, 1950–2000," in Sanneh and Carpenter, *The Changing Face of Christianity*, especially 74.

75. E.g., Jenkins, *The New Faces of Christianity*, 131.

76. E.g., Jenkins, *The New Faces of Christianity*, 134.

colonized may struggle with material such as the book of Joshua,[77] while Ecclesiastes becomes increasingly popular as efforts toward political activism and social change produce disappointment.[78] In other words, "States fail; churches flourish," and "secret police forces have to be skilled in biblical hermeneutics."[79] It is not just that in such circumstances political texts take on more poignant significance, as with Judges or Daniel; it is also that political overtones or possibilities come to light in other biblical texts. For example, "texts such as the Christological hymn in Philippians, about Christ's self-emptying and self-denial, bear a special political relevance" as models for leadership. Or Ephesians comes to transcend issues of church government and even spiritual warfare, to provide a vision for communal unity overcoming war-torn strife.[80]

On "Women and Men" Jenkins repeats his pattern of mixing Western concerns with redrawn portrayals of the global South. He notes first that "feminist theologians contribute such a sizable proportion of the literature on Third World Christianity easily available in North America" that we must move beyond what is written in order to get a complete picture of local church life.[81] And even there, "literalist readings that may appear conservative in terms of their approach to scriptural authority in practice have consequences that are socially progressive, if not revolutionary."[82] Such a passage, reflecting as it does Jenkins's own point of view to some degree, shows that his chronicle of global South Christianity involves neither uncritical naïveté nor simple cheerleading. Furthermore, he rightly points out that the Western gulf is similarly wide between academic elites and local practices or even pastoral beliefs.[83] In any case, hermeneutical differences are once more evident between the West and the South, where female circumcision becomes an interpretative issue in the Abraham narratives,

77. Jenkins, *The New Faces of Christianity*, 137–39.
78. Jenkins, *The New Faces of Christianity*, 141.
79. Jenkins, *The New Faces of Christianity*, 142–43.
80. Jenkins, *The New Faces of Christianity*, 154.
81. Jenkins, *The New Faces of Christianity*, 158.
82. Jenkins, *The New Faces of Christianity*, 159.
83. Jenkins, *The New Faces of Christianity*, 165.

or Romans 7:2 becomes a text with life-or-death significance for widows.[84]

What, then, is today's Westerner supposed to take away from this survey? According to Jenkins,

> Nobody is suggesting that in order to recreate this experience, this excitement, Christians need to return to a social order reminiscent of the first-century Mediterranean—still less to renounce modern medicine. But we can reasonably ask whether the emerging Christian traditions of the Two-Thirds World have recaptured themes and trends in Christianity that the older churches have forgotten, and if so, what we can learn from their insights.[85]

Often the questions of Christians in the global South approximate more closely the spirit of classic Christianity: "These are not just good questions, they are the same questions that agitated the early church."[86] To put the matter poignantly: "As a difficult test for Northern-world Christians, try reading two almost adjacent passages in James, one condemning the rich, the other prescribing anointing and prayer for healing, and see both texts, 'radical' and 'charismatic,' as integral portions of a common liberating message."[87] Ultimately these differences in context, along with which biblical content resonates and how it does so, point to different types of Christian community.

### Imaging God in Culture

Thus, numerous illustrations have surfaced regarding how different forms of attention to community and the variety of hermeneutical contexts shape biblical interpretation. In returning to the case study used throughout this book—the *imago Dei*—I would be foolish to act as if Westerners could simply transport themselves into a "global South" mind-set and come up with a new interpretation

84. E.g., Jenkins, *The New Faces of Christianity*, 170, 174.
85. Jenkins, *The New Faces of Christianity*, 178.
86. Jenkins, *The New Faces of Christianity*, 180.
87. Jenkins, *The New Faces of Christianity*, 183.

in that light. Nor do I have a radically different exegetical perspective to offer on this issue from non-Western theological literature. Yet it is interesting to explore the one-volume *Africa Bible Commentary* on Genesis 1:26b–27, which opposes body-spirit dualism and contains a text box regarding "New Family Relationships" on the next page. Additionally, according to the second of its three comments, the *imago Dei* "means that we should not worship any animal (Exod. 20:4; Rom. 1:21–22). Woe to the person who lowers himself to the level of animals by giving an animal or an image of an animal the place that belongs only to the Creator!"[88] Although the exegetical perspective is not that distinctive from a technical standpoint, the context of the commentary relates the concept of the *imago Dei* to unique questions and concerns.

Global concerns usually include the context within which traditional "Western" theological anthropology is set. So, for example, individualism is commonly highlighted as a problematic feature of such systematic theologies.[89] The influence of Christian doctrine, and especially the image of God concept, upon Western culture has been faulted for environmental degradation, with Genesis 1:26–31 construed anthropocentrically in terms of lordly domination rather than loving care and stewardship.[90] Meanwhile, belief in human dignity stemming in part from the *imago Dei* notion has not always extended to all persons: at times women were not taken to be divine image-bearers in the same way as men, and of course many did not consistently apply the concept to other peoples (or "races" in the modern terminology).

Particularly tragic effects of the latter occurrence include the Shoah (the Jewish term for the Holocaust), the Rwandan genocide, and the way in which the United States faces deep racial divisions, even or especially among Christians. The goal is not to blame

88. Tokunboh Adeyemo, ed., *Africa Bible Commentary* (Grand Rapids: Zondervan, 2006), 11–12.

89. See, e.g., Carver T. Yu, *Being and Relation: A Theological Critique of Western Dualism and Individualism*, Theology and Science at the Frontiers of Knowledge 8 (Edinburgh: Scottish Academic Press, 1987).

90. Most famously in Lynn White Jr., "The Historical Roots of Our Ecological Crisis," *Science* 155, no. 3767 (March 10, 1967): 1203–7.

Christian faith uniquely or to deny that the gospel contains valuable resources for addressing racial ideologies, partly through ways in which Christians could distinctively open themselves to confession and reform. To the extent that "Christian" faith contributed to the Shoah, it was a profound perversion of the gospel that did so. Nevertheless, medieval pogroms were the antecedents of that tragedy, and the case of Rwanda involved significant Christian participation in the killing.[91] Concerning race more generally, the United States may face some unique challenges and opportunities in terms of its historical origins, immigration policies, contemporary notions of pluralism, and so forth. Arguably, however, those historical origins involved genocide or its approximation, with regard to Native Americans; and of course the terrorism of the slave trade, with frequent misuse of the Bible to support it, fostered European and American economic development for hundreds of years. Moreover, evangelical religion has experienced particular forms of complex give-and-take with American racialization.[92]

The instructive point of these critical examples is that a proper historical description of a biblical concept such as the *imago Dei* does not automatically shape Christian thought and life adequately, since the church frequently lacks the virtue to recognize its implications and apply it appropriately. The pursuit of equality, for which Westerners pride themselves and Christians prize their tradition of the *imago Dei*, often gets parceled out very selectively.

We can add, though, that cultural difference shapes a recent account of the image of God significantly. Ian McFarland follows biblical scholar Claus Westermann, for whom "the assertion that

91. On genocide, see Samantha Power, *"A Problem from Hell": America and the Age of Genocide* (New York: Basic Books, 2002).

92. Michael O. Emerson and Christian Smith, *Divided by Faith: Evangelical Religion and the Problem of Race in America* (New York: Oxford University Press, 2001). For constructive theological engagement with race, see Robert J. Priest and Alvaro L. Nieves, eds., *This Side of Heaven: Race, Ethnicity, and Christian Faith* (New York: Oxford University Press, 2007). For access to the complex history and current debates regarding the Bible and slavery, see Mark A. Noll, *The Civil War as a Theological Crisis* (Chapel Hill: University of North Carolina Press, 2006); William J. Webb, "Slavery," *DTIB* 751–53.

human beings are made in God's image has the purely narrative function of setting the stage for further interaction between God and humankind. It does not imply any sort of ontological correspondence between divine and human being, but merely establishes the narrative preconditions for the story that follows. From this perspective, speculation about its material content is simply beside the point."[93] McFarland then adopts a christological approach to the content of the *imago Dei*, seeing the Pauline material as making claims about equality on that basis "rather than on any intrinsic qualities possessed by all human beings in virtue of their common descent from Adam." "In this way, the effect of the Christian confession of Jesus as the image of God is not to focus attention on humankind, but to prod people to look away from themselves to God as the source and guarantor of their identity."[94]

Yet the resulting worry is that traits of Jesus such as his maleness become definitive for human identity. To address this worry, one could restrain appeals to Jesus, only ruling out false portrayals of human identity without claiming ability to discern which of his particular characteristics manifest true universals of that identity.[95] Accordingly, "The language of Colossians 1 in particular raises the possibility that the biblical identification of Jesus as the image of God may be important less for what it tells us about humankind (including Jesus as a human being) than for what it tells us about God." In addition, "because I have no proper analogue between the Creator and any reality of which I have seen an image, I lack the conceptual framework I need in order to know how to move from the image to a true understanding of the prototype."[96] To avoid idolatry, about which considerable material appears in the Bible with respect to "images," means knowing how to learn from Jesus about God. However, even that is a tricky move: "Jesus does not come to us in isolation, but only in relation to the whole of the history he has come to redeem," which means that God's self-

93. Ian A. McFarland, *The Divine Image: Envisioning the Invisible God* (Minneapolis: Fortress, 2005), 3.
94. McFarland, *The Divine Image*, 6.
95. McFarland, *The Divine Image*, 8.
96. McFarland, *The Divine Image*, 11.

communication in Christ is "very much still in the process of being worked out" in its reception especially by the church.[97]

How can experience of other human beings give us the protocols that we need for discerning what God communicates in Christ? That is the burden of the rest of McFarland's book, in which he claims that "Jesus is not called the 'image of God' because he exhausts that image, but because he is the source of its identity and unity," the head of the body.[98] Insofar as we adopt a christological interpretation, then, we must not fill up the *imago Dei* with material content that wrongly limits what Christ's body the church contributes to our understanding of God. The image of God is not an inherent property but instead an eschatological "state into which we are gradually transformed."[99] In this way we get an illustration of how conceptual openings in biblical material can be filled out via doctrinal reflection; in the process, though, we can arrive at views that seem far away from the affirmations that certain scriptural texts seem to make.

It almost appears as if not just the image of God, but even Christ himself, becomes a bit of a formal construct, thus able to embrace material content from any and every church in any and every culture. It is not McFarland's intention to land in relativism. Still, this tension over how to fill a christological *imago Dei* concept with content highlights a perennial struggle for the interpretation of Scripture: how to remain open to the various cultural forms that the embodiment of revelation can take without losing the possibility of ascertaining and passing on enduring convictions about concrete truths.

## Preliminary Conclusions

And so this chapter evokes more questions than answers. We can affirm the need for Christians in all cultures to learn a form of "critical contextualization" or even "critical syncretism," in which

97. McFarland, *The Divine Image*, 49.
98. McFarland, *The Divine Image*, 55.
99. McFarland, *The Divine Image*, 165.

the various adjectives such as "white" or "African" or "Asian" remain "qualifiers" of our identity rather than "identifiers" that replace the gospel at the core of who we are.[100] Indeed, "the greatest missiological challenge the American church faces is not, say, the Islamic world but rather the lack of critical contextualization of the gospel in much of American cultural and political life."[101] Addressing such a challenge may require special attention to economics, acknowledging the arguably religious dimensions of market capitalism.[102]

The point is not to reject the entire Western heritage of Christian faith, as if divine providence were absent from it, but rather to recognize that the gospel is more than Western.[103] In fact, it is important to realize that the label "Western" is problematic in multiple ways. For one, the more accurate label probably is "Northern," since this provides a contrast with the global South while the issues of social class and Christian growth that are important to address do not fall as closely along any East-West divide. For another, more importantly, the Western tradition includes the influence of non-European Christians, notably African theologians such as the Alexandrians and Augustine.[104]

Mission historian Andrew Walls has highlighted that Christian faith is unique in its portability. To some degree it seems to follow the incarnation as a paradigm, taking tangible shape in a given culture through translation, institutional development, and so forth, but then emptying itself into that culture in such a way as to experience death. But its death in some of its most prominent cultural centers—Jerusalem, Antioch, Alexandria, and the like—is

100. Vanhoozer, "'One Rule to Rule Them All?'" 104, 117.

101. Ramachandra, "Globalization, Nationalism, and Religious Resurgence," 230.

102. Eloise Hiebert Meneses, "Bearing Witness in Rome with Theology from the Whole Church: Globalization, Theology, and Nationalism," in Ott and Netland, *Globalizing Theology*, 242. For an example of biblical-theological engagement with global market capitalism, see Craig Bartholomew and Thorsten Moritz, eds., *Christ and Consumerism: A Critical Analysis of the Spirit of the Age* (Carlisle: Paternoster, 2000).

103. Vanhoozer, "'One Rule to Rule Them All?'" 119.

104. For a brief spotlight on the African patristic heritage, see Grant LeMarquand, "African Biblical Interpretation," *DTIB* 31–34.

not necessarily permanent, and this death is also the occasion of new life in other places. For these cultural centers were the springboards for vibrant missionary activity elsewhere, with Christianity again planting cultural roots. Following the pattern of its Lord in this manner, Christian faith stands in marked contrast with a religion such as Islam, which involves a particular revealed language.[105]

The Christian story of creation and Pentecost affirms the possibility of legitimate cultural diversity, while the fall necessitates confronting the log in our own cultural eye before trying to remove the speck in others'. Redemption in Christ leads us to anticipate a glorious future that continues to involve culture: "The vision is ultimately one of a new humanity (not ethnic pride), a new city (not a locality), a new citizenship (not nationalism), and a new creation (not a fallen one)."[106]

As we live "between the times," awaiting this future, we must learn to deal with culture as a much more fluid concept than the modern West portrayed.[107] Globalization simultaneously confronts us more than ever with manifestations of local culture and suggests that even specific local theologies may have much more in common than they previously did.[108] These realities call for more "experience-near" theological work in tandem with the social sciences and engagement with lived Christianity.[109] It may be that

105. See, e.g., Andrew F. Walls, *The Cross-Cultural Process in Christian History: Studies in the Transmission and Appropriation of Faith* (Maryknoll, NY: Orbis, 2002).

106. Craig Ott, "Conclusion: Globalizing Theology," in Ott and Netland, *Globalizing Theology*, 336.

107. For a brief overview of this contrast between "essentialist" and "social constructionist" views, see Elizabeth Yao-Hwa Sung, "Culture and Hermeneutics," *DTIB* 150–55. At more length, though perhaps too far in a "postmodern" direction, is Kathryn Tanner, *Theories of Culture: A New Agenda for Theology*, Guides to Theological Inquiry (Minneapolis: Fortress, 1997). More practical, and with a helpful glossary, is Kevin J. Vanhoozer, Charles A. Anderson, and Michael J. Sleasman, eds., *Everyday Theology: How to Read Cultural Texts and Interpret Trends* (Grand Rapids: Baker Academic, 2007).

108. Ott, "Conclusion: Globalizing Theology," 313.

109. Robert J. Priest, "'Experience-Near Theologizing' in Diverse Human Contexts," in Ott and Netland, *Globalizing Theology*, especially 194.

Christian theologians and interpreters of Scripture could pursue forms of truly international peer review.[110] If they did, then boundaries between the academy and the church would have to become more fluid as well. All of these issues raise challenges for discernment, but they also highlight the need for courage: we must risk undertaking and undergoing catechesis so that the church in every culture finds itself accountable to discern what counts as faithfully Christian.

Beyond these formal matters of approach or method, if there is a material principle uniting many of the diverse non-Western theologies, it is perhaps an "emphasis on divine compassion and justice" along with the reality of spiritual forces and their everyday effects.[111] From postcolonial theorists we might also learn to address questions of liberation, feminism, ecology, and human rights, even if we must do so from within a more orthodox and comprehensive theological perspective.[112] Perhaps, above all, we must learn from global Christianity "that the religion does succeed best when it takes very seriously the profound pessimism about the secular world that characterizes the New Testament."[113] Such pessimism involves not the counsel of despair or simple resignation but instead a form of realism about human achievements and aspirations that is disciplined by the entire biblical gospel.

In conclusion, consider a compelling analogy from the novelist Shashi Deshpande:

> When I first begin writing, I have a huge margin, a large blank space which I know will soon fill up with alterations, corrections, new ideas and so on. And, sure enough, in time the margin is full, the words begin creeping into the centre of the page, the margin and the text merge and finally, because what I am now saying comes mostly from margin, the margin takes over, it becomes the real text.[114]

110. Ott, "Conclusion: Globalizing Theology," 330.
111. Vanhoozer, "'One Rule to Rule Them All?'" 98–99.
112. Ott, "Conclusion: Globalizing Theology," 326.
113. Jenkins, *The Next Christendom*, 220.
114. Quoted in Sugirtharajah, "Introduction: Still at the Margins," 9.

To what extent does this portray a desirable end result of Christianity's rise in the global South? That is a daunting question increasingly faced by anyone who seeks to interpret Scripture theologically. Whatever one's answer, thanks to the Holy Spirit, non-Western voices can no longer be marginal as they once were. We must listen.

# Conclusion

## In the End, God

By now, you have explored two perspectives on theological interpretation of Scripture. This book began by surveying various catalysts for the movement, such as renewed evangelical and Catholic engagement with critical biblical scholarship from the mid-twentieth century onward; the constructive theological criticism of such scholarship by Karl Barth; and hermeneutical trends sometimes labeled "postmodern," including a focus on community. Other catalysts for theological interpretation of Scripture point us to common themes within the movement: imitating the strengths of precritical interpreters such as Augustine (chap. 1); interacting with Christian doctrine, especially the trinitarian Rule of Faith that holds Scripture together around one divine story (chap. 2); and listening to others in the church as the community of the Holy Spirit, in which we are formed as virtuous readers (chap. 3). The first perspective on theological interpretation of Scripture, laid out in part 1, involved a focus on what is held in common.

Part 2 shifted the focus to continuing challenges on which the various participants in the movement either do not agree or have not clearly spoken. One of those concerns, especially for biblical scholars, is whether "biblical theology" has its proper uses, and, if so, how it should be pursued (chap. 4). A related concern, perhaps more dominant among theologians and others outside the discipline of biblical studies, is the nature of proper engagement with general hermeneutics (chap. 5). Beyond the academic guilds of the "Western" university, there is still another concern, which to this point has gone largely unaddressed by advocates for theological exegesis: engagement with the various social locations of biblical interpretation, especially in light of "globalization" (chap. 6).

From these two angles—what is held in common on the one side, and what produces continuing tension on the other side—we can gain a fairly clear picture of the movement toward recovering theological interpretation of Scripture. The goal of this final chapter is to highlight key features of that composite picture. Before that, however, it may help to sketch some of the mental moves that people make in doing theology, as a resource for undertaking theological interpretation. In this way readers may consider what it means to pursue the practice themselves.

## The Nature of Theological Reflection: Doing Theology and Imaging God

From a traditional perspective, theology is "faith seeking understanding," rooted in prayerful contemplation of God. Prayer is first theology; theology involves activity in which people become virtuous as they come to know God better. Thus, to speak of theology as "critical reflection"—very standard terminology in the modern West—could give the wrong idea, as if theology primarily involves elite academic specialists sitting around and theorizing. By contrast, in an important sense theology pertains to every activity in which Christians engage God and others, communicating and refining thereby an understanding of who God is. Theology is the practice of all Christian people growing in their knowledge of God amidst their various life activities and church practices. The academic discipline of theology is not entirely separate from, or more important than, ordinary Christian growth in biblical discernment. Rather, professional theologians ought to pursue the same practices as lay Christians but with different intensities of inquiry, amounts of time, and levels of expertise.[1]

In the modern university, theology developed more clearly into somewhat distinct subdisciplines. The resulting fragmentation of theological practice has been profoundly problematic, and many are seeking to overturn or at least relativize these disciplinary divisions. Yet they persist as facts of life that we must address, inevitable for the foreseeable future, given the way they seem natural and given the nature of academic life. So, instead of treating these exclusively as airtight specializations for scholarly experts to undertake, I suggest that we see them as offering a thinking pattern for all of us. The use of exegetical or literary, biblical, historical, philosophical, and practical categories can help us to reflect thoroughly and clearly, as well as to ask the right questions, concerning our God. The following paragraphs offer a guide to these categories and their criteria, using the *imago Dei* once again as an example.

### Exegesis

As noted early on, "exegesis" examines details of the text and seeks to interpret the "meaning" of particular passages or units of discourse using historical and literary methods. Broader approaches to meaning in general hermeneutics or theological exegesis might lead some to construe "understanding" or even "interpretation" as wider categories than exegesis narrowly defined as a scholarly practice. In any case, the point is that Christian theology at heart exists in some kind of basic relationship with biblical texts, in all their particularity.

With regard to the image of God, numerous exegetical questions surface in Genesis 1:26–27 and other texts. What is the precise nuance of the terms translated "image" and "likeness": are they basically synonymous with each other, or are they significantly different? How should we take the syntax of the relevant phrase: made "in" the *imago Dei* or "as"—to be—the *imago Dei*? Is Genesis

---

1. For a detailed exposition and defense of this view, see Daniel J. Treier, *Virtue and the Voice of God: Toward Theology as Wisdom* (Grand Rapids: Eerdmans, 2006).

1:28 about fruitfulness and dominion as consequences of the *imago Dei*, or do these instead offer an explanatory definition of the concept itself? Is the phrase in Genesis 1:27 regarding maleness and femaleness relevant to the content of the image? Some of these types of questions are very directly a function of specific textual details. Others, by contrast, are potentially broader, at least in the sense that they cannot be answered in a simply objective way based thoroughly on facts about which every interpreter agrees. To extend this example in order to see how the significance of such exegetical details can be disputable, note James 3:9–12. It clearly says that we have been made "in" God's likeness. However, is that New Testament passage relevant for the question of whether we translate "in" or "as" the *imago Dei* in Genesis 1? Exegesis strives for degrees of objectivity as much as the details of a text permit, but the resulting decisions involve varied contexts—historical, literary, and even canonical or theological—the shape of which is often up for debate. These contexts lead the interpreter to interact with several other theological subdisciplines.

### Biblical Theology

As chapter 4 explored in considerable detail, the definition and approach of biblical theology are complex matters. At a basic level, it seeks to unfold the theology of the whole Bible, depending on the degree of unity believed to be there. Biblical theology often focuses on words or concepts as an exploratory starting point and thus uses organizing principles that are as internal to Scripture as possible. This means prioritizing historical and/or literary criteria and procedures.

In the case of the *imago Dei*, one can acknowledge the relative scarcity of this terminology in Scripture, especially in the Old Testament, without considering the concept to be unimportant for a biblical anthropology. Biblical theology cannot operate simply in terms of vocabulary or the number of times a concept appears. The nature and placement of a concept are important; therefore, reference to the image of God at the beginning of the Bible, in the creation and patriarchal narratives, is significant. It might suggest that the concept operates as a background assumption elsewhere in scriptural faith. Moreover, texts such as Psalm 8 may be relevant to the doctrine without directly containing the same "image" vocabulary. Still further, the "son" or "child" of God theme—pertaining to Israel, the people of God, as a whole along with their ruler in particular—is quite significant. If we can connect it to the *imago Dei*, for instance via its connection with sonship in Genesis 5:1–3, then that might lend greater weight to humans imaging God in Old Testament anthropology.

The apparent repetition in James 3:9–12 of the sort of thinking that we see in Genesis 9:6 connects the Old Testament and the New Testament. Psalm 8 likewise seems to influence New Testament anthropology to some degree. A crucial interpretative problem or opportunity in relating the Testaments—depending on one's point of view in this key test case—concerns the passages that construe the image of God christologically. Are these "interpretations" of Genesis 1:26–27 and other Old Testament material? Or should we see them as merely applications of the language, perhaps filling out the *imago Dei* concept without interpreting those texts (wrongly, in the eyes of many biblical scholars)? Or should we instead see no coherence at all between these various biblical uses of "image" vocabulary?

Biblical theology, like exegesis more narrowly considered, pressures us to engage the details of the texts so that they shape the very patterns in which we think and live. This involves a kind of objectivity that has historical and literary dimensions, to be sure. However, if objectivity has to do with reality outside the self shaping our knowledge, then there is also a dimension in which God acts as Subject, shaping us via the Holy Spirit. Thus biblical "objectivity" incorporates methods and skills. But since these depend on how we exercise our subjectivity, they are fully reliable only to the degree that God continually reforms us by Word and Spirit.[2] Therefore they do not replace the prayerful reading of Scripture

2. For a sketch of how definitions of objectivity shifted over time, see Mark A. Bowald, "Objectivity," *DTIB* 544–46.

as part of a tapestry of Christian practices in which the church comes to know God (and yes, the Bible) better.

### Historical Theology

Another historical task involving texts is the study of previous responses to Scripture. It is now fairly commonplace to suggest that the history of the church can be seen largely as a history of biblical interpretation. Yet the history of scriptural interpretation also extends beyond the church, since ecclesiastical boundaries became ever more disputable as history progressed, and since non-Christians have always interacted with the biblical texts and their churchly readers. In the present case we are more specifically interested in the history of the church and of biblical interpretation in terms of theology—what to say about God.

Thus, historical theology is not a purely descriptive task but also contains a prescriptive dimension. Seeking to describe the theology of different persons or creeds and confessions on some question, historical theology has normative interests in terms of which questions receive study. Furthermore, we are studying in order to discern what we can learn or what we might be obligated to believe today. One might select material normative for all Christians (e.g., the Nicene Creed), for a particular tradition (e.g., Martin Luther or the Thirty-Nine Articles of the Church of England or the New Hampshire Confession), or even at variance with one's own tradition (e.g., a Calvinist studying what John Wesley says).

Regarding the *imago Dei*, the relatively universal Christian symbols—the Nicene Creed and the Chalcedonian Definition—do not seem to entail a specific anthropology, except for the way in which Jesus Christ fully shares our humanity without sin. Many denominational confessions use the image of God as an important anthropological concept; yet, while they seem to affirm some kind of metaphysical linkage between us and God in the broad sense, they do not usually take a metaphysical interpretation of Genesis 1:26–27 to the point of a necessary, clear exclusion of alternative views.

The history of precritical theological interpretation of Scripture on this concept seems to be mixed. On the one hand, we can acknowledge, in Augustine and others, the presence of a clear hierarchy in which reason has preeminent importance compared to the body, emotions, and the like. It is arguably a great virtue of critical biblical scholarship that its functional approach to Genesis 1:26–27 can highlight more clearly the significance of the human body. Such a functional view need not simply force us to choose between God having a body and humans imaging God entirely apart from their bodies. As the image of God, the human is "a representative in physical form, [though] not a representation of the physical appearance."[3] The association of idol imagery and child imagery in the background suggests that "the image of God in people provides them the capacity not only to serve as God's vice-regents (his representatives containing his essence), but also the capacity to be and act like him."[4]

Yet, on the other hand, when it comes to the *imago Dei*, I have sought to defend Augustine and other precritical interpreters at points. Undoubtedly they were influenced by cultural or philosophical presuppositions in ways of which they were not fully aware, but so are we! Moreover, they offered biblical, even detailed exegetical, reasons for these presuppositions, and for the resulting interpretations, far more often than dismissive historians and biblical scholars might lead us to believe. Even regarding the physical body, the picture is complex, since, for instance, Caroline Walker Bynum has shown the striking attention paid to resurrection, and thus the physical realm, throughout the precritical Christian tradition.[5]

Historical theology offers rich examples of taking Scripture's unity, and therefore christological interpretation of the *imago Dei* in the New Testament, very seriously. Furthermore, it offers context for relational approaches to the concept; arguably, these appropriate the classical trinitarian heritage and at the same time

3. John H. Walton, *Genesis*, NIV Application Commentary (Grand Rapids: Zondervan, 2001), 130.

4. Walton, *Genesis*, 131.

5. Caroline Walker Bynum, *The Resurrection of the Body in Western Christianity, 200–1336* (New York: Columbia University Press, 1995).

address its neglect or subsequent churchly defects, exemplified in the individual egoism criticized by Barth's generation. Historical theology helps us to see that even the words that we use to describe our interpretations do not operate in a vacuum. If that cultural background is modern Western individualism, for instance, then even the work of the biblical scholar who opts for a functional approach is not yet done. Such an interpretation must be understood and conveyed in language that accurately reflects the relational context of the biblical concept. Historical theology therefore shapes both the content and context of our theological exegesis, appropriating resources from prior insights as well as learning from previous mistakes.

### Systematic Theology

Also called "constructive theology" or "dogmatics," the discipline of systematic theology draws these other threads together, using more external principles such as logic and relevance. These principles help us both to understand and to communicate biblical teaching about God in contemporary contexts. Systematic theology does not dispense with the internal structures of biblical theology (e.g., classic categories such as "Christology" and "pneumatology" address matters in the Bible itself!), and indeed it may seek to answer questions raised by that material. But systematic theology deals with a wider potential range of intellectual tools and incorporates the perspectives of the whole canon somewhat more synthetically, sometimes less analytically or historically.

Systematic theology deals with "doctrine," which denotes teaching in general, whether the formal teaching of a church or that of a theologian who thinks that his or her teaching offers truth to the church. "Dogma" is formal church teaching that is especially binding; it cannot be refused by its members without their being counted as heretical or even excommunicated. To call this sub-discipline "dogmatics," therefore, emphasizes that theology is done by and for a particular church, which makes binding claims about the gospel and its implications for life. (This is why Barth called his great multivolume work *Church Dogmatics*.) Somewhat by contrast, labeling this subdiscipline "constructive theology" emphasizes human creativity and freedom in pursuing theological understanding; such terminology is more recent and usually reflects the pursuits of academic theologians in the modern or postmodern West.

A further subset of systematic theology is "philosophical theology," which, as one might expect, emphasizes logic more than relevance. Many questions in systematic theology have considerable overlap with those that philosophers engage as the subject of analytic philosophy of religion, and some theologians focus on this overlap in terms of specific issues and methods. Overall, despite clearly prioritizing orderly organization and explanation of our understanding of God, "systematic theology" seems to be theology's broadest or most general category. Theologies became more systematic with each phase of university life, medieval and modern. Yet Christians have always sought to understand the Bible's portrayal of God coherently and to present it using contemporary terms.[6]

Such a systematic focus challenges biblical interpreters to relate the *imago Dei* in Genesis 1:26–27 to Genesis 5:1–3; 9:6; Psalm 8; James 3:9–12; the New Testament christological texts, and so forth. Moreover, systematic theology pushes beyond the explicit statements of such passages to their logical presuppositions, entailments, and implications. Even if, for example, there is no explicit metaphysical material in Genesis 1:26–27, might not these verses still have ontological implications for how we view humans in relation to animals and angels? We must then consider whether the Bible treats angels as personal beings, although not in terms of imaging God; as a result, we might conclude that image of God and personhood are not identical concepts. We might wonder how humans and animals are distinct, and whether Genesis assumes that such distinctions provide background upon which to draw for

6. For a sketch of the increasingly systematic meaning of "systematic theology," see Colin E. Gunton, "A Rose by Any Other Name? From 'Christian Doctrine' to 'Systematic Theology,'" *International Journal of Systematic Theology* 1, no. 1 (March 1999): 4–23.

the meaning of the *imago Dei*. Since animals too have bodies, but these bodies are forbidden for use as divine images, there must be some way in which humans' nonphysical capacities are relevant. Since animals likewise are male and female, this point of contact with humans causes difficulties for at least some relational ways of interpreting the *imago Dei*. Perhaps, though, the point is that humans communicate with God in ways animals do not, and accordingly humans can communicate what God is like within the created order in ways that animals do not. The function of human beings as God's image-bearers, in other words, might nevertheless be inherently relational.

Systematic theology, by whatever name, ultimately concerns relationships between various contexts that affect, and are affected by, biblical interpretation. The goal is not to foist extraneous material on top of biblical teaching, getting in the way of Scripture having its say; instead, the goal is to ask the right questions, relating various contexts in ways that illuminate the biblical teaching and our contemporary contexts in light of it.

### Practical Theology

Also concerned with relevance is practical theology, which seeks to relate doctrinal formulations to the ministries of Christian persons and churches. Sometimes called "pastoral theology," this subdiscipline nevertheless does not focus exclusively upon what pastors do. It also addresses evangelism or mission, education, social action, counseling, and so forth. These are often studied more descriptively with the social sciences, as well as theologically, perhaps with special attention to the spiritual formation of persons and communities. Christian practices and their study create a feedback loop regarding what spiritual life and church ministry teach us about the language of our faith. They create new questions that lead us back to the scriptural texts afresh.

In the contemporary Western world the realms of bioethics, technology, animal rights, fascination with angels, and so forth generate a plethora of new questions regarding humans as the image of God.[7] Such questions, as we saw in the previous chapter, may not directly influence how one addresses historical or literary details in biblical texts. However, they remain very relevant to the theological context of interpretation, in which we make judgments about how various biblical texts relate to each other and which biblical texts pertain to different questions.

In the present case, one need not adopt a "relational" view of the *imago Dei* in Genesis 1:26–27 to believe that relationship or communion is relevant to the concept. As we understand and communicate *how* humans represent God in the created order, we may see metaphysical implications in this concept of humans having the function of representing what God is like. Humans do this as uniquely communicative beings in comparison with other creatures.[8] Ontologically, this presupposes certain capacities for communication, including reason, while entailing the importance of our bodies for fulfilling such a relational function in the created order. (It is precisely our bodies that make us fit to represent God, who is unseen, to humans and other beings that operate by sight.) Furthermore, the God whom we represent lives in communion— Father, Son, and Holy Spirit, whose love overflows to us so that we can then love God and others. Such an approach incorporates Christology: Christ uniquely mediates between the divine and the human, imaging God truly without sin and as completely as we could envision. Still, against the Western temptation to construe even Christ's imaging God in moralistic terms, we must beware of simply focusing on him living as a righteous individual. The relation between Christ, the church, and all humanity involves a

7. Many today recognize ethics as a dimension of systematic theology, and of course it can be pursued as a branch of philosophy as well. Here I do not mean to reduce such concerns entirely to matters of church practice but rather simply to illustrate how cultural engagement returns us to the biblical texts with new questions.

8. For an example of a Christian anthropology oriented around being-in-communion and communicative action, see Kevin J. Vanhoozer, "Human Being, Individual and Social," in *Cambridge Companion to Christian Doctrine*, ed. Colin E. Gunton (Cambridge: Cambridge University Press, 1997), 158–88.

thicker set of considerations. It would take more than this short chapter, or even a whole book, to do them justice.

### Imaging God and "Doing" Theology

I have portrayed these theological fields in a certain order, in light of both their historical development and logical flow, but the actual pattern of thinking often proceeds in a very different order or even quite variably. The movement of theological reflection is multidirectional, even if in a sense the line of authority moves in one direction, from the Bible to contemporary theology.[9] These subdisciplines—exegetical, biblical, historical, systematic, and practical theology—parallel broadly the frequently mentioned "sources" of theology: Scripture, tradition, reason, and experience. Regardless of how different theological traditions elucidate their precise relationships, these "sources" do not all function in exactly the same way. Scripture sits in judgment over proposals from the others, each of which plays a different but important part in the drama of biblical interpretation.[10] Accordingly, on the one hand, the order of these subdisciplines points to a certain structure in the church's theological authority; yet, on the other hand, the nature of authority does not dictate that Christians must always interact with these sources in a linear manner.

Indeed, beyond logically ordered "reflection," theology begins in the midst of active Christian practice with the questions that it generates. Thus the point here is emphatically not to suggest that one must become an expert in one or more of theology's formal subfields in order to open a Bible. As noted earlier, there are in fact

9. See, e.g., D. A. Carson, "Unity and Diversity in the New Testament: The Possibility of Systematic Theology," in *Scripture and Truth*, ed. D. A. Carson and John D. Woodbridge (Grand Rapids: Baker Academic, 1992), 65–95; "Systematic Theology and Biblical Theology," in *New Dictionary of Biblical Theology*, ed. T. Desmond Alexander and Brian S. Rosner (Downers Grove, IL: InterVarsity, 2000), 89–104.

10. For helpful reflections and analogies regarding the different functions of Scripture, tradition, reason, and experience, see N. T. Wright, *The Last Word: Beyond the Bible Wars to a New Understanding of the Authority of Scripture* (San Francisco: HarperSanFrancisco, 2005), especially 101–3.

good reasons for minimizing or even opposing the formal distinctions between them, reinterpreting what they designate once one recognizes the ways in which they overlap. It is not that theology as "theory" in an abstract sense gets formalized apart from "practice" and then simply dominates it; instead, more modestly, this sketch of theological reflection offers a pattern for thought, a set of rough-and-ready rules of thumb with which to pursue prayerful contemplation once one is already in the midst of a theological question—"doing" theology.

## The Hermeneutical Lenses of Theological Interpretation

How, then, can we sum up the essence of what it means to interpret Scripture theologically? On the one hand, we must acknowledge that its advocates draw contrasts between theological exegesis and business-as-usual in biblical studies as an academic discipline. Theological interpretation of Scripture responds to perceived problems with critical biblical scholarship. However, on the other hand, it should be clear that healthy theological hermeneutics need not involve denigrating the faithful labors and valuable contributions of biblical scholars. As we have seen, one can advocate theological interpretation of Scripture while making significant use of critical methods or in fact serving as a biblical scholar. Theoretical disagreements about the nature of proper interaction with academic biblical studies probably are healthy. Furthermore, if theological interpretation of Scripture were to define itself simply by opposing certain institutions or trends, it would not long survive, for it would depend on those perceived problems, and as soon as the institutions or negative trends change, theological interpretation of Scripture would lack coherent identity or positive momentum.

The "Scripture Project" presents nine theses that, to a large degree, could reflect the identity of theological interpretation of Scripture fairly well.[11]

11. Ellen F. Davis and Richard B. Hays, eds., *The Art of Reading Scripture* (Grand Rapids: Eerdmans, 2003), 3–5. The project involved four years of

1. Scripture truthfully tells the story of God's action of creating, judging, and saving the world.
2. Scripture is rightly understood in light of the church's Rule of Faith as a coherent dramatic narrative.
3. Faithful interpretation of Scripture requires an engagement with the entire narrative: the New Testament cannot be rightly understood apart from the Old, nor can the Old be rightly understood apart from the New.
4. Texts of Scripture do not have a single meaning limited to the intent of the original author. In accord with Jewish and Christian traditions, we affirm that Scripture has multiple complex senses given by God, the author of the whole drama.
5. The four canonical Gospels narrate the truth about Jesus.
6. Faithful interpretation of Scripture invites and presupposes participation in the community brought into being by God's redemptive action—the church.
7. The saints of the church provide guidance in how to interpret and perform Scripture.
8. Christians need to read the Bible in dialogue with diverse others outside the church.
9. We live in the tension between the "already" and the "not yet" of the kingdom of God; consequently, Scripture calls the church to ongoing discernment, to continually fresh rereadings of the text in light of the Holy Spirit's ongoing work in the world.

As this group acknowledges, however, questions arise for ongoing discussion, and the meaning of statements such as the fourth one in particular would be controversial or at least variegated for different advocates of theological interpretation. Moreover, these theses largely reflect mainline Protestant concerns, since, for example, Roman Catholics and evangelical Protestants might see the fifth

structured conversations hosted by the Center of Theological Inquiry (Princeton, New Jersey); among other participants were Robert W. Jenson, Richard Bauckham, David Steinmetz, Brian Daley, and R. W. L. Moberly.

statement as so central to their understandings of Christian faith that it goes without saying.

If we had to narrow the essential theme of much literature on theological interpretation of Scripture down to one word, the core concept might seem to be the church. Old and New Testament studies operate as guilds within the university, and so that is the public arena that defines their "best practices" and ultimate aims. Theological interpretation of Scripture need not refuse such academic practices, but its ultimate aim is to serve the interests of another public, the church. The literature on theological exegesis further explicates those interests, and the distinctive concerns of the approach that they foster, in terms of canon, creed, and culture.

"Canon" points to the fact that theological interpreters are not shy about relating particular passages to the larger context of the entire Bible. We need not ignore the historical development of words and concepts, engaging in simplistic synthetic connections that obscure the particularities of any given text. But neither should we operate as prisoners of alien standards imposed by academic guilds that tend to reject the unity of Scripture or allow passages to relate only on the narrowest criteria.[12]

"Creed" highlights the Rule of Faith as another crucial context for the church's engagement with Scripture. Narrowly speaking, this entails reading the Bible in light of the trinitarian and christological heritage of the early church that became formalized in symbols such as the Nicene Creed. More broadly, this involves approaching Scripture as members of a living tradition stemming from that earlier time period, with the practices and habits of mind that those Christians shared and passed on. Furthermore, confessions or other dogmatic symbols may extend the regulative function of doctrine into more specific churchly contexts. Such a Rule of Faith may not determine all of our exegetical decisions, but this

---

12. Before overemphasizing the dominance of "historical-critical" approaches, we must admit that the standards in academic biblical studies are increasingly pluralistic or even incoherent, as is treated at length in Markus Bockmuehl, *Seeing the Word: Refocusing New Testament Study*, Studies in Theological Interpretation (Grand Rapids: Baker Academic, 2006).

creedal context helps us to ask questions of the biblical texts, and perhaps to recognize answers, that we might otherwise miss.

"Culture" involves not only the recognition of the various contexts in which the church has read Scripture, both rightly and poorly, across history but also the acknowledgment of our own contemporary hermeneutical locations. As noted earlier, the presuppositions of interpreters have often had a bad name in biblical studies; when they are acknowledged, the admission comes grudgingly. Presuppositions are "baggage" to be set aside as much as humanly possible in a quest for "objectivity." This metaphor points to an alternative, however: baggage usually carries with us that which is essential, not that which we need to get rid of. What if presuppositions are not a threat to objectivity but rather an aid in preserving it? Indeed, presuppositions can preserve perspectives from outside our time and place and personal subjectivity, bringing them to bear on interpretation perhaps in spite of ourselves. Of course, preunderstanding can be unhealthy if it prevents Scripture from reforming human ideas; Protestant, Catholic, and Orthodox believers alike can agree on this point, regardless of their diverse approaches to the relationship between Scripture and tradition. We need to pay attention to the details of biblical texts, remaining open to their correction of our perspectives; even so, presuppositions also provide essential points of connection to the true subject matter of Scripture.

Thinking in terms of lenses may provide a useful metaphor. Although truth is comprehensive and certain in terms of God's knowledge, human perception involves finite, not to mention fallen, perspectives. Accordingly, at any given time and place we see only partially. Likewise, our reading skills and scholarly methods, even operating at their best, are divine gifts precisely in their particularity: each does some things well, but not others. The very detailed historical and literary lenses of biblical scholarship help us to see vital aspects of truth that we dare not miss. But, used exclusively, they can leave out other dimensions of the reality that we are studying. Moreover, sometimes they may obscure those theological realities by fostering a kind of myopia in which we miss the forest for the trees.

Theological interpretation of Scripture uses multiple lenses along the way but tries to integrate these various perspectives into a coherent vision of who God is and who that calls us to become in Christ.[13] This is the widest-angle lens, and it puts biblical interpretation into proper perspective. Historical and literary details may then appear in a different light; furthermore, some of those matters, while fine for scholarly specialists to pursue, may not be materially central for understanding and communicating the message of the texts. For we are studying the Scriptures to know God, not necessarily to sketch the entirety of Paul's social world or to make occasionally impossible choices between subjective and objective genitives.

The metaphor of lenses also puts interpretative difference and change in a new perspective. Some interpretations are surely wrong, while others are more or less right. But that is not the case with every interpretative difference. In many cases perspectives might be complementary rather than contradictory, a matter of various lenses enabling us to see different dimensions of the truth. In other cases, when differences do involve contradictions, still the interpretations as a whole may not be entirely right or wrong. For example, Martin Luther's breakthrough regarding Romans 1:17—he came to see the righteousness of God not as a frightening divine characteristic but instead as the gift of a righteous status before God—is exegetically questionable today in certain respects. That text probably speaks not precisely of righteousness *from* God but rather in some way of righteousness as a truth *about* God.[14] Thus, we could say that, at a certain level of detail, Luther's interpretation seems to be wrong. Yet even today scholars propose a variety of definitions for this divine characteristic and debate them with fervor. If understanding the text's basic theological message depends entirely

13. On theological vision, see Charles M. Wood, *Vision and Discernment: An Orientation in Theological Study*, Studies in Religious and Theological Scholarship (Atlanta: Scholars Press, 1985); Treier, *Virtue and the Voice of God*.

14. A survey of recent commentaries from scholars on diverse sides of debates about Pauline theology, such as Douglas Moo and N. T. Wright, would bear this out.

on a technically precise construal of this phrase, then the church remains hamstrung, unable to reach such understanding.

However, stepping back and examining how the phrase fits into the passage's message about God, we see that divine righteousness is viewed much more positively. Whatever it means exactly, it does not primarily focus on divine judgment in the sense that Luther feared. At this broader level, Luther's interpretation seems to be the proper forerunner of some contemporary perspectives. We might then conclude that God's Spirit may have blessed and advanced the church via Luther's breakthrough even if his interpretation will not win the day in every respect for all time. As interpretative lenses zoom in and out, they can be right or helpful at some levels of precision while fuzzy or inaccurate at others.

Reflecting on the activity of God in this way is at the heart of theological interpretation of Scripture. Hence, in my view, for defining this practice there is an even more important word than "church"—namely, "God." Surely, the ultimate interpretative interest of the church is to know God in a holistic sense. The risk of some theological hermeneutics literature, however, lies in neglecting a clear focus on the *divine* activity that is essential for creaturely participation in the realities the Bible addresses. At its worst, discussion regarding theological interpretation of Scripture risks criticizing academic biblical studies only to substitute too much focus on the all-too-human activity of the church. But, at its best, the discussion beckons us to view biblical interpretation from the perspective of how—via the past, present, and future activity of Word and Spirit—Scripture teaches the church to know and love God. Such a perspective requires new attention to Christian community, to be sure; yet such a communal focus must also incorporate acknowledgment of the church's weakness and need for biblical correction.

An alternative image for how various perspectives can truly work together—whether among the Bible's literary genres, through numerous scholarly methods, in different Christian traditions, or possibly between academic biblical studies and churchly interpretative interests—is the use of maps.[15] A topographical map of London, a guide to its streets, and a layout of its famous Underground provide access to aspects of the city, and they contain a certain level of coherence; still, none of these is absolutely comprehensive in and of itself, and each, if wrongly used, could be misleading. Of course, not every interpretative difference is merely a matter of complementary maps or lenses; some tensions are in fact contradictions and point to what is simply right or wrong. Yet the analogies of lenses and maps give us various perspectives with which to understand the role of various perspectives.

Speaking of maps complements the metaphor of lenses by reminding us that we are not merely spectators when it comes to Scripture, pointing us to the journey motif that is so important for understanding the church's spiritual life. Theological interpretation of Scripture, in the end, is an essential practice in the Christian pilgrimage of seeking to know God. It is that pursuit by which we endeavor to know where we are going and to catch a glimpse of what it will be like to arrive at our destination. Theological interpretation of Scripture, in other words, offers the maps and requires us to use the various lenses through which we can envision how to undertake our journey. Because the quest ultimately involves deepening love for God and neighbor, its hermeneutical point of orientation is not simply the church; rather, theological interpretation of Scripture orients the church, in a way that is both profoundly mysterious and very basic, toward seeking God.

15. Kevin J. Vanhoozer, *The Drama of Doctrine: A Canonical-Linguistic Approach to Christian Theology* (Louisville: Westminster/John Knox, 2005), especially 294–99.

# Suggested Reading

Adam, A. K. M. *What Is Postmodern Biblical Criticism?* Guides to Biblical Scholarship. Minneapolis: Fortress, 1995.

Adam, A. K. M., Stephen E. Fowl, Kevin J. Vanhoozer, and Francis Watson. *Reading Scripture with the Church: Toward a Hermeneutic for Theological Interpretation.* Grand Rapids: Baker Academic, 2006.

Alexander, T. Desmond, and Brian S. Rosner, eds. *New Dictionary of Biblical Theology.* Downers Grove, IL: InterVarsity, 2000.

Augustine. *On Christian Teaching.* Translated by R. P. H. Green. Oxford: Oxford University Press, 1997.

Barth, Karl. *The Epistle to the Philippians.* Translated by James W. Leitch. 40th anniversary ed. Louisville: Westminster/John Knox, 2002.

———. *The Epistle to the Romans.* Translated by Edwyn C. Hoskyns. 6th ed. Oxford: Oxford University Press, 1933.

Bartholomew, Craig G., et al., eds. Scripture and Hermeneutics Series. Grand Rapids: Zondervan, 2000–.

Barton, Stephen C. "New Testament Interpretation as Performance." *Scottish Journal of Theology* 52, no. 2 (1999): 179–208.

Blowers, Paul M. "The *Regula Fidei* and the Narrative Character of Early Christian Faith." *Pro Ecclesia* 6, no. 2 (Spring 1997): 199–228.

Bockmuehl, Markus. *Seeing the Word: Refocusing New Testament Study.* Studies in Theological Interpretation. Grand Rapids: Baker Academic, 2006.

Braaten, Carl E., and Robert W. Jenson, eds. *Reclaiming the Bible for the Church*. Grand Rapids: Eerdmans, 1995.

Briggs, Richard S. "What Does Hermeneutics Have to Do with Biblical Interpretation?" *Heythrop Journal* 47 (2006): 55–74.

———. *Words in Action: Speech Act Theory and Biblical Interpretation*. Edinburgh: T&T Clark, 2001.

Bruns, Gerald. *Hermeneutics Ancient and Modern*. Yale Studies in Hermeneutics. New Haven: Yale University Press, 1992.

Buckley, James J., and David S. Yeago, eds. *Knowing the Triune God: The Work of the Spirit in the Practices of the Church*. Grand Rapids: Eerdmans, 2001.

Burnett, Richard E. *Karl Barth's Theological Exegesis: The Hermeneutical Principles of the Römerbrief Period*. Grand Rapids: Eerdmans, 2004.

Carson, D. A. "Unity and Diversity in the New Testament: The Possibility of Systematic Theology." In *Scripture and Truth*, edited by D. A. Carson and John D. Woodbridge, 65–95. Grand Rapids: Baker Academic, 1992.

Charry, Ellen T. *By the Renewing of Your Minds: The Pastoral Function of Christian Doctrine*. Oxford: Oxford University Press, 1997.

Childs, Brevard S. "Toward Recovering Theological Exegesis." *Pro Ecclesia* 6, no. 1 (Winter 1997): 16–26.

Craigo-Snell, Shannon. "Command Performance: Rethinking Performance Interpretation in the Context of *Divine Discourse*." *Modern Theology* 16, no. 4 (October 2000): 475–94.

Cunningham, Mary Kathleen. *What Is Theological Exegesis? Interpretation and Use of Scripture in Barth's Doctrine of Election*. Valley Forge, PA: Trinity Press International, 1995.

Daley, Brian E. "Is Patristic Exegesis Still Usable? Reflections on Early Christian Interpretation of the Psalms." *Communio* 29 (Spring 2002): 185–216.

Davis, Ellen F., and Richard B. Hays, eds. *The Art of Reading Scripture*. Grand Rapids: Eerdmans, 2003.

Felder, Cain Hope, ed. *Stony the Road We Trod: African American Biblical Interpretation*. Minneapolis: Fortress, 1991.

Ford, David F., and Graham Stanton, eds. *Reading Texts, Seeking Wisdom: Scripture and Theology*. Grand Rapids: Eerdmans, 2004.

Fowl, Stephen E. *Engaging Scripture: A Model for Theological Interpretation*. Challenges in Contemporary Theology. Oxford: Blackwell, 1998.

———. *Philippians*. Two Horizons New Testament Commentary. Grand Rapids: Eerdmans, 2005.

————, ed. *The Theological Interpretation of Scripture: Classic and Contemporary Readings.* Oxford: Blackwell, 1997.

Fowl, Stephen E., and L. Gregory Jones. *Reading in Communion: Scripture and Ethics in Christian Life.* Grand Rapids: Eerdmans, 1991.

Frei, Hans W. *The Eclipse of Biblical Narrative: A Study in Eighteenth and Nineteenth Century Hermeneutics.* New Haven: Yale University Press, 1974.

Gadamer, Hans-Georg. *Truth and Method.* Translated by Joel Weinsheimer and Donald G. Marshall. 2nd ed. New York: Continuum, 1989.

Gracia, Jorge J. E. *How Can We Know What God Means? The Interpretation of Revelation.* New York: Palgrave, 2001.

Green, Joel B., and Max Turner, eds. *Between Two Horizons: Spanning New Testament Studies and Systematic Theology.* Grand Rapids: Eerdmans, 1999.

Greene-McCreight, Kathryn. *Ad Litteram: How Augustine, Calvin, and Barth Read the "Plain Sense" of Genesis 1–3.* Issues in Systematic Theology. New York: Peter Lang, 1999.

Greenman, Jeffrey P., and Timothy Larsen, eds. *Reading Romans through the Centuries.* Grand Rapids: Brazos, 2005.

Griffiths, Paul J. *Religious Reading: The Place of Reading in the Practice of Religion.* Oxford: Oxford University Press, 1999.

Hafemann, Scott J., ed. *Biblical Theology: Retrospect and Prospect.* Downers Grove, IL: InterVarsity, 2002.

Hahn, Scott. *Letter and Spirit: From Written Text to Living Word in the Liturgy.* New York: Doubleday, 2005.

Hauerwas, Stanley. *Matthew.* Brazos Theological Commentary on the Bible. Grand Rapids: Brazos, 2006.

————. *Unleashing the Scripture: Freeing the Bible from Captivity to America.* Nashville: Abingdon, 1993.

Jacobs, Alan. *A Theology of Reading: The Hermeneutics of Love.* Boulder, CO: Westview, 2001.

Jeanrond, Werner. *Theological Hermeneutics: Development and Significance.* New York: Crossroad, 1991.

Jeffrey, David L. *Houses of the Interpreter: Reading Scripture, Reading Culture.* Waco, TX: Baylor University Press, 2003.

————. *People of the Book: Christian Identity and Literary Culture.* Grand Rapids: Eerdmans, 1996.

Jenkins, Philip. *The New Faces of Christianity: Believing the Bible in the Global South.* New York: Oxford University Press, 2006.

————. *The Next Christendom: The Coming of Global Christianity*. New York: Oxford University Press, 2002.

Jenson, Robert W. "The Religious Power of Scripture." *Scottish Journal of Theology* 52, no. 1 (1999): 89–105.

Johnson, Luke Timothy, and William S. Kurz. *The Future of Catholic Biblical Scholarship: A Constructive Conversation*. Grand Rapids: Eerdmans, 2002.

Kannengiesser, Charles. *Handbook of Patristic Exegesis: The Bible in Ancient Christianity*. Leiden: Brill, 2006.

Kelsey, David H. *Proving Doctrine*. Harrisburg, PA: Trinity Press International, 1999.

Kovacs, Judith L., ed. and trans. *1 Corinthians: Interpreted by Early Christian Commentators*. The Church's Bible. Grand Rapids: Eerdmans, 2005.

Lacocque, André, and Paul Ricoeur. *Thinking Biblically: Exegetical and Hermeneutical Studies*. Translated by David Pellauer. Chicago: University of Chicago Press, 1998.

Levering, Matthew. *Participatory Biblical Exegesis: A Theology of Biblical Interpretation*. Notre Dame, IN: University of Notre Dame Press, forthcoming.

Lindbeck, George A. *The Nature of Doctrine: Religion and Theology in a Postliberal Age*. Philadelphia: Westminster, 1984.

Lubac, Henri de. *Exégèse médiévale: Les quatre sens de l'écriture*. 4 vols. Paris: Aubier, 1959–1964.

Lundin, Roger. *The Culture of Interpretation: Christian Faith and the Postmodern World*. Grand Rapids: Eerdmans, 1993.

————, ed. *Disciplining Hermeneutics: Interpretation in Christian Perspective*. Grand Rapids: Eerdmans, 1997.

Lundin, Roger, Anthony C. Thiselton, and Clarence Walhout. *The Promise of Hermeneutics*. Grand Rapids: Eerdmans, 1999.

————. *The Responsibility of Hermeneutics*. Grand Rapids: Eerdmans, 1985.

Martin, Francis. *Sacred Scripture: The Disclosure of the Word*. Naples, FL: Sapientia, 2006.

McCormack, Bruce L. "Historical-Criticism and Dogmatic Interest in Karl Barth's Theological Exegesis of the New Testament." *Lutheran Quarterly* 5 (Summer 1991): 211–25.

McKim, Donald K., ed. *Calvin and the Bible*. Cambridge: Cambridge University Press, 2006.

Moberly, R. W. L. *The Bible, Theology, and Faith: A Study of Abraham and Jesus*. Cambridge Studies in Christian Doctrine. Cambridge: Cambridge University Press, 2000.

Muller, Richard A., and John L. Thompson. "The Significance of Precritical Exegesis: Retrospect and Prospect." In *Biblical Interpretation in the Era of the Reformation*, edited by Richard A. Muller and John L. Thompson, 335–45. Grand Rapids: Eerdmans, 1996.

Noble, Paul R. *The Canonical Approach: A Critical Reconstruction of the Hermeneutics of Brevard S. Childs*. Biblical Interpretation 16. Leiden: Brill, 1995.

Noll, Mark A. *Between Faith and Criticism: Evangelicals, Scholarship, and the Bible in America*. New York: Harper & Row, 1986.

———. *The Civil War as a Theological Crisis*. Chapel Hill: University of North Carolina Press, 2006.

O'Keefe, John J., and R. R. Reno. *Sanctified Vision: An Introduction to Early Christian Interpretation of the Bible*. Baltimore: Johns Hopkins University Press, 2005.

Ott, Craig, and Harold A. Netland, eds. *Globalizing Theology: Belief and Practice in an Era of World Christianity*. Grand Rapids: Baker Academic, 2006.

Pelikan, Jaroslav. *Acts*. Brazos Theological Commentary on the Bible. Grand Rapids: Brazos, 2005.

Peterson, Eugene H. "Eat This Book: The Holy Community at Table with the Holy Scripture." *Theology Today* 56, no. 1 (1999): 5–17.

Radner, Ephraim, and George Sumner, eds. *The Rule of Faith: Scripture, Canon, and Creed in a Critical Age*. Harrisburg, PA: Morehouse, 1998.

Reno, Russell. "'You Who Were Far Off Have Been Brought Near': Reflections on Theological Exegesis." *Ex Auditu* 16 (2000): 169–82.

Ricoeur, Paul. *Essays on Biblical Interpretation*. Edited by Lewis S. Mudge. Philadelphia: Fortress, 1980.

———. *Figuring the Sacred: Religion, Narrative, and Imagination*. Translated by David Pellauer. Edited by Mark I. Wallace. Minneapolis: Fortress, 1995.

Rogers, Eugene F., Jr. "How the Virtues of an Interpreter Presuppose and Perfect Hermeneutics: The Case of Thomas Aquinas." *Journal of Religion* 76, no. 1 (January 1996): 64–81.

Scobie, Charles H. H. *The Ways of Our God: An Approach to Biblical Theology*. Grand Rapids: Eerdmans, 2003.

Seitz, Christopher R. "Christological Interpretation of Texts and Trinitarian Claims to Truth: An Engagement with Francis Watson's *Text and Truth*." *Scottish Journal of Theology* 52, no. 2 (1999): 209–26.

Seitz, Christopher, and Kathryn Greene-McCreight, eds. *Theological Exegesis: Essays in Honor of Brevard S. Childs.* Grand Rapids: Eerdmans, 1998.

Smith, James K. A. *The Fall of Interpretation: Philosophical Foundations for a Creational Hermeneutic.* Downers Grove, IL: InterVarsity, 2000.

Thiselton, Anthony C. *Interpreting God and the Postmodern Self: On Meaning, Manipulation and Promise.* Grand Rapids: Eerdmans, 1995.

———. *New Horizons in Hermeneutics: The Theory and Practice of Transforming Biblical Reading.* Grand Rapids: Zondervan, 1992.

———. *The Two Horizons: New Testament Hermeneutics and Philosophical Description.* Grand Rapids: Eerdmans, 1980.

Treier, Daniel J. "Biblical Theology and/or Theological Interpretation of Scripture? Defining the Relationship." *Scottish Journal of Theology* 61, no. 1 (2008): 16–31.

———. Review of *The Ways of Our God: An Approach to Biblical Theology,* by Charles H. H. Scobie. *Pro Ecclesia* 15, no. 2 (Spring 2006): 249–52.

———. "Scripture and Hermeneutics." In *The Cambridge Companion to Evangelical Theology,* edited by Timothy Larsen and Daniel J. Treier, 35–49. Cambridge: Cambridge University Press, 2007.

———. "The Superiority of Pre-Critical Exegesis? *Sic et Non.*" *Trinity Journal* 24 (2003): 77–103.

———. *Virtue and the Voice of God: Toward Theology as Wisdom.* Grand Rapids: Eerdmans, 2006.

Vanhoozer, Kevin J. "Body-Piercing, the Natural Sense, and the Task of Theological Interpretation: A Hermeneutical Homily on John 19:34." *Ex Auditu* 16 (2000): 1–29.

———. *The Drama of Doctrine: A Canonical-Linguistic Approach to Christian Theology.* Louisville: Westminster/John Knox, 2005.

———. *First Theology: God, Scripture, Hermeneutics.* Downers Grove, IL: InterVarsity, 2002.

———. *Is There a Meaning in This Text? The Bible, the Reader, and the Morality of Literary Knowledge.* Grand Rapids: Zondervan, 1998.

Vanhoozer, Kevin J., Charles A. Anderson, and Michael J. Sleasman, eds. *Everyday Theology: How to Read Cultural Texts and Interpret Trends.* Grand Rapids: Baker Academic, 2007.

Vanhoozer, Kevin J., James K. A. Smith, and Bruce Ellis Benson, eds. *Hermeneutics at the Crossroads.* Indiana Series in the Philosophy of Religion. Bloomington: Indiana University Press, 2006.

Vanhoozer, Kevin J., et al., eds. *Dictionary for Theological Interpretation of the Bible.* Grand Rapids: Baker Academic, 2005.

Ward, Timothy. *Word and Supplement: Speech Acts, Biblical Texts, and the Sufficiency of Scripture*. Oxford: Oxford University Press, 2002.

Watson, Francis. *Text and Truth: Redefining Biblical Theology*. Grand Rapids: Eerdmans, 1997.

————. *Text, Church and World: Biblical Interpretation in Theological Perspective*. Grand Rapids: Eerdmans, 1994.

————. "The Old Testament as Christian Scripture: A Response to Professor Seitz." *Scottish Journal of Theology* 52, no. 2 (1999): 227–32.

Webster, John. *Holy Scripture: A Dogmatic Sketch*. Current Issues in Theology. Cambridge: Cambridge University Press, 2003.

————. *Word and Church*. Edinburgh: T&T Clark, 2001.

Weinandy, Thomas G., Daniel A. Keating, and John P. Yocum, eds. *Aquinas on Scripture: An Introduction to His Biblical Commentaries*. London: T&T Clark International, 2005.

Wells, Samuel. *Improvisation: The Drama of Christian Ethics*. Grand Rapids: Brazos, 2004.

Williams, David M. *Receiving the Bible in Faith: Historical and Theological Exegesis*. Washington, DC: Catholic University of America Press, 2004.

Wolterstorff, Nicholas. *Divine Discourse: Philosophical Reflections on the Claim That God Speaks*. Cambridge: Cambridge University Press, 1995.

Wood, Susan K. *Spiritual Exegesis and the Church in the Theology of Henri de Lubac*. Grand Rapids: Eerdmans, 1998.

Wright, N. T. "How Can the Bible Be Authoritative?" *Vox Evangelica* 21 (1991): 7–32.

————. *The Last Word: Beyond the Bible Wars to a New Understanding of the Authority of Scripture*. San Francisco: HarperSanFrancisco, 2005.

Young, Frances M. *Biblical Exegesis and the Formation of Christian Culture*. Cambridge: Cambridge University Press, 1997.

————. *Virtuoso Theology: The Bible and Interpretation*. Cleveland: Pilgrim, 1993.

Zimmermann, Jens. *Recovering Theological Hermeneutics: An Incarnational-Trinitarian Theory of Interpretation*. Grand Rapids: Baker Academic, 2004.

# Scripture Index

# Subject Index